Warless Societies and the Origin of War

Warless Societies
and the Origin of War

Raymond C. Kelly

Ann Arbor

THE UNIVERSITY OF MICHIGAN PRESS

*444 05873

*A CIP catalog record for this book is available
from the British Library.*

Library of Congress Cataloging-in-Publication Data

Kelly, Raymond C. (Raymond Case), 1942–
    Warless societies and the origin of war / Raymond C. Kelly.
        p.   cm.
    Includes bibliographical references and index.
    ISBN 0-472-09738-5 (cloth) — ISBN 0-472-06738-9 (paper)
    1. War and society—History.   2. Warfare, Prehistoric.   I. Title.

GN497 .K45   2000
303.6'6—dc21   00-009898

To Marshall D. Sahlins

and to the memory of

Roy A. Rappaport and Eric R. Wolf

Contents

Preface   ix

Introduction   1

1. The Category of Peaceful Societies   11

2. Warless and Warlike Hunter-Gatherers:
   A Comparison   41

3. The Origin of War: A Transitional Case   75

4. The Early Coevolution of War and Society   121

Notes   163

Bibliography   177

Index   189

Preface

This book is an outgrowth of several undergraduate courses—concerned with warfare in unstratified societies—that I have taught at the University of Michigan over a number of years. I have come to believe that a thoughtful examination of the relationships between human nature, war, and the constitution of society can make a significant contribution to a general liberal arts education and that this also is an area of inquiry to which students are naturally drawn. Undergraduates invariably have certain questions in mind. They want to know if there are peaceful societies in which war is lacking and, if so, what such societies are like. They want to know whether war is a primordial and pervasive feature of human existence or a set of practices that arose at a certain time in our prehistoric past. This book is concerned to address these (and other) typical undergraduate questions as well as issues of theoretical concern in anthropology. I have also made an effort to make the discussion readily available to undergraduates whose background is limited to an introductory course in anthropology by defining terms that are not found in an abridged dictionary. Discussion of covariation is phrased so as to be readily intelligible to students lacking a background in statistics. In short, the audience I have in mind includes students (and the general reader who has some acquaintance with anthropology) as well as my professional colleagues. My principal objective is to present a general model for the initial evolution of war that is grounded in the comparative analysis of ethnographic data and then to apply this to the interpretation of pertinent data in the archaeological record. The envisioned audience thus includes colleagues in the anthropological subdisciplines of archaeology and biological anthropology as well as ethnology.

A preliminary formulation of the central argument developed in this book was originally presented in a series of five public departmental lectures at the University of Michigan in 1995. The questions and comments of my colleagues contributed to the further development of these lines of inquiry and interpretation. Michael Fleisher, Bruce Knauft, Joyce Marcus, John O'Shea, Keith Otterbein, Michael Peletz, and Polly Weissner have read earlier or later drafts of all or part of the book and have offered many valuable comments and suggestions. Thanks are also due to my daughter Gwen Kelly for help in compiling the bibliography and securing permissions for illustrations, and to Julie Raybon for typing the manuscript.

I would like to thank the following copyright holders for permission to reproduce maps, diagrams, drawings, figures, tables, and photographs included in this work.

Cambridge University Press for map 2 and figure 2, the drawing "Plan of Andamanese Village," which originally appeared in *The Andaman Islanders* by A. R. Radcliffe-Brown, copyright 1922.

Journal of the American Oriental Society for figure 1, "The Relationship between Andamanese Dialects and Languages," originally published in vol. 9, no. 4 (1989).

Vikas Publishing House for plate 5, originally published in *The Andaman Story,* by N. Iqbal Singh, copyright 1978.

The *Journal of Peace Research* for table 2, "A Summary of Common Factors of Peaceful Societies," originally published in vol. 15, no. 1 (1978).

The Anthropological Survey of India for table 11, "Seasonal Availability of the Staples of the Andamanese Diet," originally published in *The Great Andamanese Past and Present,* by Pratap C. Dutta, copyright 1978.

Mayfield Publishing Company for table 12, "An Illustration of the Relationship between Political Organization and War Motives," originally published in *Anthropology and Contemporary Human Problems,* 3d ed., by John H. Bodley, copyright 1996.

The Trustees of the National Gallery of Art for figures 3 and 4, drawings of paintings that appear on the walls of the cavern of Cougnac, originally published in *The Eternal Present: The Beginnings of Art,* by S. Giedion, copyright 1962.

This book is dedicated to three of my teachers (and subsequently my colleagues) at the University of Michigan, whose work has continued to serve as an inspiration over the years.

Introduction

The central objective of this study is to elucidate the conditions under which warfare is initiated in sociocultural contexts where it did not previously exist, and to decipher the origin of war in that sense. The investigation begins with a delineation of the distinctive characteristics of peaceful (or warless) societies that represent both a prior sociocultural disposition and the context in which primal warfare initially arises and takes shape. This analysis of peaceful societies illuminates certain key features of the transition from warlessness to warfare and provides a basis for the identification of a key transitional case in the ethnographic record. An investigation of this cluster of tribes—and the larger regional system they constitute—provides a basis for ascertaining the causes, conduct, and consequences of nascent and early warfare. This then fleshes out the picture of the origin of war and lays the groundwork for consideration of theoretical issues pertaining to the evolution of war and the coevolution of war and society.

The archaeological record provides very little clear-cut evidence of warfare within hunting and gathering populations prior to the development of agriculture. This has led to the widely held view that warfare was rare to nonexistent until quite late in human history. Roper (1975:304) denotes 7500 to 7000 B.C. as the time period of the "first generally accepted evidence of warfare in the Near East and the world" (with the exception of the Nubian site 117, reported by Wendorf (1968), that is dated to 12,000 to 10,000 B.C.; see Roper 1975:300). By 5000 to 4300 B.C., fortifications, garrisons, and site destruction at a number of locations in the Near East provide archaeological evidence for a more general prevalence of warfare (Roper 1975:323–30). By 3000 B.C., the earliest historical records document frequent warfare between neighboring Sumerian polities over land and water rights and depict the unification of Upper and Lower Egypt by conquest.

The general picture suggested by these data is one in which the origination of war in the Near East (in about 7500 B.C.) goes hand in hand with the widespread development of a sedentary agricultural existence, while the subsequent expansion of armed conflict (beginning in about 5000 B.C.) coincides with population increase, the growth of trade, efforts to control strategic sites along trade routes (Roper 1975:330), and the evolution of hierarchical and centralized forms of political organization (with the precedence accorded to these demographic, ecological, economic, and political factors being subject to divergent interpretations). The key point for our purposes is that—excepting a single late Upper Paleolithic site—archaeological evidence points to a commencement of warfare that post-dates the development of agriculture. This strongly implies that earlier hunter-gatherer societies were warless and that the Paleolithic (extending from 2,900,000 to 10,000 B.P.) was a time of universal peace. Warfare then originates rather abruptly. This is ultimately attributable to a major economic transformation that broadly alters social conditions and also facilitates the development of new forms of social and political organization. In the relatively brief span of 4,500 years, a global condition of warlessness that had persisted for several million years thus gives way to chronic warfare that arises initially in the Near East and subsequently in other regions where a similar sequence of transformative events is reduplicated.[1]

An understanding of the origin of war that takes universal peace among our Paleolithic forebears as a point of departure is not well-supported by the ethnography of hunter-gatherers recorded during the past century in all corners of the globe. In this respect the archaeological and ethnographic evidence pertinent to the origin of war are at variance. The failure of the ethnographic record to support the archaeologically derived supposition that hunter-gatherers are peaceful is brought to light by Ember (1978). Within a worldwide sample of thirty-one hunter-gatherer societies (with zero reliance on agriculture or herding),

> 64 percent had warfare occurring at least once every two years, 20 percent had warfare somewhat less often, and only 10 percent . . . were rated as having rare or no warfare . . . Even if we exclude equestrian hunters . . . and those with 60 percent or more dependence on fishing . . . , warfare is rare for only 12 percent of the remaining hunter-gatherers. (443)

If frequent warfare is commonplace among hunter-gatherers, then the origin of war very likely predates the development of agriculture and might potentially extend far back into the Paleolithic. Moreover, Ember's data contain the suggestion that the kinds of economic factors considered relevant to the origination of warfare in the Near East may not covary with the presence of frequent warfare among some hunter-gatherers in her sample, and its absence among others. A reliance on fishing characteristically entails a sedentary or semisedentary existence analogous to that necessitated by early agriculture, and there are relatively fixed subsistence resources or productive sites that are vital to the survival of resident populations in both cases. Yet Ember's data (cited above) do not show that hunter-gatherers with a heavy reliance on fishing are more likely to manifest frequent warfare and less likely to manifest rare to nonexistent warfare than hunter-gatherers lacking such reliance.[2] This casts doubt on the supposition that warfare originated as a result of sedentarism both before and after the origin of agriculture and involved similar processes in both instances. In other words, the ethnographic data are seemingly at variance with the archaeological data with respect to imputed causal factors as well as chronology, and this raises the possibility of an entirely different picture of the origin of war.

What differentiates warless and warlike hunter-gatherers? If the former were mobile and the latter sedentary, then establishing this point of differentiation would also make it possible to formulate a logically coherent and highly plausible interpretation of the origin of war in the sense defined here (i.e., the conditions under which warfare is initiated in a sociocultural context where it did not previously exist). In other words, whatever distinguishes these two classes of hunter-gatherers may quite possibly hold the key to elucidating the origination and early evolution of war. An inquiry conducted along these lines is pursued in chapter 2, following a consideration of the characteristics of peaceful societies more generally. An examination of earlier studies of peaceful societies provides important clues that point toward the sociocultural domains in which the distinctive and differentiating features of warless and warlike societies may be found—domains as potentially varied as economic organization on one hand, and child-rearing practices on the other.

Defining war and delineating the boundaries between war and other partially similar phenomena raise important issues with regard to both classifying hunter-gatherer societies in terms of the presence and frequency of warfare and ascertaining the point in a sequence of conflictual events at which war has begun. Does war of the variety manifested by hunter-gatherers represent a point on a continuum that differs only incrementally from other forms of lethal violence? Or, alternatively, does the transition to war constitute a watershed event that institutes practices governed by a distinctively different logic? I will argue that the latter is the case and that there is a turning point in human history (or prehistory) marked by the origin of war.

There are also transitional cases among ethnographically described hunter-gatherers and hunter-horticulturalists that are very instructive. They allow us to hear the words of social actors in situations of conflict that have reached a critical juncture. I will introduce this testimony after presenting the definitional features to which it pertains.

War entails armed conflict that is collectively carried out. It differs from other (often antecedent) forms of conflict such as disputes and altercations by the fact that participants employ deadly weapons with deadly force. One of the key features of war is that the deaths of other persons are envisioned in advance and this envisioning is encoded in the purposeful act of taking up lethal weapons.

War is an organized activity that requires advanced planning. The most elementary form of warfare is a raid (or type of raid) in which a small group of men endeavor to enter enemy territory undetected in order to ambush and kill an unsuspecting isolated individual, and to then withdraw rapidly without suffering any casualties. Achieving the essential element of surprise precludes undertaking such a raid as an immediate and spontaneous expression of anger in response to whatever events precipitated the conflict. This tactical requirement (of surprise) enforces protracted intervals between engagements and thus ensures that emotions have cooled well before a raid commences, and that a considered decision to elect this course of action has been collectively made through discussion among potential participants. Moreover, undertaking even the most elemental raid requires setting a date and time; planning a route, an objective, and a pattern of deployment; and (potentially) designating a scout, point, and individual to cover the rear, or otherwise allocating specialized roles among participants. War entails a division of labor that goes beyond that based on age and gender alone. The inevitable intervals between acts of primitive war provide scope for rational calculation, planning, organization, and the foregrounding of the predominantly instrumental character of war. This instrumentality contrasts with spontaneous forms of collective violence such as brawls and riots, where the intentionality centers on expressing anger rather than causing previously envisioned deaths to fulfill a purpose (although deaths may occur during spontaneous violence and the purposes of a raid may encompass fulfillment of the deferred gratification of emotionally satisfying revenge).

War also differs from other forms of violent conflict in that the use of deadly force is seen as entirely legitimate by the collectivity that resorts to arms. The deaths of other persons are not only envisioned in advance but are also believed to be both morally appropriate and justified by circumstances or prior events. The ancient principle of lex talionis—an eye for an eye and a tooth for a tooth—is an example of a concise statement of event-based moral justification for the legitimate use of force.

Moral appropriateness is integral to the collective nature of the activity of making war. Social actors are explicitly recruited to the project of causing the deaths of other persons on the grounds that it is proper and legitimate to do so. War is collectively sanctioned, and participation is laudable. Thus the men of a local group who take part in a retaliatory raid on their neighbors are esteemed by their coresidents and earn prestige.

"Murder" (or homicide) contrasts with war in that the killing is negatively valued by the social collectivity that constitutes the killer's (or killers') reference group. Murder is culturally disapproved, stigmatizing rather than prestigious, and falls somewhere along an evaluative scale that extends from regrettable to heinous, depending on the circumstances. Such illegitimate killing is a criminal act (by definition) and is characteristically regarded as warranting retribution. This often takes the form of the death penalty (or capital punishment), defined as the appropriate killing of an individual whose criminal responsibility has been established in advance.[3] Since the kinds of societies with which we are concerned lack judicial and penal institutions, the execution of a murderer is carried out by the homicide victim's aggrieved next of kin and his supporters. The kin and coresidents of the murderer often render tacit assistance by withholding support and thus facilitating the execution. A recidivist murderer (including the witch and sorcerer who kills by supernatural means) may even be killed by his or her own kinsmen.[4]

There are many similarities between war and capital punishment when the latter is carried out by the aggrieved next of kin and his supporters. In both cases the collective use of deadly force is considered to be morally appropriate, justified, and legitimate so that participation constitutes an honorable fulfillment of civic duty. From the standpoint of observable behavior the two may also appear very much alike: a party of armed men employs the element of surprise in order to kill an individual caught unawares. However, there is one very critical difference between capital punishment and war: the death penalty is only applicable to a specific individual, the perpetrator of a prior criminal homicide. In war the killing of any member of the enemy group (or any of a class of members such as adult males) is considered legitimate. War (including feud) is grounded in application of the principle of *social substitutability* and is thus governed by a distinctive logic that is entirely foreign to murder, duel, and capital punishment.[5]

In war and feud, the killing of an individual is perceived as an injury to his or her group. The same logic engenders the companion concept of holding a group responsible, so that any member of the killer's collectivity is a legitimate target for retaliatory blood vengeance (rather than the specific killer alone). The principle that one group member is substitutable for another in these contexts underwrites the interrelated concepts of injury to the group, group responsibility for the infliction of injury, and group liability with respect to retribution. War is thus cognitively and conceptually (as well as behaviorally) between groups. It is consequently critical that war be analyzed as meaningfully entailed social action (intelligible from the actor's point of view) rather than simply in behavioral terms.

While capital punishment removes a wrongdoer whose responsibility for causing the death of another person has been established, war and feud do not excise killers from society but instead target other individuals who

are innocent of direct responsibility for prior deaths. "In societies characterized by feuding, blood revenge is often taken by a small group of men
who lie in ambush and kill an unsuspecting relative of the man whose act
of homicide is being avenged. The victim is usually alone and has little
chance of escape" (Otterbein 1968:279). It is important to notice that such
blood vengeance entails a radical emotional displacement absent in capital
punishment. In the latter case the anger a man feels toward the individual
who slew his brother is directly expressed. But in war and feud the anger is
redirected to an entirely different individual, and one who is sufficiently
peripheral to be unsuspecting. Meanwhile, the actual killer of one's
brother lives on. Yet such vengeance is experienced as emotionally gratifying.

This displacement of vengeance also requires a more complex scheme
of moral legitimation. The logic of "an eye for an eye" is a straightforward
logic of first-order identity, not one of substitution. In itself, it would provide no warrant for the type of blood vengeance described above but
would rather nominate the perpetrator of the initial homicide for like
treatment. Substantial cultural elaboration is required to make the killing
of an unsuspecting and uninvolved individual "count" as reciprocity for
an earlier death, and to make it morally appropriate as well as emotionally
gratifying and socially meaningful. The meaning system of war (and feud)
is quite distinct from the meaning system of the death penalty, and the
movement from the latter to the former constitutes a jump in level with
respect to elaboration of the group concept. This entails not only an ideol-
ogy of the group, but also the kind of internalization of a group identity
illustrated by the statement "I *am* an American" (as opposed to "I live in
America" or even "I am a citizen of the United States of America"). The
substitution of one person's death for another, a substitution that is central to war and feud, is rendered intelligible by elucidating these underlying concepts.

Although war entails lethal violence between individuals who reside
in separate social groups, not all acts of intergroup lethal violence exhibit
the full ensemble of distinctive features that characterize war. Distinguishing war as a specific form of intergroup lethal violence is essential to elucidating the initial evolution of war in that the distinctions provide both a
means of recognizing antecedent forms of collective violence and a point
of departure for identifying critical variables in the developmental process
that pertain to the emergence of the concepts of injury to the group, group
responsibility for counteraction, and group member liability to retribution.

The boundary between war (including feud) and other similar phenomena such as collective execution can thus be very precisely specified in
terms of the presence or absence of a calculus of social substitutability (see

table 1). The emergence of this calculus and its companion concepts is clearly a watershed event in human history in that it creates the preconditions for a more general deployment of lethal violence as *an instrument of the social group* and a legitimate means for the attainment of group objectives and interests. The origin of war thus brings into being an instrument of power that has the latent potential to transform society. This marks the beginning of a coevolution of war and society that shapes the future course of sociocultural development.

The ethnography of the Gebusi provides accounts of social conflicts that aptly illustrate the important conceptual difference between collective execution and war. In 1986 the Gebusi were a cultural/linguistic group numbering about 450 persons who lived in small longhouse communities of close kin and affines (averaging 27 residents) scattered across a 65-square-mile territory within the lowland tropical rain forest of south-central Papua New Guinea, in the watershed of the Strickland River (Knauft 1985:16–31; 1987:459). The Gebusi are hunter-horticulturalists who rely on hunting, foraging, processing wild sago palms, and the shifting cultivation of bananas (as staple crop). Social conflict among the Gebusi is largely a product of sorcery attributions, and these eventuate in a substantial incidence of executions (Knauft 1985:113–56). Deaths that follow from illness are believed to be due to sorcery. Typically the sorcery suspect is identified by an entranced spirit medium during the illness, and the alleged sorcerer is entreated to withdraw his or her sorcery so the ill individual can recover (100–101). When a sick person subsequently dies, it is evident that the source of illness was not withdrawn. The spirit medium then conducts a spirit inquest that confirms the guilt of the alleged sorcerer. This is typically followed by several types of divination (including corpse divination in which the deceased is shaken by the suspect and the corpse may emit signs taken to confirm guilt; see Knauft 1985:38–39).

TABLE 1. Distinguishing Attributes of Capital Punishment, Feud, and War

	Capital Punishment	Feud and War
1. Collective armed conflict	variable	+
2. Collectively sanctioned by participants' community	+	+
3. Morally justified in participants' viewpoint	+	+
4. Participants esteemed by others of their collectivity	+	+
5. Entails organized, planned, and premeditated attack(s)	+	+
6. Serves identifiable instrumental objectives (e.g., defense, revenge, excision, appropriation)	+	+
7. Social substitution governs the targeting of individuals for lethal violence	–	+

The spirit inquest and divinations establish criminal responsibility for a death. This provides a warrant for execution of the guilty sorcerer that the aggrieved kin of the deceased may or may not carry out (in all, 56 of 211 alleged sorcerers in Knauft's sample were killed; see Knauft 1985:124–25). If the next of kin are able to elicit sufficient support for an execution, an all-night séance is held to solidify a consensus of justifiable anger prior to a planned ambush of the sorcerer.

> The spirits [of the entranced medium] roundly condemn the suspect as an irremediable sorcerer and a continuing threat to the community. The audience becomes caught up in escalating rounds of whooping, hollering, and joking, amid which the medium's spirits may present plans for the attack. At dawn, bonded in vitality and without sleep, the men go out to stage the ambush. In some cases they have been aided by complicity among the suspect's close kinsmen, but even when this is not the case, only the alleged sorcerer is attacked, leaving his or her kinsmen unharmed. Some resistance may be encountered from the suspect's agnates and other close kinsmen. Seeing that they are outnumbered, however, they almost invariably flee, leaving the alleged sorcerer to his or her fate. The suspect is shot with arrows or clubbed to death, then butchered and taken in net bags back to the settlement to be cooked and eaten. (102)

Communal consumption of the butchered sorcerer entails communal acceptance of the moral appropriateness of the execution and is also regarded as a component of just retribution.

When a sorcery execution party encounters resistance, fighting may ensue that resembles warfare. However, the shouted comments of the parties on both sides make it clear that the concept of killing a member of the sorcerer's group in lieu of the sorcerer himself (or herself) is never entertained. The following case is particularly instructive with regard to this point (the account of the execution is provided by the sister's son [ZS] of the slain sorcerer, who is reciprocally the mother's brother [MB] of the informant).

> A man had been accused of sorcery and suspected that there might be an attempt on his life. He therefore sent word out to all his kinsmen, some of whom came to stay with him in a show of support. In the evening, however, a group of visitors that included the accuser entered the village with the ostensible reason of requesting a curing séance for the accuser's sore foot. Since the visiting party was large, the suspect and his supporters did not dare turn them away; they welcomed and shook hands with the visitors, sitting down all together on the longhouse

porch. After talking a while, the accuser suddenly jumped up and grabbed a large piece of firewood; others among the visitors held the suspect and restrained his kinsmen. The suspect was clubbed over the head and killed. His kinsmen broke free and, obtaining their bows and arrows, staged a battle against the visitors outside the longhouse. Though one or two people received minor wounds, the fight was quickly over. As my informant (the ZS of the slain man) stated, "It was getting dark and we could not see to fight. The women and the wife of my MB [the wife of the man killed] shouted to us, 'Don't let anyone else die; they came to shoot my husband; now that he's dead, let that be enough!' The visitors shouted, 'We didn't come to shoot at you!' And so we stopped shooting." (Knauft 1985:123)

The events described here culminate in an armed conflict between men of two communities that has all the observable characteristics of warfare except group liability for the infliction of injury by a group member. Although the execution party gains a momentary advantage over the accused sorcerer's kin and coresidents, they utilize this only to *restrain* the sorcerer's supporters, not to dispatch them. Only the sorcerer himself is killed. The kin of the executed sorcerer then initiate an exchange of arrows as an expression of their anger and sorrow at their loss. This expressive—rather than instrumental—violence is a short-lived outburst. The expressive character of these acts is evident from the fact that there is no subsequent retaliation by the executed sorcerer's kin. They do not seek to take vengeance upon the executioner and/or his supporters at a later date (as would be characteristic of war). This is due to the fact that the slain sorcerer's kin ultimately accept the legitimacy of such executions knowing that the sorcerer's criminal responsibility for a death has been established in advance by the conventional equivalent of "due process," that is, a spirit inquest and divination.

This acceptance of the execution is verbally expressed by the women of the community, and especially by the slain sorcerer's wife, who speaks as one of the potentially aggrieved next of kin. She acknowledges the selectivity of the execution and essentially expresses the view that there is no injury to the group. Moreover, she explicitly rejects a payback. Although one might well expect her to be one of the persons most likely to cry out for blood vengeance, she instead says "don't let anyone else die." The members of the execution party then affirm that they have no quarrel with the slain sorcerer's community or kinsmen, and the exchange of arrows ends.

The execution party then withdraws, and there are no further hostilities between these two communities. In all such instances this is invariably the case. Even though the close agnatic kin of an executed sorcerer sometimes do not accept the validity of the precipitating sorcery attribution, and may consequently desire revenge for what they regard as a miscarriage of justice, this desire remains unrealized due to "the near-impossible task of organizing collective retaliation against men from another community" (Knauft 1985:130).[6]

The Gebusi collective armed conflict described here is not war but rather the administration of capital punishment by a sorcery victim's aggrieved next of kin and his supporters (cf. Otterbein 1987:484). It is distinguishable from war because only the perpetrator of a crime is targeted for killing. The calculus of social substitution that is the hallmark of war is clearly absent. The Gebusi case studies of sorcerer executions presented by Knauft (1985) thus exemplify the boundary between war and phenomena that are partially similar (particularly from a strictly behavioral perspective). Delineating this boundary makes it possible to rigorously discriminate between warless societies and those in which warfare is present. This, in turn, lays the groundwork for an analysis of the characteristics of warless (or peaceful) societies and for pinpointing the features that differentiate these from societies characterized by frequent warfare.[7]

CHAPTER 1

The Category of Peaceful Societies

Every theory of the origin of war necessarily forecasts the characteristics of peaceful (or warless) societies. If the development of a significant degree of dependence upon agriculture is implicated in the origination of warfare, then peaceful societies should be hunter-gatherers. If a sedentary existence precludes the curtailment of conflict by the simple expedient of moving apart to effect spatial separation, then peaceful societies should evidence a capacity for mobility that readily facilitates disengagement from conflict situations. If resource competition promotes warfare, then warless societies should enjoy a sufficiency of resources (relative to population). In short, peaceful societies should lack whatever instigates war (or manifest this to a significantly lesser degree than warlike societies).

The study of peaceful societies is thus critical to the development of a theoretical understanding of the origin and early evolution of war. However, scholars concerned with war have, not surprisingly, focused on those cases where the phenomenon of war was present (and generally well-developed as well). Paradoxically, many scholars engaged in peace studies also share this same focus, as Sponsel (1994:6) points out:

> Their working assumption is that a knowledge of the causes and functions of war will help to reduce the frequency and intensity of war and [help] to find alternative ways of conflict resolution that will lead to a more peaceful world. This preoccupation with war over peace is found in most of the peace studies literature. For instance, in a review of the contents of the *Journal of Peace Research* from 1964–1980, Wiberg (1981:113) observes: "For it turns out that out of approximately 400 articles, research communications, etc. published over seventeen years, a single one has been devoted to the empirical study of peaceful societies with a view to find out what seemed to make them peaceful" [the article referred to is by Fabbro (1978)].

Thus the important questions of (1) isolating the distinctive features of peaceful societies and (2) identifying the critical differences between peaceful and warlike societies remain largely unexamined, although Fabbro's (1978) contribution constitutes a potential bridge to such inquiry.

Fabbro's article presents a systematic, ethnographically based comparative analysis of peaceful societies that represents a foundation on which to build. It is a logical point of departure for my own inquiry into the distinctive features that differentiate warless and warlike societies, and for my efforts to profile the likely precursors of the societies in which warfare originated. Although I will seek to revise and transcend Fabbro's work, I want to begin by acknowledging the stimulating and pathbreaking nature of his contributions.

Fabbro seeks to identify a set of peaceful societies and to compare them in order to determine what characteristics they have in common. His larger objectives are to contribute to an understanding of "the social preconditions of peace" and also to remedy the tendency for peace to be treated in the literature as "an abstraction and/or utopia," by the antidote of presenting "a number of concrete examples of peaceful societies" (Fabbro 1978:67). He begins by establishing "criteria of peace" that can serve as a basis for the selection of societies to be included in his study:

> There are a number of levels or intensities of peace which members of a society may experience. In ascending order of comprehensiveness these would include:
> 1. The society has no wars fought on its territory;
> 2. The society is not involved in any external wars;
> 3. There are no civil wars or internal collective violence;
> 4. There is no standing military-police organization;
> 5. There is little or no interpersonal physical violence;
> 6. There is little or no structural violence;
> 7. The society has the capacity to undergo change peacefully;
> 8. There is opportunity for idiosyncratic development. (67)

Fabbro (1978:67) is critical of past studies that have relied exclusively on a behavioral definition of peace (as merely the absence of war, criterion 1) because this leads to a "study of stable empires and states rather than an analysis of social structures and organizations which minimize both direct and structural violence." He consequently expands his criteria so as to preclude isolating cases of highly efficient oppression (see criterion 4) and to instead encompass those in which peace is accompanied by social justice and minimal social and economic inequalities (i.e., little or no structural violence, criterion 6).

The position adopted by Fabbro engages his project in a dilemma that is to some degree inherent in peace studies. He does not want to define "peaceful societies"—as an ideal type—so as to accommodate (and enshrine) anything that is less than desirable as a societal goal and objective. Although this is understandable and commendable from one perspective, it inevitably leads to a utopian delineation of the category of peaceful societies. But one cannot realistically expect to find utopia in the real world of human imperfection. A difficulty then emerges: there are no concrete examples of societies that entirely fulfill our highest aspirations for peace, nonviolence, equality, and social justice. This formulation of the category of peaceful societies is consequently conducive to the disappointing conclusion that there are no qualified candidates that might be included in it. In short, a concrete empirical study of utopia is a contradiction in terms. What can be located empirically is, at best, a rather pale reflection of utopian conditions.

Fabbro finesses this dilemma by maintaining his full list of eight criteria, as an ideal, but at the same time selecting societies for inclusion in his study that meet the lesser standard of fulfilling the first five criteria and manifesting at least partial conformance to the sixth. Criteria 1, 2, and 3 preclude inclusion of societies that have engaged in external or internal war. However, this standard is somewhat relaxed in practice insofar as a society that "at one time engaged in acts of violence against white colonisers" (Fabbro 1978:68) is selected on the grounds that this was a response to external stimuli rather than an indigenous characteristic. In addition, physical violence that does not take the form of organized warfare may not disqualify a society since criterion 5 allows for "*little or no* interpersonal physical violence" rather than none at all. Within these degrees of latitude, Fabbro then selects a set of societies for examination. These are "the first seven to meet these criteria [1 to 5] from a collection of possible societies drawn from various works which make references to societies lacking in warfare or other forms of violence (Benedict 1935; Davie 1929; Fromm 1973; Mead 1961; Otterbein 1970; Sipes 1973)."

In effect, Fabbro's selection procedure rounds up "the usual suspects" of the anthropological literature. For example, the !Kung are the subject of an ethnography entitled *The Harmless People* (Thomas 1959) and the Semai are the subject of a book subtitled *A Non-Violent People of Malaya* (Dentan 1968). Also included are the Mbuti, Siriono, and Copper Eskimo, of similar reputation, and two utopian-oriented societies ("established . . . with specific social structures designed to achieve definite goals"; Fabbro 1978:81) that have come into being in recent centuries: the Hutterites and the South Atlantic island society of Tristan da Cunha. Fabbro thus gathers together a collection of well-known cases of reputedly peaceful societies in order to determine what they may have in common.

In order to facilitate systematic comparison, Fabbro (1978:68) generates a list of fourteen areas of investigation that serve to guide his inquiry into the available sources for each society. The results of this comparison are summarized in a table (reproduced as table 2) that is keyed to his fourteen domains. The specific questions he poses are:

General
1. In what type of natural habitat does the society reside?

2. How is subsistence gained?
3. What is the prevailing ideology-cosmology-world view of the society? What are the core or paramount norms which act as the basis of regulation in social intercourse?
4. On what basis is the society integrated?

Direct Violence

5. What are the major characteristics of the child socialisation process?
6. Does physical violence exist? If so, what forms does it take?
7. What conflict resolution processes exist? Are they institution- alised or informal?

Structural Violence

8. Is there any division of labour and if so does it lead to specialisa- tion?
9. Are there any forms of socially coercive organisations which are capable of gaining compliance on the basis of power?
10. Are there any forms of hierarchy? If so are they exclusive or restrictive?
11. Who participates in decision-making concerning the society as a whole? Is such participation direct or mediated?
12. Who exercises social control?
13. What forms does social control take?
14. Are there any forms of discrimination which militate against an equal distribution of self-respect between individuals? (Fabbro 1978:68)

In his concluding discussion (following a concise review of the ethno- graphic data pertaining to each case), Fabbro summarizes his main findings. He had already noted earlier that the five traditional societies represent egal- itarian band societies in Fried's (1967) evolutionary typology, and they manifest the accompanying similarities linked to an absence of stratification and of notable material inequalities. However, the full complement of all seven peaceful societies inhabit dissimilar ecological niches and also lack a common hunting and gathering mode of production, so that the similarities they manifest with respect to the criteria of peacefulness cannot be attrib- uted to such ecological and economic factors. For example, two of the egal- itarian band societies are hunter-horticulturalists, so that there is no covari- ation between a hunter-gatherer economy (lacking agriculture) and peace, even when the comparison is restricted to traditional societies.

All the peaceful societies are characterized by "small face-to-face com- munities" that facilitate "egalitarian decision-making and social control processes" (Fabbro 1978:80). The traditional band societies uniformly experience seasonal fluctuations in group membership. The ease of individ- ual movement between groups facilitates a dissociative mode of conflict res- olution and undercuts social control systems based on "lineal leadership."

TABLE 2. **A Summary of Common Factors of Peaceful Societies**

Groups / Items	Semai	Siriono	Mbuti	Kung	Copper Eskimo	Hutterites	Tristan
1 Habitat	Tropical Rain Forest	Tropical Rain Forest	Tropical Rain Forest	Hot Desert	Arctic Tundra	Temperate Grassland	Temperate Grassland
2 Subsistence	Hunting-Gathering, Swiddening	Hunting-Gathering, Swiddening	Hunting-Gathering	Hunting-Gathering	Hunting, some Gathering	Mixed Agriculture	Mixed-Subsistence Agriculture
3 Cosmology	Ideational*	Ideational	Ideational	Ideational	Ideational	Ideational	Idealistic
4 Integration	Kinship & Interest	Kinship & Interest	Kinship & Interest	Kinship & Interest	Kinship & Interest	Interest & Kinship	Interest & Kinship
5 Socialisation	Permissive	Permissive	Permissive	Permissive	Permissive	Authoritarian	Authoritarian
6 Physical Violence	Little, Lethal	Little, non-lethal	Little, non-lethal	Little, non-lethal	Some, Lethal	Some, non-lethal	Some, non-lethal
7 Conflict Resolution	Individual & Group	Individual some Group	Individual & Group	Individual & Group	Individual some Group	Group	Individual
8 Division of Labour	Yes	Yes	Yes	Yes	Yes	Yes + Specialisation	Yes
9 Coercive Organisation	No	No	No	No	No	Perhaps	No
10 Hierarchy	Yes, non-restrictive for males	No	No	Yes, non-restrictive for males	No	Yes, non-restrictive for males	No
11 Decision	All adults	All adults	All adults	All adults	All adults	All male adults	All adults
12 Social Control	All	All	All	All	All	All male adults	All adults
13 Forms of Social Control	Usually psychic	Usually psychic	Usually psychic	Usually psychic	Psychic & Physical	Psychic	Psychic
14 Discrimination	Yes	Yes	Yes	Yes	Yes	Yes	Yes

* Used in Sorokin's (1962: 55–102, Vol. I) sense.

Source: Fabbro 1978:79–80, photographically reproduced by permission of the *Journal of Peace Research.*

In keeping with Fried's (1967) observations concerning egalitarian band societies, Fabbro (1978:80) confirms that the five traditional societies produce little surplus so that there is no basis for significant material inequalities or the development of leadership with coercive powers (i.e., powers based on the potential use of physical violence). However, he notes that the Hutterites produce a significant surplus without this leading to material inequality. What is produced is equitably distributed in all seven cases. He then concludes:

> The cases of Tristan da Cunha and the Hutterites demonstrate that it is possible for a society to produce a surplus and still retain a fairly egalitarian social structure which is not maintained by the use or threat of physical violence. (Fabbro 1978:81)

Thus attainment of peace is not confined to non-surplus-producing hunter-gatherers and hence to an unrecoverable evolutionary past. Moreover, Tristan and the Hutterites suggest that peaceful societies can be created in modern times. The main point Fabbro emphasizes in his conclusions is that his comparison shows that peace is not incompatible with social justice, equality, surplus production, and the historical present. The production of peace is thus an obtainable goal (81).

In a nutshell, Fabbro successfully shows that a peaceful human past is reproducible in the future by his ingenious juxtaposition of traditional band societies (representing an early evolutionary stage) and modern, created, utopian-oriented societies. He also shows that, by and large, an absence of structural violence can be seen to go hand in hand with an absence of direct violence in both types of societies. There is thus the implication that equality and social justice engender peace.

An inspection of Fabbro's summarizing table shows that virtually every attribute characteristic of the five band societies is found among one or the other of the two created societies—or, conversely, that what is characteristic of the created societies is practiced to at least some degree by one or two of the traditional societies (e.g., agriculture). But there is one striking exception to this general pattern of correspondences: socialization is uniformly "permissive" for all five hunter-gatherer societies but "authoritarian" for both the Hutterites and Tristan (see item 5). Fabbro directly takes up this troubling incongruity that runs counter to the underlying theme of his concluding observations (and to the interpretive key in his analysis of the comparative data).

> The differences in child-rearing practices between the traditional and created societies are open to a number of possible—and contradictory—explanations. Firstly, it could be argued that the latent "violence" of the created societies—the existence of surplus which does not produce material inequality—manifests itself in their authoritarian child-rearing methods. Alternatively,

their violent socialization ways are a product of their historical background. Their respective conceptions of human nature—natural carnality or willful behavior—are only a reflection of their Western European Christian origin which emphasizes control rather than development and as such directly influences the way they rear their children. Another possible explanation derives from their mode of subsistence. Both Tristan da Cunha and the Hutterites have sedentary farming lifestyles which are incompatible with independent adventurous personalities which permissive child socialization processes tend to create. (1978:81).

These explanations have an ad hoc, epicycle-like quality that renders them unconvincing. An alternative conclusion suggested by the comparative ethnographic data is that there is, in fact, no straightforward one-to-one relationship between violent forms of child socialization on one hand and adult physical violence (including war) on the other.

The critical issue that arises at this juncture is whether one form of violence begets another. Fabbro implicitly assumes this is the case, and he is thus led to the expectation that societies that entirely lack war will also lack other forms of physical violence (including physical punishment of children). However, this expectation is not borne out by the ethnographic data Fabbro presents. As Fabbro goes over each case, he briefly records the forms of physical violence that are ethnographically reported to be present. These can readily be summarized (although Fabbro does not himself do so). Four of the seven societies employ some degree of physical punishment of children as a component of socialization (the Mbuti, Copper Eskimo, Hutterites, and Tristan), with a more extensive reliance on this among the two created societies. In the case of Tristan, physical punishment increases in severity as the age of the child increases.

> Paradoxically it is through threats or acts of physical punishment that children are inculcated with the importance of non-violent behavior. (Loudon 1970:307, cited in Fabbro 1978:78)

Among adults, Fabbro notes that physical violence between husband and wife is reported for three of the seven societies (the Mbuti, Copper Eskimo, and Tristan). In the case of the Siriono, fighting between adult women is not uncommon.

> Males seldom express direct aggression against other males. Neither do males beat their wives, but there are apparently quarrels among women, frequently culminating in fighting with digging sticks. (Fabbro 1978:71)

In another context, Fabbro also indicates that Siriono men engage in supervised wrestling matches as a form of conflict resolution. Fighting between adult males is reported to be virtually absent in two cases (the

Hutterites and Tristan), rare in four cases (the Semai; Siriono, excepting wrestling; Mbuti; and !Kung), and somewhat more prevalent in one case (the Copper Eskimo). Homicide is said to be "quite frequent" among the Copper Eskimo, rare among the Semai and !Kung, and not noted for the Siriono, Mbuti, Hutterites, and Tristan (see item 6 in Fabbro's summary table). War and other forms of collective violence are not mentioned (with the exception of Siriono acts of violence against colonists) and would be assumed to be absent insofar as these societies are said to meet the first three criteria of peacefulness that preclude war.[1] (However, some qualifications with respect to Fabbro's assessments are introduced further along; see also note 1.)

It must be noted here, as an aside, that these findings are certainly disappointing from the standpoint of the idealistic, utopian expectations created by Fabbro at the outset. Having selected seven societies that are reputedly among the most peaceful ones known (out of a potential pool of about 5,000), and having been led to expect that they meet a criterion of "little or no interpersonal physical violence," we then find instances of harsh physical disciplining of children, violence between spouses, women fighting each other with digging sticks, and men committing homicide. It is perhaps especially disappointing that in the one society where there is reportedly no physical punishment of children, nor spousal abuse, nor male-male homicide, women commonly fight among themselves with heavy implements. However, the source of these understandable disappointments is clearly the unrealistically high expectations that are intrinsic to an effort to locate concrete instances of utopia in the real world. It is arguably somewhat unfair to expect other societies to exemplify our highest aspirations (which we ourselves cannot meet) and to then fault them and be disappointed in them when they invariably come up short.[2] Given these pitfalls, one can understand the paucity of peace studies of this kind (noted earlier). Nevertheless, there is much to be learned from the kind of comparative analysis of peaceful (or warless) societies that Fabbro pioneers, even though the inquiry may be discomforting in some respects. The issue is too important to limit ourselves only to knowledge that makes us feel good, and to consequently fail to consider all the relevant data.

There is, unfortunately, further disappointment in store. This arises from a reevaluation of the levels of interpersonal violence in these societies, based on both a reconsideration of the original sources employed by Fabbro and an examination of additional sources, including those published in the twenty years since Fabbro's article was written.[3] These data will be introduced further along. At this juncture I am primarily concerned to examine the relationship between the data Fabbro presents and the conclusions he draws.

The striking conclusion suggested by the comparative ethnographic data Fabbro assembles is that societies lacking war are not necessarily nonviolent in other ways and consequently are not invariably "peaceful" in this expanded sense of the term. Thus societies initially selected on the grounds that they were warless may fail to entirely fulfill the additional criterion of "little or no interpersonal physical violence." While this point runs counter to Fabbro's expectations and is downplayed, it emerges quite clearly from his data. They do not show that there is a strong pattern of covariation between one form of violence and another. Thus female physical violence may occur in relative isolation, as among the Siriono. Although it is counterintuitive that Siriono women frequently come to blows in their quarrels with each other while they engage in "little or no physical punishment of children," this is indeed what Fabbro (1978:185) reports. Similarly, his data show that homicide and fighting among adult males are virtually absent in the two cases where the physical punishment of children is most severe (Tristan and the Hutterites). There is an inverse rather than one-to-one relationship between this "authoritarian" socialization (present) and lethal violence (absent) (see items 5 and 6 of the summary table). One can conclude that the attainment of societal peace in the form of an absence of war is not contingent upon an absence of other forms of physical violence. Achieving utopian levels of human perfection is fortunately not a prerequisite for peace (in this sense).

These conclusions are significant for an inquiry into the origin of war because the assumption that one form of violence begets another implies a cumulative process of origination. A null hypothesis based on this assumption of linkage between forms of violence could be formulated as follows: that societies with frequent external war would tend to have frequent internal war; that societies with frequent internal war would tend to have a high frequency of feud; that societies with frequent feud would tend to have a high incidence of individual homicides; that societies with a high rate of individual homicides would tend to have a high frequency of dyadic (one-on-one) fighting between adult men; that societies with a high frequency of adult male fighting would tend to have a high frequency of spousal violence; that societies with a high frequency of spousal violence would tend to have a high frequency of adult female fighting; that societies with frequent female fighting would tend to employ physical punishment of children as a means of socialization. This hypothesis would be supported if the forms of violence found in a cross-cultural sample of societies were Guttman-scaleable (either in this posited order or in some other order). This would confirm that violence begets violence and is cumulative. War would then be found to have its roots in harsh child socialization and/or spousal violence (i.e., violence within the nuclear or extended family context). But it is evident both from the data Fabbro assembles and from other studies that no such consistent pattern of linkages between forms of violence obtains. Knauft's (1987) study "Reconsidering Violence in Simple Human Societies" is particularly important with respect to this issue and to the more general question of the evolution of violence (further considered in Knauft 1991).

Knauft is concerned to distinguish the patterns of violence that are characteristic of "simple foraging and non-intensive foraging/horticultural societies" from those of sedentary agricultural societies with more developed forms of social and political organization (1987:457). Simple societies are decentralized, "lack recognizable leadership roles and status differentials among adult men," and manifest pervasive egalitarianism and communal food-sharing (Knauft 1991:392–93). Although the sociopolitical attributes are diagnostic, simple societies also tend to be characterized by an absence of:

> Population densities greater than 2–3 per km², year-round residence at a single site, pronounced food storage (Testart 1982), substantial delayed-return reciprocity systems (Woodburn 1980, 1982, 1988), substantial material wealth, and intensive reliance upon domesticated animals or fishing. (392)

The ethnographic cases Knauft focuses on as examples include the !Kung, Semai, Mbuti, and Central Eskimo (encompassing the Copper Eskimo) as well as the Hadza and Gebusi. Thus Knauft (1987) provides an independent analytic appraisal of violence in four of the five traditional band societies in Fabbro's category of Peaceful Societies. This will facilitate a more fine-grained assessment of the incidence of lethal interpersonal violence in these ethnographic cases, in keeping with the investigative agenda for the comparative analysis of peaceful societies mapped out by Fabbro.

Homicide rates in simple foraging societies are considerably higher than those reported for agricultural societies with more developed forms of sociopolitical organizations. The !Kung homicide rate, calculated in terms of an inclusive fifty-year period, is 29.3 per 100,000 per annum, while the earlier 1920–55 segment of this time period that is more indicative of indigenous (precolonial) conditions evidenced a rate of 41.9 per 100,000 per annum (Lee 1979:398, cited in Knauft 1987:458). Although Dentan (1978:98) notes that there were only two documented homicides among the Semai between 1955 and 1977, Knauft (1987:458) points out that this indicates a rate of 30.3 per 100,000 per annum for the study population of 300. A similar calculation could be made for the Mbuti, who are reported to execute sorcerers as well as incorrigible thieves and those who do not appropriately participate in the important *molimo* ceremonies (Turnbull 1965:186, 190, 236; cited in Otterbein 1986:52). If only one instance of each of these types of homicides occurred during the past thirty years within the band of 252 persons that comprised Turnbull's study population, this would yield a rate of 39.7 per 100,000 per annum. Among the Copper Eskimo,

Rasmussen (1932:17) conducted a survey of the adult men of one community and found that 60% (9/15) had committed one or more murders of adults and an additional 13% (2/15) had attempted killings without success. He concludes, "There was not a single grown man who had not been involved in a killing in some way or another." (Knauft 1987:458)

This parallels Knauft's (1985:132) finding that 64.7 percent (11/17) of a sample of Gebusi men over thirty-five years of age had committed homicide (e.g., served as primary executioner of a sorcerer). The overall Copper Eskimo homicide rate (which isn't provided by Rasmussen) therefore is very likely to be of the same order of magnitude as the Gebusi homicide rate (for 1963–82) of 419 per 100,000 per year. Taken together, these data indicate a strikingly bimodal distribution of homicide rates for simple societies, viz., 30 to 42 per 100,000 per annum for the !Kung, Mbuti, and Semai and ten times this rate for the Copper Eskimo and Gebusi.[4] In contrast, homicide rates for a sample of African agricultural societies cluster in the 4.0 to 6.0 per 100,000 per annum range (Knauft 1987:458; Lee 1979:398).[5] It is clear that homicide rates are considerably higher in simple foraging societies than in some sedentary agricultural societies with more developed forms of sociopolitical organization.

Fabbro's Peaceful Societies thus are not characterized by a comparatively low incidence of lethal interpersonal violence (and the Copper Eskimo are not an exception in this respect, as he imagined). More specifically, Fabbro's expectation that warless societies would have "little or no" homicide (item 6) is disconfirmed. The critical feature that distinguishes warless from warlike societies therefore cannot be a low incidence of homicide. This in turn casts doubt on the conventional wisdom that one form of violence begets another, as applied to the origin of war, since it is evident that a high homicide rate does not engender a warlike society. The Gebusi case, discussed in the introduction, shows that a very high homicide rate does not even lead to feud in which the principle of social substitution and the attendant concepts of injury to the group and group liability are applied. These data are conducive to a more general conclusion: *war is not related to violence as simply more of the same, but instead entails the deployment of violence in accordance with a distinctive logic, contingent upon concepts rooted in the sociocultural system.* Moreover, the absence of a relationship between war and interpersonal physical violence is expectable given the instrumental and collective nature of war.

The lack of covariation between low homicide rates and the absence of warfare undercuts the logic of seeking to account for the character of peaceful (or warless) societies through recourse to child socialization practices. It would be difficult to envision the mechanisms by which the indulgent, affectionate, permissive, and nonauthoritarian child-rearing practices characteristic of the five traditional band societies and the Gebusi might contribute to an absence of war if they also covary with exceptionally high homicide rates. Knauft (1987:473–75) details the difficulties that the ethnographic data on the !Kung, Semai, Central Eskimo, and Gebusi pose for theories that attempt to link child socialization to the incidence of lethal violence.[6] This amplifies the point noted earlier with regard to Fabbro's compilation, which shows that "permissive" socialization does not covary with an absence (or lesser degree) of lethal interpersonal violence.

Although homicide rates are comparatively high in Fabbro's selected sample of peaceful societies, this does not necessarily mean that interpersonal violence is invariably pervasive. Only one homicide every fifteen to twenty years within a social universe of 150 persons (residing in a number of small, neighboring groups) yields a homicide rate of 33.3 to 44.4 per 100,000 per annum, roughly comparable to the rates that prevail among the !Kung, Semai, Mbuti, and Siriono. Thus the general tenor of daily social relations observed by the ethnographer can readily be a strongly positive one of friendship, camaraderie, and communal sharing that is very rarely disrupted by argument or physical fighting (see Knauft 1987:476). Alternatively, altercations and outbursts of ill-feeling may be commonplace. The !Kung, Semai, Mbuti, Siriono, and Copper Eskimo do not conform to a monolithic pattern in terms of the levels of interpersonal conflict and violence that are observable on a day-to-day basis.

A more detailed and comprehensive review of the available data on physical violence and conflict in these Peaceful Societies is warranted given the absence of "common features" anticipated by Fabbro. This will, at the same time, provide a context in which Fabbro's findings can be updated by consideration of ethnographic reports published since his mid-1970s assessment of interpersonal violence in these five traditional band societies. Moreover, Knauft's (1987) analysis of male-male interpersonal violence in simple societies needs to be supplemented by consideration of male-female and female-female physical violence. This in turn raises questions concerning the extent to which all of Knauft's simple societies conform to the single ideal type he proposes in which there is "a high ratio of lethal violence to aggression despite a low overall incidence of aggression" (1987:459).

In the Semai case quarrels are reportedly "uncommon" and physical violence "very rare" (Dentan 1979:57). But the picture is quite different among the Siriono, where "quarreling and wrangling are ubiquitous. Hardly a day passes among them when a dispute of some kind does not break out" (Holmberg 1969:153). Quarrels not uncommonly result in "minor assaults," which among men take the form of wrestling or tussling (without punching) (152). Spouses quarrel frequently. Mild quarrels entail verbal disparagement and name-calling. If a man's anger intensifies, he may "smash one of [his wife's] pots . . . tear her hammock to shreds, chase her out of the house with a firebrand, or even turn his anger against himself and break his bow and arrows. He never beats her, however" (127–28).

During Siriono drinking feasts (of which there are about a dozen a year), men commonly insult and pick fights with each other. These take the form of wrestling matches in which a man tries to throw his opponent to the ground repeatedly.

> Since the contestants are usually so drunk that they cannot stand up, these wrestling matches frequently terminate with both of them passed out on the floor, much to the merriment of the spectators. (Holmberg 1969:95)

These fights are often between in-laws. The women, who do not participate in the drinking, are upset to see their husband and brother, or husband and father, fighting. The women cry and attempt to stop these fights, whereupon they are "not infrequently struck forcibly by their husbands" (95).

In Holmberg's account, drinking feasts are represented as a context in which the expression of anger and ill-feeling between individuals is both facilitated and contained. Subjects of contention are aired and "the disputes are settled by wrestling matches, and are usually forgotten after the period of drunkenness is over" (1969:156). The potential for serious injury is reduced by the constraint of rules limiting the acceptable forms of fighting and by the presence of numerous onlookers. However, injuries are sometimes incurred when wrestlers fall into cooking fires, and ill-feeling may then carry over beyond the festive context (96). In addition, one of the two homicides Holmberg reports entailed a man shooting and killing his wife at a drinking feast (see note 4). Leaving aside these exceptions, Holmberg argues that the expression of antagonism in physical violence is both constrained within the context of drinking feasts and also largely confined to that context (156–57). Thus men may strike their wives during such feasts but not otherwise. Likewise, although quarrels leading to "minor assaults" between men are not uncommon, fighting with weapons is "rare," and no male-male homicides (i.e., male killing of a male) were recollected going as far back as fifteen to twenty years before study.

The fighting that occurs between Siriono women contrasts with supervised male wrestling in that implements are employed as weapons and an effort is made to time an attack so as to preclude intervention that could limit its severity. Characteristically, female fighting entails a woman attacking a cowife with a digging stick or spindle at a time when their common husband is absent and thus cannot interfere (Holmberg 1969:127). The aggressor is typically an aging first wife who is being sexually displaced by a younger wife. Access to critical resources is at stake since the wife or wives "with whom the husband most frequently has sex relations are the ones who generally get the most to eat" (126). The senior wife thus seeks to maintain her "dominance in the family" and her "economic rights" through recourse to physical violence and intimidation (126–27). The attack entails utilization of implements and timing conducive to the infliction of injury. This is consistent with instrumental objectives that go beyond the mere expression of ill-feeling or jealousy.

The !Kung are intermediate between the nonviolent Semai and the frequently quarreling Siriono in terms of levels of interpersonal conflict and violence, but closer to the Siriono end of this range of variation. Lee (1979:370) recorded 58 conflicts (verbal and/or physical) during a three-year period among a study population that varied between 379 and 457 persons. Comparatively, Holmberg recorded 75 conflicts (excluding those that took place at drinking feasts) in sixteen months among a study population that varied from 325 (at one location) to 152 (at another). However, Holmberg's data on disputes pertain almost entirely to the eight months he resided with two bands (of 99 and 58 persons) that lived well-removed from the Bolivian government Indian school and mixed Bolivian-Indian village where he initiated language study and preliminary ethnographic inquiry. Thus Holmberg recorded approximately one noteworthy dispute every three days in this context while Lee recorded one conflict every nineteen days (within a larger study population). While neither ethnographic account claims an exhaustive tally, these figures are nevertheless useful in showing that interpersonal conflict is rather commonplace and readily observed within Fabbro's Peaceful Societies. While the Siriono are depicted as constantly "wrangling," the !Kung are described as rather argumentative (Lee 1979:372). The verbally aggressive "ribbing" of others is also said to be a regular feature of daily interaction.

Among the !Kung, 58.6 percent (34/58) of the recorded conflicts proceeded beyond the verbal level to physical fighting. These included 11 instances in which a male attacked a male, 14 in which a male attacked a female, 1 in which a female attacked a male, and 8 in which a female attacked a female (Lee 1979:377). In all, 11 of the 15 male-female fights involved spouses, with husbands initiating these fights by a ratio of 10 to 1. "Despite the higher frequency of male-initiated attacks, women fought fiercely and often gave as good or better than they got" (377).

Allegations of adultery were a factor in 5 of 8 female-female fights but only 2 of 14 male-female and 2 of 11 male-male fights. The causes of the remaining conflicts were not readily apparent. Comparatively, only 19 of the 75 altercations Holmberg recorded were "over questions of sex," and these also were almost entirely between women (including cowives) and between spouses rather than between men (1969:156). However, the majority of the Siriono disputes (44 of 75) were over food and entailed allegations of failure to share, hoarding, hiding, improperly distributing, or stealing food (154–55). These allegations were predominantly between members of the same uxorilocal extended family (composed of a mother, her daughter(s), and the husbands of these women), this being the unit within which food is shared. In contrast, Lee (1979:201) sees a lapse in the usual sharing of mongongo nuts between the families of a camp as a result, rather than a cause, of conflict: "When conflict breaks out, sharing breaks down." On the other hand, stinginess or impropriety in game distribution is sometimes alleged and may itself be a source of ill-feeling (247). In societies where food-sharing is a central value, slights in sharing both express and exacerbate disruptions in social relations.

All of the physical fights that occurred among the !Kung during Lee's three-year fieldwork period were limited conflicts that did not involve recourse to deadly weapons (poisoned arrows and spears). At this restrained level of conflict, wrestling combined with punching predominates and implements (a stick or riding crop) were employed in only 6 of the 34 fights. Injuries were confined to minor cuts and scratches in 32 of the 34 cases (1979:377). However, fights with deadly weapons occurred in earlier times, and Lee collected accounts of 37 such conflicts that took place between 1920 and 1955. These fights resulted in 22 fatalities that provide the basis for calculation of the homicide rate (discussed earlier).

A substantial proportion of these homicides occurred in conjunction with efforts to kill individuals who were the perpetrators of prior homicides. Specifically, 4 of the 22 instances were executions of a killer, while 4 participants and a bystander were also killed in the effort to carry out these executions. In all, 9 of the 22 homicides were capital punishment–related, 4 were attributable to adultery, and 4 occurred in general brawls (including the death of one bystander). One of these brawls arose out of a dispute over which of two young men would marry a young woman, while the causes of the others are not reported. One of the 5 remaining homicides arose out of a minor quarrel over the collection of bush foods, while the causes of the others are not determinable from Lee's (1979:382–400) extensive treatment of the subject. He emphasizes the noninstrumental character of !Kung fighting and the fact that

> In the majority of cases *the victim was not a principal in the verbal conflict that led up to the actual killing with arrow or spear.* In only 8 of 18 cases on which I have data was the victim a principal in the previous argument. In 10 other killings, the victim was struck more or less at random: in 3 cases a man came to the aid of another and was killed; in 4 cases a peacemaker was fatally wounded; and 3 victims (2 of them women) were bystanders. (392; italics in original)

These data show that a fight with deadly weapons between principals generates the involvement of a number of other people as peacemakers, defenders, and bystanders, all of whom are evidently within a few arm's lengths of the principal combatants. Side fights may also develop between those trying to aid or separate the opposed principals and a kind of general melee thus ensues. A somewhat similar pattern of brawls is described for the Mbuti, although deadly weapons are eschewed and no fatalities are reported.

Among the Mbuti, as among the Siriono, quarrels and trivial disputes are a feature of everyday life.

> A headache, a hungry stomach, a painful leg, a leaking hut or a damp forest—almost any kind of discomfort is likely to make an Mbuti irritable, and he will pick a quarrel with ease and readiness so that he can make his heart feel better, as they say. It is known to be bad to keep things concealed, so there is no particular disgrace in voicing suspicions and revealing antagonisms, particularly if it is done quietly. Few, however, managed to make their heart feel better without creating a great deal of noise and making everyone else feel considerably worse. Most such disputes, and there were likely to be several every day, died as they began, in complete indecision. (Turnbull 1965:212)

In all, Turnbull recorded the details of 124 noteworthy disputes over a fourteen-month period within a study population of 252 persons, or about one every three and a half days (215,326). Of the 124 disputes, a representative sample of 34 are described in some detail (191–214; see also Turnbull 1961:108–26), and these provide a basis for enumerating the general features of interpersonal conflict in Mbuti society that follow. Fifteen of the 34 disputes (or 44 percent) progressed from a verbal to a physical altercation. In 10 of these instances the physical violence was limited to the principals alone, while in the other 5 cases, 2, 3, 4, or 5 pairs of individuals were involved. The use of implements is rare in single-dyad conflicts (1 in 10 cases), but stout sticks (four inches thick and three feet long) or firewood logs are typically employed in multiple dyad conflicts (4 or 5 cases). An escalation in the number of participants and in the degree of severity thus go hand in hand. However, restraint is enjoined even in these instances:

> It is perfectly proper to hit someone with anything wooden; it is not at all proper to draw blood, nor to hit anyone on the forehead, which is considered a dangerous spot. In the frequent marital disputes, any man who hits his wife on the head or in the face promptly loses any sympathy he might have had from his fellows. A dispute that follows such lines almost invariably ends with an elder, male or female, physically interposing himself between the disputants, who then revert to hurling abuse which

becomes more and more exaggerated until it is so humorous that even they join in the laughter. Alternatively they may lapse into a sulk, which will last for the rest of the day and through the evening, but will be gone in ample time for the next day's hunt to take place as though nothing had happened. (Turnbull 1965:189)

It is also noteworthy that intervention by third parties is progressively more likely as one moves from verbal disputes (5 of 19 cases) to physical altercations (8 of 15 cases) and is typical of physical conflict in which implements (logs) are employed (4 of 5 cases), even when appropriate restraint is practiced. This intervention may be by elders, seniors, kin, neighbors, "clowns" (1965:182), or the camp as a whole.

In all, there were 21 dyads involved in 14 of the 15 physical conflicts (excluding one unusual melee in which fighting broke out between 5 young men and their respective girlfriends over male reluctance to wed; Turnbull 1965:205). Six of these sets of combatants were pairs of females, with two cases entailing implements. Ten conflicts were between a male and a female, with logs used in three. Six of these episodes were spousal violence, and in all six the husband initiated the physical violence. In one case the wife retaliated by hitting her husband with a log; otherwise no implements were used in spousal conflict. In 2 of 4 cases of nonspousal male-female violence the female initiated the attack and employed a log. In one of these instances an old widow attacked a young man for slapping his wife too hard, hitting him over the back with a burning log. (Most spousal violence is between teenage newlyweds who "beat each other." If this "gets too severe then the older women intervene, slapping both boys and girls soundly" [201].) In the remaining 2 of 4 cases of nonspousal male-female violence a male struck a female, without an implement. Thus firewood logs are used only by females in male-female conflicts (3 of 10 cases) and never by males. The only conflict that went beyond the conventional limits of restraint noted above was a fight between a married woman and a young girl whom she accused of adultery. The wife who initiated the assault lost three teeth, so that both blows to the face and blood loss were clearly in evidence (although there is no mention of the use of logs; 1965:206). Wrestling, punching, slapping, kicking, biting, and scratching are all mentioned, with "tooth and nail" fighting evidently restricted to female-female conflicts. Turnbull describes several instances where deadly weapons (spears) were brandished or used threateningly (1961:110, 122), but in none of these instances were they used to strike a blow. In one case the threat led to a fight, but one in which only stout sticks were actually employed.

Turnbull (1965:216) categorizes the distribution of his 124 disputes in terms of issues as follows: food, 67; sex, 37; Bantu village relations, 11; theft, 5; territory, 4. There are "innumerable petty squabbles over division of food" and many "trivial domestic disagreements" (197, 201) in which complaints over male failure to procure game, flawed female cooking, and the like are voiced. Discontent over individual labor contributions and the degree of participation in collective net hunting is also commonly expressed. Within the realm of sexual behavior there is considerable latitude both in the Mbuti case and in the other Peaceful Societies considered here. Generally there are sexual relations outside of marriage that are either permitted or tacitly accepted (Holmberg 1969:165–69; Lee 1979:373–75; Balikci 1970:160–61). Among the Mbuti, discreet adultery and premarital fornication are not sources of conflict, but the same behaviors ignite disputes when public fondling occurs, when fornicating youths awaken parents, or when a woman flaunts her adulterous liaison in the presence of her lover's wife. Only 2 of 34 Mbuti conflicts involved adultery (one between spouses and one between a wife and her younger sexual rival). The other main area of difficulty in this category ("sex" issues) involves male procrastination and/or reluctance to wed a lover, or a husband's neglect of one of multiple wives. Other less prominent sources of dispute are occasional thefts of food or implements and a few conflicts over trespass between band sections. Turnbull (1965:210, 216) also includes several spousal disagreements concerning decisions to reside with one group rather than another under his category of disputes related to territory.

There are similarities between the Siriono, Mbuti, and to a somewhat lesser extent, the !Kung, in the commonplace occurrence of low-level physical violence (in which lethal weapons are eschewed and no serious injuries result). These are also three of the four ethnographic cases in which homicide rates are in the 30 to 53 per 100,000 per annum range. The other half of the bimodal distribution of homicide rates for simple societies is represented by the Copper Eskimo and Gebusi (in the 400 per 100,000 per annum range), and these cases present a significantly different pattern with respect to interpersonal violence. Among the Gebusi, violence is infrequent, short-lived, often extreme in form, and subsequently downplayed or ignored (Knauft 1987:475). There were only three instances over a twenty-two-month period in which a dispute engendered open antagonism between men within a village of 46 persons, and in only one of these three cases did the antagonists come to blows (Knauft 1985:73–75, 271). Spousal violence, which takes the form of asymmetrical wife-beating, is somewhat more frequent (but unquantified) while female fighting is unreported (Knauft 1985:32; Cantrell n.d.).

On a day-to-day and week-to-week basis, anger and aggressiveness are strikingly absent; aggression is rare, even though it is extremely violent when it does occur. Homicide tends to occur in a highly delimited and socially sanctioned context: The attribution of sorcery following the sickness death of someone in the community. (Knauft 1985:475)

The Copper Eskimo and other Central Eskimo groups are similar to the Gebusi in that disputes are comparatively infrequent but tend to be associated with more extreme violence when they do occur. This is well illustrated by Balikci's account of a conflict between two Netsilik[7] women that arose over a trivial incident.[8]

> Innakatar was an elderly woman with a little adopted girl and a grown-up son who was living as a second husband with a younger woman named Itiptaq in an adjoining igloo. One day Innakatar's little daughter pissed on Itiptaq's bed, wetting the sleeping skins. Itiptaq scolded the girl, who started crying. Her mother didn't like this and started a quarrel with the younger woman. Itiptaq lost her temper and Innakatar answered: "Don't scold my little girl, just come and fight with me." They started hitting each other on the face, just like men. Soon cuts and blood covered their faces and they fought noiselessly on. After a while Itiptaq said: "You are getting in a bad shape, bleeding a lot, I don't want to hit you any more" (meaning that Itiptaq was getting scared and in pain and wanted to find a way to give up the fight). Innakatar, feeling strong, answered: "If I feel anything I will give up, just hit me a few more times." Innakatar was the obvious winner, although both of them were badly cut up around the face. (1970:173)

In this type of fighting, which is also (and more typically) practiced by men, an individual accepts his or her antagonist's "best shot" in the form of a single closed-fist blow to the face (directed toward the temple), and then delivers one's own "best shot" in return. The exchange of blows continues until one of the antagonists elects not to retaliate for the last blow received (186).

Men also engage in song duels in which each contestant derides his opponent before the assembled community in a lengthy composition that contains a litany of "various accusations of incest, bestiality, murder, avarice, adultery, failure at hunting, being henpecked, lack of manly strength, etc." (186). Public mockery and derision of others was also practiced informally on a regular basis. While ill-feeling was aired and given controlled cathartic expression by these means, there was also the possibility that the target of repeated acts of derision would develop deepseated resentment, anger, and lasting hatred. This might then subsequently be expressed in homicide (Rasmussen 1932:20–21; Balikci 1970:147, 169–71, 174). Balikci (1970:179–80) discusses seven murders that took place in the 1950s in which the homicide victim was killed from behind (six cases) or shot in his sleep (one case) as a preplanned endeavor. The motives included wife-stealing as well as resentment of mockery or bullying. The man shot in his sleep was killed by his wife, who desired to leave him. In contrast, Rasmussen (1932:18) describes the spontaneous killings of an earlier era in which "a mere trifling incident often gives rise to a fight, which is nearly always to the death." However, both ethnographers emphasize the potential for the unexpected occurrence of lethal violence, whether preplanned or spontaneous. Apart from the controlled exchange of blows described above, fighting between men evidently tended to entail recourse to lethal weapons (often knives) and was carried out with lethal intent. This presupposes that such fighting could not have been frequent. In other words, the Copper Eskimos conform to the pattern identified by Knauft (1987) in which day-to-day tranquillity is punctuated by widely spaced episodes of extreme violence.

Briggs (1970, 1982) emphasizes the tranquil side of Central Eskimo social life and argues that individuals "manifest a horror not only of killing but also of much milder forms of aggression, such as striking a person or even shouting" (1982:115, also cited in Knauft 1987:475). This fear of low-level aggression would be understandable if there is a pattern whereby trivial conflicts may rapidly escalate to a homicidal conclusion. Unfortunately, there is no quantification of the frequency of conflict and violence compared to that available for the other societies under consideration. Balikci (1970:170) does note that "repeated wife beatings and jealousies and hatreds involving brothers and cousins seem to have been numerous." However, these jealousies and hatreds were "often concealed for long periods" (171). Thus, while the frequency of spousal violence may not differ greatly from that of Fabbro's other Peaceful Societies, the frequency of physical violence between men, between women, and between men and women not related by marriage appears to be significantly lower among the Copper Eskimo, as among the Gebusi.

Knauft (1987) formulates a single ideal type in order to capture the distinctive form and character of violence in egalitarian "simple societies." He argues (476) that the pattern delineated is applicable to the Gebusi, Central Eskimo, Semai, !Kung, "probably" the Hadza, and "possibly" the Mbuti and Waorani. On the contrary, I have argued that there is considerable variation in patterns of violence in these kinds of societies. I would locate the Siriono and Mbuti at one end of the spectrum of variation and the Gebusi and Central Eskimo at the other, with the !Kung intermediate, but considerably closer to the Siriono-Mbuti pattern. In these first three ethnographic cases, verbal disputes and minor assaults are a commonplace occurrence, but these do not so often progress to more severe forms of physical violence and only infrequently escalate further, entailing use of weapons. The contrasting pattern is characterized by a virtual absence of minor assaults (apart from regulated and constrained contestlike fighting) since trivial conflicts have the potential to escalate into lethal violence or to be expressed in sorcery accusations and executions. Frequent low-level violence is not present (with the possible exception of spousal conflicts). I have also suggested that these two patterns covary with a bimodal distribution of homicide rates, which are high in comparative (cross-cultural) terms for all these cases, but nevertheless vary by a tenfold difference between them. The Siriono, Mbuti, !Kung, Gebusi, and Copper Eskimo cases are consistent with this hypothesized covariation, but the Semai constitute an exception. They are characterized by infrequent conflict (like the Copper Eskimo and Gebusi), but manifest a lower homicide rate, consistent with the range applicable to the societies that have frequent low-level violence (the Siriono, !Kung, and Mbuti). Nevertheless, the applicability of this hypothesized covariation to five of six cases is sufficient to encourage further exploration of the posited connection within a wider sample in the future. However, my central objective here is not to account for differences in homicide rates but to characterize interpersonal violence in Fabbro's sample of Peaceful Societies. In effect, I am trying to provide a detailed, comprehensive, and updated answer to item 6 of Fabbro's (1978:182) list of questions: "Does physical violence exist? If so, what forms does it take?" Knauft (1987) has likewise sought to characterize violence in many of these same societies and has made a significant contribution to answering this important question. I seek to extend his efforts by subdividing his broad ideal type into several variants (and also attempting to link these subtypes to differences in homicide rates). However, Fabbro's question continues to be the central focus of my inquiry.

It is evident that violence does indeed exist in Fabbro's Peaceful Societies, that is, in a sample of societies selected on the grounds that they have not participated in warfare. A reappraisal, based on both new sources (published since Fabbro's 1978 article) and a reexamination of the original sources Fabbro employs, leads to the conclusion that the five traditional egalitarian band societies do not for the most part fulfill Fabbro's (1978:180) utopian criterion of "little or no interpersonal physical violence." Most notably, they all manifest comparatively high homicide rates. With the exception of the nonviolent Semai, less extreme forms of interpersonal physical violence are also a regular occurrence between men, between women, and between men and women in these societies (although male-female physical violence is reportedly limited to the context of drinking feasts among the Siriono). When numerical data are available, these indicate that violence between males and females is the most prevalent of the three types (44 and 48 percent of incidents of physical violence among the !Kung and Mbuti, respectively). The bulk of cross-gender violence is between spouses (60 percent for Mbuti, 73 percent for !Kung). It is typically initiated by the husband (often as an escalation of a verbal quarrel) but then becomes reciprocal. Bare-handed blows (e.g., slaps) are typical and the use of implements is comparatively infrequent (though reported for both genders). The violence tends to be restrained in level of intensity, although expressive in character, and injuries are not noted. Moreover, very few spousal homicides are reported in sample data. Only one of twenty-two !Kung homicides involved spouses (with a man killing his wife for adultery). Only one of seven circa 1950s Netsilik Eskimo homicides was spousal (with a woman killing her husband). However, one of two Siriono homicides was spousal (with a man killing his wife). Nearly all homicides involve males killing males (although two !Kung women were killed as bystanders in male conflicts and both Siriono homicides involved female victims).

While male-female (typically spousal) conflicts are the most prevalent variety of interpersonal violence (excepting the Siriono), fighting between men is only a little more frequent than fighting between women. Female fights account for 24 percent of incidents of physical violence among both the Mbuti and !Kung while male fights account for 29 and 32 percent, respectively. Female fighting is reported to be particularly prevalent among the Siriono and also occurs among the Netsilik. Siriono female fighting between cowives is more instrumental than expressive and is carried out with the intent to inflict injury in order to secure economic position (i.e., conjugal provisioning). The only Mbuti fight (of thirty-four in all) that resulted in noteworthy injuries was between two women (over the flaunting of adultery) and three of five female-female Mbuti fights entailed either use of implements (two instances) or notable injuries (one instance). Less than half of Mbuti fights between women would be classified as minor conflicts, and in other cases (e.g., the Siriono) "minor assault" is unreported for women, although commonplace among men.

Excepting the Netsilik, rule-governed contestlike combat between women is also absent. Thus the physical violence that does occur between women is likely to be disproportionately of the more severe variety. Although no instances of female-female homicides are reported in these five societies, they have been noted in other band societies and in other societies more generally (see Lee 1979:388 for a comparison of the percentages of female killers and female victims in a number of different societies). The Ingalik and Yahgan (both discussed in the next chapter) illustrate the pattern of female killing in those band societies in which it occurs. Among the Yahgan, there is fighting between cowives, similar to that reported for the Siriono, and "it often happens that a young and beautiful wife has to pay with her life for the preference with which she is treated by the common husband" (Bové 1884:191). Similarly, an Ingalik woman "very rarely commits a murder but she may do it out of jealousy" (Osgood 1958:54). This pattern of killing sexual rivals is consistent with the fact that adultery (or the flaunting of adultery) is the cause of much nonlethal female fighting in the band societies under consideration (e.g., 63 percent of female-female fights among the !Kung).

In contrast, adultery, sexual rivalry, and jealousy are much less frequently a source of male-male fighting and of male-male homicide,
although the Central Eskimo are an exception. Among the !Kung, only
two of eleven male-male fights concerned adultery, and in the Mbuti case
none were attributable to adultery. The Siriono are very similar to the
Mbuti. Adultery and sexual rivalry also lead to conflict that is almost
exclusively between women and between spouses, rather than between
men. The Central Eskimo present an unusual configuration of features
that is concisely described by Balikci (1970:161).

The Netsilik, then, were free concerning sexual matters. Besides
the possibility of engaging in casual affairs there was also the
previously described custom of wife exchanges, which could
afterwards lead to the establishment of quasi-marital ties. Jealousy was expressed much more often by men, but there were
cases of wives getting angry over the behavior of their adulterous
husbands. Though lovers and cuckolded husbands often fought
with fists, adultery never led to murder. It was simply not considered important enough. One killed to obtain a wife but not to
get sexual access to a woman.

Several of the seven circa 1950s Netsilik murders were motivated by
wife-stealing (Balikci 1970:232). This was a product of a substantial rate
of female infanticide that produced a chronic shortage of marriageable
women (1970:148). These underlying conditions did not obtain in any of
the other cases. However, adultery was a factor in one of two reported
Semai homicides (Dentan 1978:98; 1979:133). Among the !Kung, only
15.8 percent (3/19) of male-male homicides were attributable to adultery.
Adultery is not one of the reported causes of male-male homicide among
the Mbuti, and no such homicides are recollected by the Siriono. Overall, adultery, sexual rivalry, and jealousy are a comparatively unimportant source of male fighting in all but one case (the Central Eskimo,
where this leads to a regulated exchange of blows). Likewise, these
related phenomena are a motive for only a small proportion of male-
male homicides in all but two cases (Central Eskimo and Semai), and in
the Eskimo case the motive is more accurately described as wife acquisition, which is in turn related to the economic contribution a wife can
potentially make (Balikci 1970:161). The pattern of same-sex violence
and homicide is thus quite different for males than it is for females,
where sexual rivalry is the paramount issue (although connected to economic provisioning as well).

The data pertaining to these societies do not support the common
view that male-male conflict is predominantly "over women," in the sense

that males are engaged in an effort to secure and maintain a monopoly over sexual access to their wives through recourse to acts of physical violence against sexual rivals. No such monopoly is culturally postulated in four of these five societies. The exchanges of blows between men that occur in the Central Eskimo case are over "unauthorized" adultery rather than adultery per se. Wife-exchange partnerships encompass authorized extramarital copulation, and a wife's casual affairs may also be tacitly accepted by her husband (Balikci 1970:161). Among the Siriono,

> a woman is allowed to have intercourse not only with her husband but also with his brothers, real and classificatory, and with the husbands and potential husbands of her own and classificatory sisters. Thus, apart from one's real spouse, there may be as many as eight or ten potential spouses with whom one may have sex relations. (Holmberg 1969:165)

When conflicts arise, these involve "excessive" adultery, or sexual neglect of a spouse, rather than extramarital activity per se. This neglect is "what adultery amounts to among the Siriono" (167). It is entirely consistent with this that conflict occurs between spouses, not between men. In the absence of a formulated monopoly over sexual access, a husband's rights are not infringed by other men who copulate with his wife. Among the Mbuti and Semai extramarital sexual relations are not enjoined but are tacitly accepted with equanimity provided that they are transitory. Turnbull (1965:122) reports that there was not a single instance in which the men of the Epulu band came into conflict with each other over spousal infidelity. Semai extramarital sexual relations are characterized as the "loan" of a spouse, and any illegitimacy that may result is not considered problematic (Dentan 1979:74). However, these cases are not exceptional in that the absence of a one-to-one relation between sex and marriage is as ubiquitous as the institution of the family itself (Lévi-Strauss 1971:346).

The !Kung differ from these other four cases in that a theoretical monopoly over sexual access to a spouse is postulated. Adultery is thus regarded as consequential and is associated with dissolution of the union. Howell (1979:230) reports, "We frequently see married people becoming involved in a sexual relationship with someone outside the marriage, and divorcing and remarrying the new partner simultaneously." This betokens an effort to engender an alignment between marriage, on one hand, and an exclusive sexual relationship, on the other. Adultery is consequential in this ethnographic case because it poses the threat of potential loss of a wife. A man who seeks to prevent this loss may then attack a sexual rival, and there is consequently some degree of conflict between men over adultery (although this is the cause of only 18 percent of the reported instances of male-male physical violence as noted above). However, one has the overall impression that only a quite small percentage of extramarital contacts eventuate in a man being subject to physical violence at the hands of a jealous husband. It is surprising that only three !Kung male-male homicides over a thirty-five-year period were related to adultery despite the fact that adultery is characteristically part of the transition from one marriage to another among women who have been married for more than five years, and 14 percent of marriages of this duration ended in divorce (Howell 1979:237). This suggests that there were many divorces in which adultery didn't precipitate extreme violence between a woman's husband and the husband's successor. In other words, there is a substantial incidence of situations in which !Kung men are in competition over sexual access to a woman, but only a small proportion of these entail recourse to physical violence on the part of these men. In this respect, the !Kung are not so different from the other four cases. Thus the findings for all five societies pose difficulties for theories that attempt to link male aggression to competition involving sexual reproduction (e.g., Manson and Wrangham 1991). On the contrary, these data suggest that the underlying issue of importance to male social actors is maintaining a relationship with a coproducer within the framework of a gendered division of labor that makes the husband-wife team an important unit of production.[9] Adultery is of concern to a husband when it threatens continuation of the union, especially when the female contribution to subsistence is high, as among the !Kung. However, it is of concern to a wife when it affects conjugal provisioning, irrespective of the potentiality for divorce. Hence the observed difference between the genders in fighting over the issue of adultery.

Fighting that is rule-governed, contestlike, carried out in the presence of an audience of onlookers, and constrained in terms of the forms of violence considered acceptable is a specific type of physical violence that is distinctive to male-male conflicts. Netsilik women constitute an exception, but when they fight in this way they are said to be "fighting like men." Lee (1979:376, 379–81) labels this "play fighting" and describes it as involving "tests of strength" between the combatants, young males between the ages of eighteen and thirty-five. Among both the Siriono and Netsilik such fighting reportedly constitutes a cathartic form of conflict resolution. Ill-feeling is expressed and dissipated. Many of the male-male physical conflicts described for the Mbuti also manifest the above noted attributes that comprise this pattern.

There is a much wider range of forms of male-male violence than of female-female violence. These forms include low-level physical violence that does not result in serious injuries, on one hand, and potentially lethal violence, carried out with deadly weapons, on the other. In between these two extremes is an intermediate form of violence in which implements are employed and there is a potentiality for inflicting injuries that are neither lethal nor permanent, but nevertheless go beyond the minor scrapes and bruises likely to result from wrestling and punching. Female-female violence tends toward this intermediate level. Play fighting and tests of strength are unreported. Moreover, women do not own or routinely use deadly weapons such as bows, arrows, and spears (and an absence of recourse to these may account for the low rate of homicides perpetrated by females). The implements women fight with tend to be those they regularly employ in their labors, such as digging sticks. It is also noteworthy that bare-handed female fighting not infrequently includes facial scratching, or blows to the face, seemingly directed to the objective of marking or disfiguring the opponent. This may be related to the fact that sexual rivalry is the preeminent cause of physical violence between women.

A great deal of low-level physical violence between men appears to be directed to the cathartic venting of ill-feeling arising from minor grievances and slights that are subsequently forgotten. At the same time, the initiator of the episode establishes that he is an individual to be reckoned with and a man among men. In other words, low-level male violence is a component of a militant egalitarianism in which a slight constitutes less than equal treatment that can be rectified by an equal exchange of blows or a bout of inconclusive wrestling. Equality is thereby established.[10]

The critical point to be noted here is that all physical violence is not the same thing. The development of a theoretical understanding of violence requires an appreciation of differences between the forms of violence present in the same society (e.g., differences between male and female violence) as well as an account of differences between societies (in the occurrence of war, in homicide rates, in the presence or absence of spousal violence, etc.). An effort can then be made to identify covariants and to formulate a series of hypotheses that might account for the presence or prevalence of each form of violence under certain conditions. This would entail an implicit definition of violence as something akin to a pathogen that occurs in an array of forms under a specifiable set of conditions and is amenable to an epidemiological investigation. However, defining violence as akin to a pathogen is not intended to in any way make it appear excusable or unavoidable, since the precipitating conditions are social conditions that are created or socially reproduced by human agency. The moral condemnation of interpersonal violence certainly continues to be justified. However, moral condemnation does not lead to an understanding of the phenomena that could contribute to the development of preventatives or countermeasures that might reduce the incidence of any specific form of violence. For example, if spousal physical violence is absent among the Siriono (except where wives attempt to intervene in male wrestling matches during drinking feasts), then there are clearly social conditions conducive to precluding or minimizing such violence.[11] A broader comparative study could thus potentially lead to an identification of these covarying conditions. The present work constitutes this type of effort in that it entails an attempt to isolate the covariants of warlessness.

The misconception that violence is a unitary phenomenon underwrites the mistaken notion that war is related to violence as simply more of the same. A systematic appraisal of the forms of physical violence present in Fabbro's five traditional Peaceful Societies—selected on the basis of their nonparticipation in warfare—clearly shows that the ethnographic data do not support either of these commonplace (mis)understandings of violence. By the same token, these ethnographic data show that violence does not beget violence in a lockstep manner. Female fighting can in fact co-occur with permissive child rearing and an absence of physical punishment of children. (Indeed women may come to blows over the verbal reprimand of a child.) The same societies that eschew war may be characterized by high levels of interpersonal physical violence, rather than "little or none," with violent episodes occurring weekly within each small face-to-face community. Likewise, the same societies that eschew war may evidence homicide rates that are quite high—or even extraordinarily high—by comparative standards. (In the Gebusi case homicide traditionally accounted for nearly a third of all adult deaths [Knauft 1985:116] and the situation among the Copper Eskimo was probably comparable.) Moreover, these exceptionally high homicide rates are found in conjunction with day-to-day tranquillity and the lowest reported incidence of interpersonal physical violence. This is precisely the opposite of what would be expected if it were the case that violence begets violence.

If there is no cumulative relationship between one form of violence and another at the societal level, then there is no reason to expect, as Fabbro does, that societies lacking war will manifest little or no interpersonal violence. The envisioned concrete examples of utopian peaceful conditions under which an absence of physical punishment of children and of spousal conflict is associated with rare adult male fighting which in turn correlates with a virtual absence of homicide topped off by a lack of participation in warfare cannot be found (although a single ethnographic case, the Semai, comes closest to fitting these specifications). However, warless societies *do* exist and, in fact, are not scarce in the world ethnographic sample. This is to say that societies in which war is rare to nonexistent can readily be found but they are not Peaceful Societies in Fabbro's expanded sense of that term. Such societies are thus more appropriately designated simply as warless societies.

The central orienting questions of this study can thus be more precisely phrased as follows: What are the distinctive features of those societies in which warfare is rare to nonexistent, and what are the critical differences between warless and warlike societies (especially among those with little or no dependence upon agriculture)? The second question requires comparative consideration of societies with regular or frequent warfare (as well as consideration of those lacking war) and thus cannot be addressed within the kind of framework Fabbro employs. However, Fabbro's framework (and study) can be utilized to rule out a number of potential hypotheses concerning the distinctive features and covariants of warlessness in traditional band societies, or simple societies. Warless band societies are not characterized by a low incidence of spousal physical violence, or a low incidence of male-male or female-female fighting. Warless societies likewise are not characterized by comparatively low homicide rates.

A detailed examination of conflict in the five traditional band societies Fabbro selects also shows that there is no distinctive mechanism of conflict resolution they share in common. Among the Mbuti there are a number of categories of individuals who may intervene in a conflict— elders, seniors, kin, neighbors, "clowns," or the local group as a whole. Moreover, intervention is progressively more likely at each stage of escalation (from verbal to physical conflict, and from bare-handed to log fighting). Intuitively, one might readily imagine that such a pattern of third-party intervention in escalating conflict would covary with an absence of war. The Semai are somewhat similar to the Mbuti in that elders may mediate quarrels (Dentan 1979:57). However, none of the other three warless band societies in Fabbro's sample manifest anything comparable to the Mbuti pattern. Among the !Kung, attempts at intervention lead to side fights, and peacemakers are sometimes killed in the general melee that results from the third-party intervention of kin on both sides. Among the Siriono and Central Eskimo, those present when low-level violence breaks out typically constitute themselves as an audience and eschew any intervention. Supervised physical violence in the form of wrestling or the exchange of punches *is* conflict resolution in these cases. Moreover, Siriono wives who attempt third-party intervention in fights between their husband and their brother (or father) are themselves likely to be struck. As among the !Kung, intervention merges into participation and is not held distinct. A survey of conflict resolution processes (Fabbro's item 7) thus fails to turn up a set of practices characteristic of warless band societies (other than the mechanism of spatial dissociation between individuals who find themselves in conflict, as noted earlier).

As Fabbro's table (reproduced earlier) shows, there are a number of features that are common to his Peaceful Societies, particularly the five traditional band societies. However, these common features are not distinctive features of warless band societies but are rather characteristic of unstratified band societies more generally. For example, kin-based forms of social integration (item 4) are typical of all unstratified band societies, as are the exertion of social control through public opinion (item 12), a corresponding absence of coercive organization (item 9), and the participation of all adults in decision making (item 11). Four of Fabbro's five traditional Peaceful Societies rely principally on hunting and gathering and have little or no dependence upon agriculture (item 2), while the Semai, who constitute an exception, have become more dependent upon agriculture only in recent centuries. All five societies manifest a division of labor based on age and gender and the absence of a more specialized division of labor (item 8). However, both of these economic commonalities are widespread among warlike unstratified band societies as well as their warless counterparts. It is evident here that the type of approach adopted by Fabbro can only serve as a means of advancing our understanding of warless societies up to a certain point. In order to carry the inquiry further, it is necessary to switch gears and undertake a comparative analysis of warless and warlike societies so that the distinctive covariants of warlessness can be definitively established. Such an analysis is the subject of the next chapter.

CHAPTER 2

Warless and Warlike Hunter-Gatherers: A Comparison

War is grounded in the application of a calculus of social substitution to situations of conflict such that these are understood in group terms. The killing of a coresident is thus perceived and experienced by his or her fellows as an injury to the homicide victim's community or residential group. The entity considered responsible is likewise the killer's local group, any member of which may then legitimately be killed in retaliation. Thus what characterizes Fabbro's Peaceful Societies is not an absence of homicide (which is comparatively prevalent), but rather a response to homicide that is devoid of the concept of social substitution. There is no sense that anyone other than the specific perpetrator of a homicide is responsible for the death, and no effort is made to take retaliatory blood vengeance against anyone else. Among the !Kung a bystander, a peacemaker, or an individual who comes to the aid of a murderer who has been targeted for revenge may potentially be killed in the melee that ensues when execution of a murderer is attempted. However, the deaths of individuals who intervene do not constitute retribution. They are not conceptualized in these terms. They present a very striking contrast to the killing of an isolated "unsuspecting relative" characteristic of blood vengeance. Moreover, the death of a bystander or supporter does not eliminate the murderer, who is considered to be a continuing threat to others, nor do such deaths bring conclusion to the conflict arising from a homicide. Conclusion is reached when a killer is killed.[1]

Alternatively, there may be no sequel to an individual homicide in warless societies. The victim's next of kin express their grief and sorrow at the loss but take no action (cf. Knauft 1987:477). This is the more typical outcome in these five ethnographic cases. Among the Mbuti, the execution of sorcerers, incorrigible thieves, and those guilty of sacrilege prompts no reported counteraction. None of the recollected homicides that occurred among the Semai and Siriono were followed by retaliation against the killer, nor was the theoretical possibility of this envisioned. The Netsilik and other Central Eskimo groups are more similar to the !Kung in that family members or other close kinsmen of a homicide victim may express a desire to avenge themselves by executing the killer. However, accounts of revenge actually being accomplished are very scarce and none of the seven circa 1950 homicides discussed by Balikci (1970:179–81) involved or engendered a sequel.[2] This is equally true of the homicides recorded by earlier ethnographers.

> Strangely enough, in all the historical cases recorded not a single instance of successful physical revenge occurs, although intentions for revenge are clearly expressed by close relatives of the victim even years after the murder has taken place. (181)

In sum, retaliation following a homicide is rare in practice among the Central Eskimo and not envisioned by the Mbuti, Semai, and Siriono. Among the !Kung, retaliation is more frequently undertaken, but with the murderer alone targeted for execution. The application of group concepts to the situation of homicide is thus uniformly absent in the ethnographic cases that comprise Fabbro's Peaceful Societies.

We have seen that a selected sample of societies that lack war is not, in fact, characterized by low levels of predisposition to aggression and physical violence. On the contrary, both the impulse to express ill-feeling in interpersonal physical violence and the enactment of this impulse—in one form or another, for example, wrestling matches or striking a spouse—are relatively commonplace. Moreover, extreme violence in the form of homicide is comparatively frequent (in cross-cultural terms). In other words, these societies are not warless as a consequence of features of enculturation that (1) preclude or diminish the experience of anger at the psychological level, or (2) suppress the expression of angry feelings in interpersonal violence, or (3) effectively limit such expression to nonlethal forms of violence. Moreover, these societies are not warless as a result of effective mechanisms of conflict management or conflict resolution, such as third-party intervention (see Koch 1974:26–35). The intervention by third parties that does occur either takes the form of participation or is likely to be interpreted by one of the principals as participation, so that dyadic interpersonal violence tends to escalate into a melee or brawl when the ingredients for this potential form of conflict management come into play. Thus violence is not nipped in the bud by potent modes of conflict resolution in these warless societies. On the contrary, physical violence is itself a principal vehicle of conflict resolution, as manifested in regulated, contestlike fighting and in the removal of a killer or sorcerer by execution. However, what warless societies do uniformly manifest are intrinsic limitations on the extent to which one act of lethal violence leads to another. When felt anger or ill-feeling is expressed in interpersonal violence, the expressive action typically runs its course (despite any attempted intervention) and may potentially culminate in murder. However, the violence that occurs is specific, not generalized, and it does not escalate beyond a sequence of events that encompasses homicide followed by execution of the killer. Typically, a murder is an isolated event with no sequel.

These findings very strongly suggest that the origin of war—in the sense of the initiation of warfare in a sociocultural context where it did not previously exist—entails a transition from one form of collective violence to another, rather than a transition from peaceful nonviolence to lethal armed conflict. The main contours of this postulated transition are also indicated by the reappraisal of interpersonal violence in Fabbro's selected sample of Peaceful Societies carried out in chapter 1. The transition entails a shift from: (1) individual homicide followed by the execution of the killer, carried out by the homicide victim's aggrieved next of kin and the latter's supporters, to (2) war (including feud) in which an "unsuspecting relative" or coresident of the perpetrator of an initial homicide is killed in blood vengeance by the homicide victim's aggrieved next of kin and the latter's supporters or coresidents, triggering a like desire for vengeance and thus underwriting reciprocating episodes of lethal armed conflict between two social groups or collectivities. The critical change from individual to group responsibility overrides the intrinsic self-limiting features of violence in warless societies.

The ethnographic findings summarized here also very strongly suggest that the distinctive features of warless societies are organizational and are linked to an absence of certain group concepts, or a lack of application of such concepts to the context of homicide. The transition from capital punishment to feud or war—that is, the transition that encapsulates the origin of war—is thus contingent upon the development of the companion concepts of injury to the group and group liability that provide grounds for generalized, reciprocating collective violence that takes the form of raid and counterraid. The hypothesis that emerges from a Fabbro-inspired effort to delineate the central characteristics of warless societies is that such societies manifest a set of organizational attributes connected to an attenuated cultural conception of social substitutability. The key question that then arises is whether or not warless societies can also be differentiated from warlike societies by these specifiable organizational attributes, especially among those societies with little or no dependence upon agriculture.

We have seen from Ember's (1978) cross-cultural study that frequent warfare is evident among 64 percent of a worldwide sample of 31 hunter-gatherers, while warfare is rare or nonexistent in only 10 to 12 percent of those cases (as noted in the introductory chapter). This prompts the question: what differentiates warless from warlike hunter-gatherers? The potential differentiating features range from child socialization patterns, conflict management practices, and the structural violence of hierarchy to population pressure, resource competition, and sedentarism. However, the results of the inquiry conducted in the preceding chapter suggest that the key differentiating features are essentially organizational. Thus we now need to determine the extent to which specifiable organizational attributes covary with the frequency of warfare among a representative sample of hunter-gatherers with little or no reliance on agriculture.

There are no human societies in which social groups are absent so that there is no potentiality that warlessness simply covaries with group-lessness. However, there is a range of variation in the extent to which group concepts are elaborated and in the delineation of some but not other social situations as group concerns, including various situations of conflict. Moreover, there is variation in application of the much more precise concept of social substitution whereby one individual takes the place of another in certain specifiable social situations (e.g., one brother succeeds to aspects of the social position of another upon the latter's death). Social substitution establishes an identity between a pair of individuals (or the comembers of a set of individuals) both from the external standpoint of other persons and in terms of the way in which they view themselves and view each other. This contains the kernel of an operational collective identity, that is, of a group identity capable of being realized in social action, as well as the kernel of a sense of interests or projects in common that transcend the individual level. In contrast, a group identity based on a shared similarity (such as a common language) does not intrinsically contain any basis for collective action, nor does a shared similarity necessarily entail a common interest. While no societies are groupless, there is thus very substantial variation with respect to the development of group concepts. A general appreciation of this ethnographic range of variation informs the delineation of a type of society characterized by the minimum degree of elaboration of social groups. This type may conveniently be labeled by the rubric *unsegmented societies.*

Unsegmented societies are characterized by the minimal complement of social groups. They manifest only those social groups that are cultural universals, present in every society, and nothing more. Local groups composed of cooperatively linked coresiding individuals are present, but these local groups are not combined into any higher order organizational entities. In other words, there is no level of organization beyond the local community (although there is a sense of shared language and culture that extends outward to adjacent communities, and diffusely beyond these as far as is known and is applicable). Within the local group, families are generally identifiable as detachable constituent subunits. Although social life is in many respects communal, families often occupy a separate, spatially distinct sleeping place, windbreak, hut, or hearth.[3] They may also operate independently in food procurement during certain seasons.

The forms of the family that may be present include independent

monogamous nuclear families, independent polygynous families (composed of a man, several spouses, and their children), and extended families
that are manifested during a certain period (or periods) of an individual's
life course. For example, a married daughter and her husband might live
and work in close association with her parents for a period of time during
the early years of the marriage, but then live separately (as a nuclear family) for more than a decade before being joined by their own married
daughter's family for several years later in life. Unsegmented societies lack
extended families that persist continuously over the full term of a marriage. Thus an extended family that included two married siblings and
their parents would dissolve upon the death of the parental pair, generat-
ing two nuclear families. The independent nuclear family is thus always a
phase in the developmental cycle of domestic groups in unsegmented societies. It is typically the most protracted phase. At any given time, nuclear
families tend to predominate within the local group.

The culturally recognized coactive groups found in unsegmented societies are thus limited to the family and local community. There is also
recognition of something akin to neighborhoods, typically designated as
"the people of such and such a place" (e.g., the Honey Creek Valley),
although the boundaries of these neighborhoods are quite vague. Contiguous local groups are likely to aggregate during periods of seasonal
abundance, with these gatherings providing an occasion for socializing,
exchange, courtship, ritual performance, or some combination of these.
The scope and composition of these aggregations tend to vary from year to
year, rather like attendance at a traditional summertime county fair.

Unsegmented societies contrast with segmental societies, so it will be
useful to briefly sketch the outlines of this counterpoint in order to make
the thrust of this axis of differentiation entirely explicit. Segments are units
that are equivalent in structure and function. Segmental organization is
the combination of these like units into progressively more inclusive
groups within a segmentary hierarchy. The combination of a set of town-
ships into a county and a set of counties into a state provides a familiar
example of a segmental type of organization in modern American society.
In unsegmented societies there is no specific set of families that constitutes
a given local group, and a local group is not a subunit of any larger organizational entity. The families that are identifiable as constituents of a
local group are simply whatever families are coresiding at the moment.
This contrasts with a segmentary hierarchy in which *specified* families
comprise the constituents of a patrilineage, certain *designated* patrilineages make up a subclan, and so forth. A house-group composed of the
families of a pair of married siblings who live together throughout their
lifetimes and are replaced in turn by their married children also represents
an elementary form of segmental organization in that particular nuclear

families are combined into a higher order grouping that is not transient (i.e., the corporate extended family). A community may then be made up of certain house-groups incorporating specific families. However, this is precisely the type of extended family that is absent in unsegmented societies. Unsegmented societies thus lack any social groups that manifest the distinctive features of segmental organization.

The category *unsegmented societies* is largely defined by what is not present (or, differently put, by the features that preclude any potential ethnographic candidate from being admitted). These absent features encompass not only the extremely widely distributed attributes of segmentation outlined above, but also a number of features connected with the broad recognition of social substitutability within a sociocultural system. Often attributes of segmentation and social substitutability go hand in hand. Thus descent groups, such as clans, are nearly always delineated as being made up of component subgroups (i.e., either local branches or subclans) and are thus culturally formulated within the framework of a segmental design. Descent groups also embody the identity and social substitutability of same-sex siblings. As Fortes (1969:77) aptly puts it, "the mutual substitutability of like-sex siblings in jural and ceremonial relations . . . follows from their identification in the structure of the lineage." In other words, the specific families that constitute a patrilineage are those headed by the sons and son's sons of a set of brothers, thereby encoding the structural equivalence of these same-sex siblings. One brother in an antecedent generation is equivalent to another as a link between an individual patrilineage member and an ancestor, just as one patrilineage is equivalent to another in a segmentary hierarchy of progressively more inclusive groups whereby a set of patrilineages make up a subclan.

Unsegmented societies lack patrilineal descent groups, matrilineal descent groups, and ancestor-based restricted cognatic descent groups. They are instead characterized by the egocentric bilateral kin networks or kindreds found in every society. An individual characteristically maintains some level of social relations with relatives by marriage, as well as relatives on his/her mother's and father's side. While there is overlap between the kin networks of separate individuals, no two persons share identical kin networks (since same-sex siblings have different spouses and different relatives by marriage, although they share the same maternal and paternal kin). There is consequently no structural basis for either the explicit social identification of same-sex siblings as a unit, or the sense that they share a common social position or social fate. Bilateral kin networks or kindreds thus do not intrinsically contain the seeds of the concept of social substitutability in the way that descent groups do. Descent groups are amenable to the formulation of group interests, or collective interests, while bilateral kin networks are compatible with a notion of shared interests that link one individual to another. A homicide is consequently likely to be perceived and experienced as an individual loss shared with some kin rather than as an injury to a group. The de facto "group" of mourners is contextually generated by the event and lacks any independent existence apart from that context.

A calculus of social substitutability is built into classificatory kinship terminologies that equate same-sex siblings and also treat them as uniquely equivalent as linking relatives. This would include bifurcate merging terminologies in which mother and mother's sister on the maternal side are designated by a common term, as are father and father's brother on the paternal side. When the children of these pairs of same-sex siblings are also equated, then sister and mother's sister's daughter are included within a common category (while the children of cross-sex siblings, such as mother's brother's daughter, are distinguished from these by a separate term). Similarly, brother and father's brother's son are terminologically identified, while father's sister's son is differentiated. These features are central to the Iroquois, Crow, and Omaha types of classificatory kinship terminology but are not found in Eskimo or Hawaiian type terminologies. Unsegmented societies—in which the concept of social substitutability is absent or attenuated—lack the types of classificatory kinship terminology that encompass and accommodate this concept. That is, they manifest the Eskimo or Hawaiian type of classificatory system in which same-sex siblings are not bracketed, and treated as a unit distinct from all siblings, in their role as linking relatives. These two types of classificatory kinship terminologies are also consistent with the social contours of the egocentric bilateral kindreds described above. Within a circle of kin with whom ego maintains social relations, maternal and paternal "sides" are not differentiated.

In unsegmented societies marriages are contracted by individuals and by families. Marriage links a husband to his wife's family and a wife to her husband's family, as is culturally universal. Each becomes a relative by marriage to the family of orientation of the other. However, marriage is not also formulated as a transaction between more encompassing social groups (such as local communities) even though intermarriage between members of two different local groups engenders affinal and kin relations that span communities. In other words, marriage is not conceptualized as an exchange between groups. In contrast, when a woman of one group is given in marriage in exchange for a woman of another group, this expresses a number of group-level concepts that are common to segmental societies (but foreign to unsegmented societies). Marriage as an exchange between groups entails both collective interests and the notion that a person is a representative of a collectivity in these matrimonial transactions. For the purposes of reciprocation, one female group member is the substitutable equivalent of another. These concepts are strictly commensurate with the concepts of loss or injury to the group, group responsibility to retaliate, and group liability that provide the basis for collective violence which takes the form of feud or war. Unsegmented societies lack this formulation of group concepts within the realm of marital transactions that might serve as a basis for their extension into the domain of reaction to a homicide.

Unsegmented societies also lack a number of widespread features of social organization that entail or embody the concept of marital exchange between groups, namely, moieties, preferential cousin marriage, and marriage payments (other than token gifts). Moieties conceptually formulate all marriages as exchanges between two intermarrying groups. By the same token, preferential cousin marriage—when combined with local exogamy—is typically a component (and marker) of group-to-group marital exchange relations and the collective interests these incorporate. Marriage payments likewise instantiate collective responsibility for and involvement in the social transaction of matrimony. In a standard bridewealth payment, the groom's kin contribute bridewealth valuables that the groom subsequently presents to the bride's father or brother. The transfer of valuables typically takes place in the context of a public event. The recipient then redistributes these valuables among the bride's family and kin, who have foregathered to witness the transaction. The marriage is thus formulated as a group project that consequently links the participating kin groups, rather than simply as a family concern.

In unsegmented societies, marriage characteristically involves no significant transfer of valuables. However, in some of these societies marriage does entail the transfer of labor and/or gifts from the groom to his wife's parents. What is given is a product of the groom's own efforts, such as portions of game he himself has procured or items he has manufactured. There are no significant material contributions by the groom's kin, and the redistribution of valuables among the bride's kin that forms a counterpart to such contributions is also absent. The transaction that marks a union is thus consistent with the character of marriage described above, that is, a man is conjoined with his wife and brought into relationship with his wife's family. Often the couple will reside with the wife's family initially, for a period of several years. This may form a component of customary practices included under the rubric of "brideservice," that is, the labor contributions, services, and gifts of food a groom/husband renders to his bride's/wife's family during a time period that may extend from somewhat before to several years after the initiation of cohabitation.[4]

It is important to note that brideservice tends to separate brothers, since each is drawn into the orbit of his respective wife's family for a time, and thus may interfere with fraternal coresidence during the formative period of early adulthood. The relation that epitomizes social substitutability in those social systems in which it is well-developed is thus undercut by the marriage practices of unsegmented societies, or a significant subset of unsegmented societies. Brothers are drawn to the only set of relatives they do not share in common, that is, relatives by marriage.

The category *unsegmented societies* is an organizational type that has been very precisely defined here in terms of attributes coded in the *Atlas of World Cultures* (Murdock 1981). Of the 563 societies in this representative world sample there are only 32, or 5.68 percent, that manifest the combination of features delineated in the preceding pages (and specified by codes in note 5).[5] However, most of Fabbro's seven Peaceful Societies are unsegmented societies, namely the !Kung, Mbuti, Copper Eskimo, and Tristan da Cunha Islanders. The eastern Semai (described in Dentan 1968) manifest all of the requisite attributes except one: corporate extended families are not absent. However, the Semang, or western branch of the Semai, who differ from the eastern Semai in that they have little dependence on agriculture, do lack such extended families and are among the 32 unsegmented societies. The Semang and Semai are equally peaceful and nonviolent (Dentan 1968:4). With respect to the other two of Fabbro's Peaceful Societies, the Siriono differ in organizational design[6] and the Hutterites are not coded in the *Atlas of World Cultures* (and are in any case an enclave society within and under the protection of a powerful state). This covariation therefore strongly supports the deduction that warless (or "peaceful") societies can be differentiated from warlike societies in terms of organizational characteristics. The societies that Fabbro selected on the grounds that they were warless tend, very disproportionately, to be unsegmented societies even though the latter are only a small fraction of the world sample. These results are summarized in table 3.

TABLE 3.   The Covariation between Fabbro's Peaceful Societies and the Category Unsegmented Societies within Murdock's (1981) Representative World Sample

Societies in the *Atlas of World Cultures:*	Societies Classified by Organizational Type:	
	Unsegmented Societies	Other Organizational Types of Societies
Fabbro's Peaceful Societies	• !Kung • Mbuti • Copper Eskimo • Tristan da Cunha • W. Semai (Semang) 5	• Siriono • E. Semai (Senoi) 2
Other societies	27	529

Note: In Murdock's (1981:44) *Atlas* the eastern Semai are labeled the Senoi (identity code E24b) and the western Semai are labeled the Semang (identity code E24a).

The 563 societies in table 3 have not been systematically classified in terms of the frequency of warfare. Thus while it is apparent that the warless societies selected by Fabbro tend to be unsegmented societies, we do not yet know whether the 27 remaining unsegmented societies are warless, or have a lower frequency of warfare than the other 529 societies that are not of the unsegmented organizational type. However, there is a way to address this question, because there are representative world samples that have been coded with respect to the frequency of warfare and other forms of violence. These representative samples are derived from the "Standard Cross-Cultural Sample" devised by Murdock and White (1969). These authors analyzed 1,250 ethnographically described societies and classified them into clusters, that is, "groups of contiguous societies with cultures so similar, owing either to diffusion or recent common origin, that no world sample should include more than one of them" (1969, 5). Clusters that were sufficiently similar in language and culture to "raise the presumption of historical connection" were then grouped together into 200 sampling provinces. Further considerations of similarity led to some additional reduction of these and to the formulation of 186 "distinctive world areas." The standard sample was then drawn by picking one society from each of these distinctive world areas, this generally being the society for which the most comprehensive ethnographic data were available at that time. From this representative world sample a half-sample of 93 societies may be drawn by selecting every other society. This is equally representative but more manageable in terms of the task of coding a range of variables.

The codes developed by Ross (1983) to measure various dimensions of armed conflict are particularly useful for the purpose of addressing the critical question of what differentiates warless from warlike societies among those societies with little or no dependence on agriculture or herding. Ross selects a standard half-sample of 93 societies from which 3 cases are then dropped due to inadequate information on conflict. Within Ross's coded sample of 90 societies, there are 25 foraging societies, that is, societies whose subsistence economy entails a 75 percent or greater combined dependence upon collecting wild plants and small animals, hunting, trapping, and fishing, and a 25 percent or less combined dependence upon agriculture, horticulture, shifting cultivation, and/or domestic animals. (This information on the relative contributions of various components of the subsistence economy is provided by Murdock's [1981] *Atlas,* column 7; see also Murdock and White [1969].) Of these 25 foraging societies, 8 are of the unsegmented organizational type and 17 do not conform to this organizational design (i.e., are to some degree segmental, and/or manifest attributes associated with social substitutability).

These two subsets thus provide a means of examining the relationship between organizational type and frequency of warfare among foragers.

Ross (1983:179, 182–83) codes each society for the frequency of internal warfare (between communities of the same society) and the frequency of external warfare (with components of other societies) on a scale of 1 to 4, with 1 denoting the occurrence of warfare yearly or more frequently, 2 denoting warfare at least once every five years, 3 denoting warfare at least once every generation, and 4 indicating that war takes place "rarely or never." In table 4, I have combined these codes to create a scale from 2 to 8, with 2 denoting comparatively warlike societies in which both internal and external warfare occur yearly and 8 denoting comparatively warless societies where both kinds of warfare rarely or never occur. A code of 7 denotes societies in which one type of warfare or the other occurs once a generation. Codes of 7 and 8 thus divide off those societies in which warfare is relatively infrequent or nonexistent. Codes 6, 5, 4, 3, and 2 indicate that warfare occurs fairly to very frequently, that is, at least twice a generation. However, in all but a few cases one or another form of warfare occurs once every five years, or more often (i.e., there is a code of 1 or 2 for either external or internal war whenever there is a code of 5 or less and in many cases where there is a code of 6 as well).

Table 4 shows that there is a very strong association between the unsegmented organizational type and a low frequency of warfare (codes 7 and 8) among foragers. Warfare is comparatively infrequent in six of eight unsegmented foraging societies but equally infrequent in only one of seventeen other foraging societies. The answer to the critical question of what differentiates comparatively warless from warlike hunter-gatherers is thus readily apparent. The former lack the organizational features associated with social substitutability that are conducive to the development of group concepts.

Four of the six comparatively warless unsegmented foraging societies in table 4 are already quite familiar to the reader since they are among Fabbro's Peaceful Societies, namely, the Mbuti, Semang (western Semai), Copper Eskimo, and !Kung. These societies are included in the standard cross-cultural sample (from which Ross draws his half-sample) because they are the best described cases in one of the 186 "distinctive world areas." The contextualization of these societies within a representative world sample makes it possible to address the question of whether the common features of peaceful (or comparatively warless) foraging societies are distinctive features of warlessness rather than common features of foraging societies more generally. For example, kin-based forms of social integration (Fabbro's item 4) are typical of all foraging societies while the distinction between unsegmented and segmental types of kin-based organization differentiates these in terms of the frequency of warfare.

The two cases of unsegmented foraging societies that are coded for frequent warfare require some discussion. On checking the original

TABLE 4. Combined Internal and External Warfare Frequency for Unsegmented and Other Foraging Societies

	Warless Both "rare or never" (code 4+4)						Warlike Both "yearly" (code 1+1)
	8	7	6	5	4	3	2
Unsegmented Foraging Societies (n = 8)	Mbuti Semang C. Eskimo	!Kung Ingalik Yahgan			Andamanese	Slave	
Other Foraging Societies (n = 17)		Warrau	Gilyak Yurok Yokuts Gros Ventre Eyak	Saulteaux Bellacoola Comanche Chiricahua Tiwi	Nambicuara		Ainu Klamath Shavante Aweikoma Abipon

sources it is evident that the annual external warfare reported for the Slave consisted of attacks by the Cree that were largely a product of disruption engendered by the Canadian fur trade in the region west of Hudson Bay.

The warlike Cree, particularly after they secured firearms, carried their raids far up into the Great Slave Lake region, spreading blind terror among the less courageous Athapaskans in their greed for scalps. Every person in this region, day and night, lived in mortal terror of enda, the enemy. In practically every case, probably the Cree were the aggressors. Tradition has it that the Chipewyan and Beaver defended their territory well, the Yellowknife and Dogrib less so, while the Slave were abject cowards.

In war only men were killed, women and children [were] kept as slaves. Scalps and heads were not [traditionally] taken in warfare. The Chipewyan warred upon the Slave and Dogrib in which wars they are said to have been assisted by the Cree. (Mason 1946:35–36)

Although the Slave were subject to external war in the form of raids carried out against them by the Cree (and Chipewyan), they did not counter-raid these tribes or offer any defense other than flight. They were called the Esclave by the early French explorers because so many of their women and children were taken captive by the Cree. The name is a translation of the Cree word for captive. These data suggest that the Slave would have been a warless society if left alone, and that the description of them as "abject cowards" could alternatively be rendered as "peaceful." Internally, homicide occurred, deaths attributed to witchcraft led to execution of the witch, and strangers encountered while hunting might be ambushed and killed for fear that they had come "with evil intent" (Mason 1946:36). However, raids by members of one Slave band against another are not reported.[7] In other words, there is no evidence of internal war as defined in this study, although homicide and execution of a killer (including a witch) does occur. The Slave case is thus consistent with the proposition that unsegmented foraging societies are comparatively warless.

In contrast, the Andaman Islanders are appropriately coded as a society in which warfare occurs with some frequency. They represent an important case that provides insights into the question of the origin of warfare and will be discussed at length in the next chapter.

Ross's (1983) codes are generally quite consistent with those that would be assigned based on the distinction between war and capital punishment employed in this study. This is due to the fact that Ross distinguishes between organized armed conflict (internal and external war), on one hand, and physical violence (including homicide and vengeance killing), on the other, and codes each separately (see Ross 1983:174,

177–79). This provided scope for Ross's three coders to differentiate the collective execution of a killer from warfare. In contrast, Ember and Ember's recent (1992) coding of all the societies in the standard cross-cultural sample with respect to warfare is not very useful due to the definitions employed. Ember and Ember (1992:172) formulate a behavioral definition of war as "socially organized armed conflict between members of different territorial units." However, a one-sided attack is sufficient, so that "a warfare event could involve the ambush of a single person" of another community (172). Thus the execution of the perpetrator of a homicide by the victim's surviving kin is not distinguished from warfare. The collective execution of a witch or sorcerer is also indistinguishable from war.[8]

The relationship between organizational type and the response to the killing of a group member can be directly assessed by comparing the unsegmented foraging societies with the other (segmental) foraging societies in Ross's (1983) sample. The results, presented in table 5, are based on codings contained in Ericksen and Horton's (1992) cross-cultural study of variations in kin group vengeance.[9] This study proceeded from consideration of the following question: "What happens if a consanguineal kin group member is killed, injured or insulted by a member of another kin group?" (60). Ericksen and Horton evaluated both group responsibility and group liability, coding dimensions of each separately. For our purposes, the critical distinction with respect to group responsibility turns on recognition of a kin group as having some obligation to avenge transgressions against a group member, as opposed to an absence of such recognition (and the presence only of "individual self-redress," code 6).[10] With respect to group liability, Ericksen and Horton's (1992:62) distinctions between legitimate targets of vengeance are especially pertinent. They differentiate between (1) those societies in which the malefactor alone is the legitimate target of vengeance, (2) those in which any member of the malefactor's group is a legitimate target, and (3) those in which vengeance is preferentially directed against the malefactor, but may be exacted against any group member if this preference cannot be realized. These codes for both group responsibility and group liability are incorporated into table 5.

These data show that unsegmented societies uniformly lack the concept of group liability. Retaliatory vengeance is only directed against the perpetrator of a homicide (or of an injury or insult), not against a member of the perpetrator's family, bilateral kindred, or local group. In six of eight cases, there is also no formulation of responsibility to carry out vengeance on behalf of a group member, based on the concept that an injury to any member is an injury to the group as a whole. This is entirely consistent with the earlier observation that there is typically no sequel to a homicide in unsegmented societies.

When there is a recognized group responsibility to exact vengeance, as among the Copper Eskimo and Yahgan, this devolves upon coresident close relatives, that is, coresident members of the homicide victim's family or kindred.[11] However, it is important to note that this ideologically legitimated vengeance obligation (i.e., the attribute coded by Ericksen and Horton) may be infrequently carried out in practice. In the Eskimo case, the expression of a desire for vengeance is accompanied by mutual avoidance that inhibits the potential for its realization. Among the Yahgan interpersonal physical violence occurred relatively frequently, and homicide rates were quite high.[12]

> When a murder occurred, the friends and relatives of the victim would take revenge, but the family of the murderer abandoned him and made no effort to defend him. (Lothrop 1928:165)

However, this acceptance of retaliation against a family member guilty of homicide appears to have been at least partly predicated on the expectation that he might not in fact be killed.

TABLE 5. Variations in Kin Group Vengeance for Unsegmented and Other Foraging Societies

Kin Group Responsibility for Vengeance	Target of Vengeance	Organizational Type	
		Unsegmented Foraging Societies	Other Foraging Societies
Absent (n = 11)	Not applicable	Mbuti Semang !Kung Ingalik Andamanese Slave	Warrau Saulteaux Bellacoola Nambicuara Tiwi
Present (n = 13)	Malefactor only (n = 3)	Copper Eskimo Yahgan	Yokuts
	Malefactor if possible (n = 3)		Yurok Gros Ventre Eyak
	Any member of malefactor's group (n = 5)		Gilyak Comanche Klamath Shavante Aweikoma
	Not determinable (n = 2)		Chiricahua Abipon
Uncodable (n = 1)			Ainu

Sometimes [the] murderer is allowed to live, but he is much
beaten and hurt and has to make presents to all relatives of the
dead all his life. (Gusinde 1931:885)

In this case retaliation takes the form of a severe beating and compen-
satory payments rather than blood vengeance (as would be in accordance
with the principle of lex talionis). Nevertheless, recognition of the legitimacy of retribution is clearly in evidence. Thus, the execution of an individual whose criminal responsibilities have been established (i.e., capital
punishment), or other punishment of the malefactor, is simply accepted by
the killer's kin, as it is among the Gebusi. In either case it is readily apparent that there is no capacity for violence to escalate beyond a sequence of
events in which homicide is followed by the execution of the killer. Moreover, this characterization is uniformly applicable to all the unsegmented
societies in Ross's (1983) representative world sample.

A kin group responsibility to exact vengeance is manifested in 69 percent (11/16) of the other (segmental) foraging societies, and in 89 percent
(8/9) of these societies members of the malefactor's group are a potential
target of vengeance (omitting from the second calculation the two cases
where group responsibility for vengeance is attested but the target of
vengeance is not determinable from the sources). Thus group liability
tends to covary with group responsibility for vengeance among segmental
foragers.

Ericksen and Horton (1992:73–74) also note: "Controlling for all
other factors, individual self-redress [i.e., absence of kin group responsibility for vengeance] is seven times more likely to be used in hunter-gathering
societies than in any others." It is consequently not surprising that there are
a number of foraging societies that lack the concept of group responsibility.
However, 9 of the 11 foraging societies that do manifest kin group responsibility for vengeance are segmental in organizational design. The organizational distinction developed in this study thus covaries with patterns of
kin group vengeance among foraging societies (with little or no dependence
upon agriculture) just as it covaries with the frequency of warfare among
these same societies. This supports the general proposition that the origination of war entails a transition from execution of the perpetrator of a homicide to blood vengeance directed against a relative of the perpetrator.

The distinctions developed by Ericksen and Horton suggest a logical
sequence of developments that constitute a progressive transition from
warlessness to war (or, more precisely, blood feud). The ethnography of
homicide in warless societies presented earlier elucidates these changes in
social responses to the killing of a group member. The point of departure
for this developmental progression is a societal condition in which murder
is an isolated event that does not engender a sequel. The violent death of

an individual is experienced as a relational loss—the loss of a father, mother, sister, brother, cousin, or others of like kind—rather than as the diminution of the kindred as a conceptualized group (or abstract group concept). The composition of the actual local group of which the deceased was a member undergoes both regular seasonal fluctuations and frequent residential relocations, so that it has no fixed membership that could be perceived as being depleted. There is consequently no sense of a loss to a group that would serve as the basis for the conceptualization of an injury to the group. Individuals are licensed to personally seek redress for wrongs they have suffered at the hands of others. But when homicide occurs, the individual licensed to act on his or her own behalf is deceased. Thus murder leads to a public expression of grief by relatives but precipitates no counteraction by the living, although the spirit of the deceased may take vengeance. As we have seen, this public inaction is the typical response to a homicide in unsegmented foraging societies.

The first embryonic step in the development of collective violence is the verbal expression of a desire for revenge on the part of family members of a homicide victim. The empathetic ratification of the appropriateness of a revenge killing by relatives and coresidents constitutes an incipient form of legitimation. However, this endorsement of retribution does not entail any commitment to participate in its realization at this stage in the developmental progression. The concept of a vengeance *obligation* is as yet underdeveloped. Any kinsman of the deceased who is individually moved to take vengeance can be assured that his action will receive public approbation after the fact. But there is no group or individual whose failure to act would be subject to disapproval. No one is mobilized. Thus the expressed desire for vengeance is infrequently consummated.

When a killer is in fact killed, this is typically accomplished by a single individual acting alone. Although the reciprocal killing may be planned, it may also occur spontaneously, at a later time, when a minor disagreement triggers recollections of the past loss of a relative. It may also occur opportunistically, as when the murderer, in an unguarded moment, kneels to drink at a stream and inadvertently presents his back to a close relative of the person he killed. Sometimes the execution of a recidivist murderer becomes a collective act when one man takes the initiative and others who are sympathetic to the objective join in the attack on an impromptu basis once the murderer has been wounded.[13] However, none of these modes of vengeance connotes group responsibility. Legitimation of capital punishment in the realm of public opinion thus precedes the development of an entity responsible for carrying it out. This state of affairs is also typical of unsegmented foraging societies. Some small proportion of murders are avenged, but with the perpetrator alone being targeted.

A vengeance obligation stipulated in terms of kinship generates a de facto vengeance group. For example, the obligation to avenge the death of a father or brother would effectively instantiate the extended family as the core entity responsible for exacting socially legitimated vengeance. A coresident sister's husband would be likely to be part of this endeavor, as a member of the extended family, and other relatives might also elect to participate once a node of responsibility to take action is definitively established by kinship obligation. Collective responsibility that devolves upon several kinsmen (e.g., the brother and son of a homicide victim) necessitates a coordinated effort that in turn requires discussion, preplanning, and premeditation. All of these features contrast with the typical pattern of relatively spontaneous, self-generated individual action characteristic of the previous state, so that a kin-based vengeance obligation is readily identifiable ethnographically, as exemplified by the Yahgan. The Gebusi execution of a sorcerer described in the introductory chapter also constitutes an ethnographic example, but for a segmental society.

Preplanned collective efforts to exact vengeance are rare in unsegmented societies. Lee (1979:390) describes an "expedition" to kill the multiple murderer ǂGau that was an outgrowth of an unsuccessful attempt on the part of Debe's family to avenge Debe's death at the hands of ǂGau. However, this expedition also failed to accomplish ǂGau's execution (although ǂGau killed one participant and two members of his local group were also killed, in an exchange of poisoned arrows). At a later date, a young man with whom ǂGau was in conflict (unrelated to the earlier conflicts) stabbed him in the heart with a spear while he slept. Thus ǂGau's death conformed to the pattern characteristic of unsegmented societies in that the killing was carried out by an individual acting alone, relatively spontaneously, prompted by self-generated motives and operating in an opportunistic mode. The act met with general approbation, but the actor was not actually an individual who was carrying out a vengeance obligation. The multiple murders ǂGau had committed made him eligible for legitimated capital punishment that might be carried out by anyone. But this is not the same thing as the accomplishment of kin group responsibility for vengeance (which was attempted but was unsuccessful). Thus while there is some evidence of incipient kin group responsibility for vengeance among the !Kung, vested in the extended family or kindred, only one of the twenty-two homicides Lee (1979:382–400) describes represents fulfillment of vengeance by members of the responsible group. Moreover, !Kung informants almost exclusively describe loss in relational, rather than group terms. The concept of injury to the group is not detectable in the ethnographic description. This shows that kin group responsibility for vengeance may develop, in embryonic form, on a relational basis, prior to the conceptualization of injury to a group. An obligation to avenge the death of a father or brother is a relational formulation, logically distinguishable from an obligation to avenge the death of a member of the extended family (qua group), even though the same core personnel are mobilized. The relational form of the vengeance obligation could readily be present in unsegmented societies without contradiction. A kindred- or extended family-based form would also be consistent with the social contours of this organizational type, although only incipient ethnographic examples are presented in the cases under consideration. For example, Lee (1979:390) describes "Debe's family" as the entity initially seeking to avenge his death.

Kin group responsibility may be socially established even though the companion concept of kin group liability is unrecognized. In this case vengeance is enacted by members of the kin group, but only the perpetrator of a homicide is liable to retribution. It may also be the case that vengeance is enacted by relatives of the deceased, acting in their capacity as kinsmen rather than in their capacity as group members, as explained above. The difference between these two modes is difficult to establish ethnographically, because they are behaviorally indistinguishable and also grade into each other as points on a developmental continuum. A vengeance obligation stipulated in terms of kinship generates a de facto kin group that may also become conscious of its status as a collective entity through the social action of conflict. However, insofar as the local group is in a constant state of flux due to residential mobility, the extended family persists only episodically as part of the developmental cycle of domestic groups, and the kindred of each individual is distinct from that of every other, it is difficult for incipient group-level conceptualizations to jell. A sense of bounded social groups is not reinforced by day-to-day experience. This accounts for the asymmetry of the social condition in which group responsibility is evident but group liability is absent, since the former logically implies the latter as its reciprocal. The fact that only three of the twenty-two (coded) foraging societies in table 5 evidence this asymmetrical combination also suggests that it is a transitional form of comparatively limited duration in evolutionary terms.

Kin group liability expands the target of legitimate vengeance to include members of the malefactor's kin group. The killing of such individuals is either morally appropriate or morally imperative in "classic blood feud" (Ericksen and Horton 1992:63). This leads to the assassination of an isolated "unsuspecting relative" of a murderer, which is significantly different from the slaying of a bystander, peacemaker, or supporter who comes to the aid of a kinsman beset by a vengeance party. The intermediate form is one in which the murderer is the preferred target of vengeance but selected members of his group may be substituted if these are accessible and the perpetrator is not. These three modes by which a kinsman of a murderer may be killed also represent points on a developmental continuum. The endpoint is full social substitutability.

There are thus six incremental stages of development that can be logically formulated as the constituents of a progressive transition from an absence of counteraction following a homicide to capital punishment to classic blood feud. Blood feud entails the morally legitimated use of deadly force in preplanned armed conflict between political units and is a form of warfare. It is usefully distinguished from internal war only in those cases in which the political units in conflict are components of a more encompassing political entity such as a confederacy, chiefdom, or state. In that case feud typically constitutes a somewhat more constrained form of internal war. For example, the killing of only one person, or a small number of persons, in any given raid may be taken to satisfy vengeance requirements. Thus the six identified stages effectively encompass the transition from warlessness to internal war (including feud as a subvariety of the latter). The first four stages are particularly germane to the social contours of unsegmented societies. These are: (1) no counteraction, (2) the legitimation of capital punishment through public opinion in the absence of specification of a party or entity responsible for its achievement, (3) the stipulation of relational, kin-based vengeance obligations that generate a de facto vengeance group, and (4) kin group responsibility for carrying out vengeance against the malefactor (alone) vested in the extended family and/or kindred of the homicide victim. The transition to kin group member liability—in which the malefactor is the preferential but not the only recognized target of vengeance (stage 5), or in which any member of the killer's group is susceptible to vengeance (stage 6)—constitutes a watershed in that these stages are restricted to societies with segmental forms of organization (as shown in table 5). This suggests that the development of kin group member liability goes hand in hand with the development of descent groups and the conceptualization of marriage as a transaction between social groups, that is, with the attributes that are notably absent in unsegmented societies.

There is a very strong pattern of covariation between kin group member liability to vengeance and the conceptualization of marriage as a group transaction in our representative sample of foraging societies. This is shown in table 6. The accumulation, transfer, and redistribution of bridewealth formulates marriage as a group project that links participating kin groups (as explained earlier). The reciprocal exchange of valuable gifts between relatives of the bride and groom likewise encodes the same formulation (see Murdock 1981:92 for definitions of codes B and G). The presence of either of these features of marriage (or spouse acquisition) thus serves as a marker for the conceptualization of marriage in group terms. When these are absent, kin group member liability to vengeance also tends to be absent, and when these are present, kin group member liability to vengeance also tends to be present (in 17/22 or 77 percent of the codable ethnographic cases).

There is a weaker pattern of covariation between kin group liability and descent groups in this sample of foraging societies. Both are absent in ten cases and both are present in three, so that, in all, 13/22 or 60 percent of the societies conform. The same result obtains if one includes corporate extended families together with matrilineal, patrilineal, or cognatic descent groups (other than kindreds). In other words, the presence or absence of any one of these social forms covaries with the presence or absence (respectively) of kin group liability for vengeance in thirteen of the twenty-two codable ethnographic cases. However, there is only one case (the Aweikoma) in which kin group liability for vengeance is present when both marriage payments and descent groups (and/or corporate extended families) are absent. There are likewise only two cases (the Bellacoola and Tiwi) in which kin group liability is absent while marriage payments and/or descent groups are present. Thus, the conceptualization of marriage as a transaction between social groups, and/or the presence of

TABLE 6. **The Covariation between Marriage Payments and Kin Group Member Liability to Vengeance in a Representative Sample of Twenty-five Foraging Societies**

Kin Group Member Liability to Vengeance	Marriage Payments	
	Absent	Present
Absent ($n = 14$)	Mbuti	Bellacoola
	Semang	Tiwi
	!Kung	
	Ingalik	
	Andamanese	
	Slave	
	Warrau	
	Saulteaux	
	Nambicuara	
	Yokuts	
	Copper Eskimo	
	Yahgan	
Present ($n = 8$)	Comanche	Yurok
	Shavante	Gros Ventre
	Aweikoma	Eyak
		Gilyak
		Klamath
Not determinable ($n = 3$)		Chiricahua
		Abipon
		Ainu

descent groups, does empirically go hand in hand with the development of kin group liability for vengeance in nineteen of twenty-two foraging societies (or 86 percent of the cases).

Marriage is the most potent factor in this social transformation (to stages 5 and 6) because the exchange of women between groups directly encodes the key concepts of social substitutability, of the person as representative of the group, of collective interests and projects, and of the "loss" of a group member that diminishes the collectivity. Moreover, these key social conceptions are palpably presented to and experienced by social actors repeatedly, every time a marriage occurs. The potency of marital forms in social transformation that is indicated by these data is consistent with the generalizable conclusion, reached in another study of war in a tribal society, that "marriage transactions convey particularly compelling representation of the social order" (Kelly 1985:298) and that these transactions also shape the forces that engender organizational change (226–52). Within their full sample of 186 societies, Ericksen and Horton (1992:72) also find that "classic blood feuds occur within the context of marriage linkages between kin groups" and are related to various features of marriage payments and marriage transactions (e.g., a concern with premarital chastity on the part of daughters).[14]

Marriage practices pertaining to exogamy are also related to the frequency of warfare in foraging societies (with little or no dependence upon agriculture). This is shown in table 7. When the frequency of marriages between (rather than within) local communities rises above 60 percent, the frequency of warfare is at the low end of the scale (codes 8, 7, and 6 for the combined frequency of internal and external war). When the frequency of intermarriage between local communities falls below 40 percent, the frequency of warfare is at the high end of the scale (codes 5, 4, 3, and 2). When there is an intermediate frequency of exogamy (40 to 60 percent)— that is roughly equal proportions of endogamous and exogamous unions—the full range of frequencies of warfare obtain. Only one of the twenty-five foraging societies (the Warrau) is at variance with this overall (three-part) pattern. This covariation is consistent with Tylor's (1889) insight that outmarriage functions to blunt violence between local groups—an insight that represents one of the earliest formulations of anthropological theory.[15]

The frequency of exogamy is intermediate or higher in all 8 unsegmented foraging societies, while the 17 segmental foraging societies display the full ethnographic range of variation in frequencies of exogamy (from 11 to over 90 percent). Among the unsegmented societies, marriage does not engender political alliances between communities because it only joins individuals (and makes a man a member of his wife's extended family and she a member of his). In this type of society, there is consequently

TABLE 7. The Covariation between the Percentage of Exogamous Marriages and the Combined Frequency of Internal and External Warfare in a Representative Sample of Twenty-Five Foraging Societies

Exogamy: The percentage of marriages outside the local community	**Warless** Both "rare or never" (code 4+4)						**Warlike** Both "yearly" (code 1+1)
	8	7	6	5	4	3	2
90–100%	Mbuti	Yahgan	Gros Ventre				
61–89%	Semang	!Kung	Yurok Yokuts				
40–60%	C. Eskimo	Ingalik	Gilyak Eyak	Tiwi	Andamanese	Slave	Klamath Shavante Abipon
11–39%		Warrau		Saulteaux Bellacoola Comanche Chiricahua	Nambicuara		Ainu Aweikoma
0–10%							

Note: The frequency of exogamous unions is derived from Murdock and Wilson's codes for societies in the standard cross-cultural sample (1972:262, see column 11).

no intrinsic capacity for intermarriage to amplify the scale, intensity, or duration of intergroup violence. The consequences of exogamy are thus that the resulting kin ties spanning local communities can only have positive effects conducive to visiting, socializing, feasting, exchange, and joint participation in ritual. This generation and amplification of positive social interactions between the members of neighboring social groups contributes to the maintenance of a low frequency of warfare (codes 8 and 7).

In segmental foraging societies, intermarriage creates group-to-group relations. Thus these same links between communities produced by exogamous unions are potentially a vehicle for military alliance in which a pair of local groups join together to raid others, or to defend themselves against external attacks. Warfare between neighbors may also engender long-standing enmities that preclude intermarriage in those quarters. There is the potential for the development of a positive feedback cycle in which warfare leads to enmities that are conducive to elevated rates of endogamy and a diminution of social interaction between communities, creating a fertile ground for conflicts to take root and flourish in the absence of the countervailing tendencies generated by kin relations that link members of neighboring local groups. Thus the frequency of exogamy would fall as the frequency of warfare increased and rise as the frequency of warfare decreased. Similarly, the likelihood of an outbreak of armed conflict between local groups, and thus the frequency of warfare, would be decreased by a high rate of exogamy and increased by a low rate, so that mutual-causal relations would amplify a trend in either direction (in the incidence of armed conflict between the communities of a social system) that was generated by other factors. The pattern of covariation for segmental societies in table 7 is consistent with this type of mutual-causal interrelation.

The isolation of a representative world sample of hunter-gatherer societies that differ in terms of coded frequencies of internal and external warfare makes it possible to test the underlying propositions contained in a number of explanatory frameworks that have been put forward to account for the origin, development, and/or intensification of warfare. One of the most prominent and durable sets of propositions links warfare to aspects of sedentarism such as a reliance on relatively fixed subsistence resources or productive sites. This line of reasoning is attractive on several grounds. First, it is logical to suppose that fixed subsistence resources upon which a local group depends are vital and must be defended. Second, the archaeological record provides scant evidence of warfare prior to the development of agriculture and the sedentarism this entails (as noted in the introductory chapter). Third, ethnographic studies of hunter-gatherers repeatedly document dissociative mechanisms of conflict resolution (as Fabbro reports). Conflict often leads the family of one party to move away and join another band, and conflict between mobile bands often results in each giving the other a wide berth. A transition from a mobile to a more sedentary existence would thus undercut the principal mechanism for defusing conflicts among hunter-gatherers by inhibiting the capacity to move apart. One might then envision warfare arising out of emergent needs to defend critical food resources, combined with the debilitation of a conflict resolution mechanism that had formerly been effective in limiting the frequency and scale of physical violence (in terms of prolongation and escalation, respectively). This explanation essentially represents anthropological received wisdom with respect to a posited origination of warfare among heretofore warless hunter-gatherers (see Wolf 1987; Carneiro 1994).

The extent of covariation between frequency of warfare and degree of residential mobility among foragers is shown in table 8. The twenty-five foraging societies in the representative sample are classified in terms of settlement pattern codes provided by Murdock (1981:99) and Murdock and Wilson (1972). There are four categories that represent a graded progression from a fully mobile to a fully sedentary existence. If this progression covaried with an increased frequency of warfare, then the explanatory framework outlined above could be considered to be consistent with the comparative ethnographic data, and consequently regarded as a plausible developmental model. More specifically, one would expect a tendency for societies with fully migratory bands to manifest a low frequency of warfare (code 7 or 8), while fully sedentary societies, with nucleated permanent settlements, would be characterized by a high frequency of warfare (code 3 or 2). Similarly, one would expect seminomadic foragers—who move in migratory bands for six or more months of the year, but occupy fixed settlements seasonally—to manifest an intermediate frequency of warfare (code 6 or 5). Likewise, semisedentary foragers—who occupy permanent quarters for most of the year, but disperse seasonally to smaller camps—should evidence a somewhat more elevated intermediate frequency of warfare (code 5 or 4).

The shaded cells of table 8 depict this hypothesized pattern of progressive covariation. It is evident that the cross-cultural data are not supportive. Only seven of the twenty-five cases (or 28 percent) fall into the shaded cells, while the latter comprise a comparable proportion of the total number of cells (i.e., 8/28 or 28.6 percent of the cells are shaded). In other words, the number of ethnographic cases that "fit" is not greater than what would be expected if each case were assigned a place on the grid by rolling dice.

A closer inspection of the distribution of ethnographic cases in table 8 reveals some interesting subpatterns. The ethnographic cases that are arguably the most widely utilized as exemplars of hunter-gatherers—the

TABLE 8. Combined Internal and External Warfare Frequency for Foraging Societies with Varying Degress of Mobility

	Warless Both "rare or never" (code 4+4)						Warlike Both "yearly" (code 1+1)
	8	7	6	5	4	3	2
Fully migratory or nomadic bands	Mbuti Semang	!Kung Yahgan	Gros Ventre	Tiwi Comanche Chiricahua			Aweikoma Abipon
Migratory (6+ months) with seasonal permanent quarters	C. Eskimo	Ingalik	Gilyak Yokuts	Saulteaux	Andamanese Nambicuara	Slave	Klamath Shavante
Semisedentary with seasonal dispersion to camps		Warrau	Eyak				Ainu
Nucleated permanent settlements			Yurok	Bellacoola			

!Kung, Mbuti, and Semang—are both mobile and comparatively warless (and are, of course, also among Fabbro's selected Peaceful Societies). This may account for the common perception that these attributes covary. However, some of the most warlike foragers are also fully migratory (the Aweikoma and Abipon). Moreover, three additional cases of mobile hunter-gatherers exhibit yearly warfare, either external or internal (i.e., the Tiwi, Comanche, and Chiricahua Apache).[16] Thus less than half of the mobile foragers conform to the expectations of anthropological received wisdom regarding warfare frequency, while the remainder exhibit unanticipated high levels of conflict in the form of annual raids. More specifically, these data indicate a marked tendency toward a bimodal distribution of fully migratory foragers with respect to frequency of warfare.

However, the bimodal distribution is readily resolved by consideration of organizational type. The comparatively warless mobile foragers are all unsegmented societies, while the mobile foragers characterized by annual warfare are all segmental societies.

Seminomadic foragers who occupy fixed settlements seasonally manifest the full range of variation in terms of frequency of warfare. In other words, there is no incidence of warfare that could be said to be characteristic of this particular settlement pattern. Wide variation is characteristic. However, it is noteworthy that the one unsegmented society with a comparatively high frequency of warfare—the Andamanese—is seminomadic rather than mobile.

Sedentary and semisedentary societies with little or no reliance on agriculture do not tend to have incessant warfare as anticipated by received wisdom. All five of the societies in the lower half of table 8 rely on fixed resources or productive sites they would be expected to defend, yet only one of these evidences frequent warfare (the Ainu). These data indicate that there is a tendency toward intermediate levels of warfare among sedentary and semisedentary foragers, that is, the occurrence of warfare several times a generation is most typical.

All sedentary and semisedentary foraging societies are segmental in organizational design; conversely, all unsegmented foraging societies are either fully migratory or seminomadic. The frequency of warfare is thus low among unsegmented mobile foragers, intermediate among semisedentary and fully sedentary segmental foragers, variable among seminomadic foragers (of both organizational types), and high among mobile and seminomadic segmental foragers. Although sedentarism—considered independently—does not differentiate warlike from warless hunter-gatherers, a consideration of settlement pattern in conjunction with organizational type suggests the intriguing possibility that a low frequency of warfare might be a prerequisite for the development of sedentarism, or that sedentarism entails a reduction in the level of warfare, rather than an increase.

These possibilities will be explored in the context of consideration of other potential economic and demographic covariants of warfare frequency.

The development of a significant capacity for food storage on the part of hunter-gatherers is widely regarded as a pivotal point in cultural evolution (Testart 1982:524). Food storage both limits the mobility of foragers and renders full nomadism unnecessary. It facilitates a degree of sedentarism that is a necessary precursor to the development of agriculture (524). It stimulates population increase followed by a stabilization at higher densities. It lays the groundwork for the development of wealth accumulation and economic inequality (525–26).

The development of food storage also transforms the character of warfare because substantial dependence upon stored food during a seasonal period of scarcity makes a local population exceptionally vulnerable to the effects of raids, at the same time that the possibility of plundering food stores creates an additional inducement for carrying out forays against neighboring social groups. When food is stockpiled, it inevitably becomes a key military objective of raiding parties. Prior patterns of warfare are thus recontextualized so as to greatly amplify their material consequences. Consider, for example, a simple raid carried out to secure blood vengeance. A raiding party surprises an unsuspecting small settlement at dawn and succeeds in killing one or two residents while the remainder flee into the forest. But now the raiding party is also in possession of the settlement's food stores, as an unintended consequence of an effort to avenge a death. The looting and/or destruction of these food supplies that have fallen into the hands of the raiding party can cause famine-related mortality among the residents of the raided community far in excess of the casualties inflicted by the attack itself. The loss of essential food stores may also compel the displaced residents to take refuge with relatives at other locations and consequently yield territory.[17] Population movements and territorial changes thus become an intrinsic consequence of warfare once dependence upon food storage is a feature of the economy. Moreover, these augmented economic consequences of established raiding practices impinge on residential groups, whose members' food reserves are all equally at risk (whether stored communally or in each household). Coresidents thus have a common economic interest in defense that necessarily raises warfare to the level of a residential or territorial group concern, rather than merely a matter of kin group vengeance. At the same time, stored food may facilitate larger residential aggregations that are less vulnerable to attack. Since flight and subsequent reoccupation becomes an unattractive option for a food-storing community subject to raids, recourse to defensive fortifications such as palisades may develop. Subsistence patterns may also be altered for defensive purposes. In short, a new phase of the coevolution of war and society is triggered by substantial reliance on food storage.

The relationship between intensive food storage and the frequency of warfare among foragers is shown in table 9. The criteria for inclusion in the food-storing category are those developed by Testart (1982:529): seasonal and/or annual variation in food resources, adequate storage techniques, and lack of substantial dependence on land-animal hunting (which makes large-scale storage unnecessary). This table resolves the classification based on four degrees of mobility/immobility presented in table 8 into two categories that are especially pertinent to the question of the presence of vital stationary resources that cannot be abandoned or lost to theft without incurring serious food shortages. Thus the seminomadic Gilyak and Yokuts and the semisedentary Eyak and Ainu are grouped together with the fully sedentary Yurok and Bellacoola. It is evident here that food storage is strongly associated with intermediate frequencies of warfare among hunter-gatherers rather than either frequent warfare or an absence of warfare. (The warlike Ainu constitute the sole exception.)

Endemic warfare may well preclude the development of intensive food storage among hunter-gatherers, because this practice entails too great a risk when raiding is prevalent and the looting of caches is a distinct possibility. It is especially important to note that reliance on substantial food storage would be likely to be initiated under conditions entailing a less than fully sedentary settlement pattern. As Testart (1982:524) notes:

> The usual residence of hunter-gatherers practicing storage is a village or a permanent camp built around food reserves from which seasonal expeditions, requiring a certain mobility, such as hunting, are launched. What characterizes this residence pattern is not so much the total absence of mobility, but, first, a greater sedentarism than in the case of non-storing hunter-gatherers, which is frequently reflected in the nature of dwellings, and secondly, permanence of residence during the season of scarcity.

This partial sedentarism may entail the risk of leaving stored food resources vulnerable during certain periods. For example, the Chugach Eskimos timed their pillaging of Ahtna riverine settlements, and the looting and destruction of their fish caches, at the time the Ahtna were away hunting in the mountains (De Laguna and McClellan 1981:642). This untenable situation prompted the Ahtna to unite on a sufficient scale to carry out effective countermeasures.

> After several such [Chugach] raids, the Ahtna claim to have slaughtered the Chugach on Mummy Island in Prince William Sound, thus ending the Eskimo attacks and justifying the composition of several victory songs. Although these raids occurred

TABLE 9. Combined Internal and External Warfare Frequency for Food-Storing and Nonstoring Foraging Societies

	Warless Both "rare or never" (code 4+4)						Warlike Both "yearly" (code 1+1)
	8	7	6	5	4	3	2
Nonstoring foraging societies	Mbuti Semang C. Eskimo	!Kung Ingalik Yahgan Warrau	Gros Ventre	Saulteaux Comanche Chiricahua Tiwi	Andamanese Nambicuara	Slave	Klamath Shavante Aweikoma Abipon
Food-storing foraging societies			Gilyak Yurok Yokuts Eyak	Bellacoola			Ainu

some time in the nineteenth century, the two peoples remained unfriendly in the mid-twentieth. (642–43)

The Ahtna case thus illustrates the tendency toward periodic rather than endemic warfare, as well as the vulnerability of a partially sedentary hunter-gatherer population that relies on food storage. It is also evident that the material consequences of warfare engendered by substantial food storage prompt military engagements that are conclusive. Conversely, annual raiding over a protracted period is much more likely to be associated with inconclusive outcomes that do not significantly alter the status quo (in the case of foraging societies).

None of the unsegmented foraging societies are food-storing societies. Thus food storage and a segmental organization go hand in hand. While substantial food storage is likely to arise in a context where warfare is infrequent—that is, within a regional system of unsegmented hunting and gathering societies—it engenders changes in political economy that are eventually conducive to organizational change, especially under conditions of an increased frequency of warfare. The transformation of the character of warfare brought about by food storage may very well play a role in bringing about these changes. In other words, the inception of food storage constitutes a watershed in the coevolution of war and society.

The degree of covariation between population density and the frequency of warfare within this representative sample of foraging societies is shown in table 10 (the categories and codes for population density are derived from Murdock and Wilson 1972:254–95). The shaded cells map the pattern of progressive covariation that would be expected if an increase in the frequency of warfare went hand in hand with an increase in population density. As in table 8, only seven of the twenty-five societies conform to this postulated progressive covariation, this being identical to the number expected on a random basis. Population density therefore does not provide a means of accounting for observed differences in the frequency of warfare among foraging societies as a group. This finding is consistent with Keeley's (1996:118) conclusion "that absolutely no correlation exists between the frequency of warfare and the density of human population" within cross-cultural samples that encompass all types of societies.

However, if we restrict the comparative analysis to unsegmented foraging societies a very different picture emerges. Seven of the eight unsegmented foraging societies have population densities of less than one person per square mile, and all seven of these have infrequent warfare (code 7 or 8), excepting the Slave, who were the victims of unreciprocated external attacks and would otherwise have had a comparably low frequency of warfare. The only society of this organizational type with a comparatively high frequency of warfare is thus the Andamanese, who also evidence a higher population density (more than twice that of the other unsegmented

TABLE 10. Combined Internal and External Warfare Frequency for Foraging Societies Classified by Population Density

Population Density	Warless Both "rare or never" (code 4+4)						Warlike Both "yearly" (code 1+1)
	8	7	6	5	4	3	2
Less than 0.2 per M²	Semang C. Eskimo	!Kung Ingalik	Gilyak Gros Ventre Eyak	Saulteaux Comanche Chiricahua			Shavante Aweikoma
0.2 to 1 per M²	Mbuti	Yahgan Warrau		Tiwi	Nambicuara	Slave	Ainu Klamath Abipon
1.1 to 5 per M²			Yurok	Bellacoola	Andamanese		
5.1 to 25 per M²			Yokuts				

foragers). Thus warless and warlike unsegmented hunter-gatherer societies *can* be differentiated by population density, suggesting that an increase in population density may play a role in the origination of warfare within a regional system composed of such societies. This covariation also highlights the significance of the Andaman case as an ethnographic and archaeological site of particular interest with regard to the origin of war. The next step in our inquiry is thus to investigate this key case in detail. This will provide insights into the relationship between resource competition and collective armed conflict between local groups that are further developed in the concluding chapter.

The central conclusion reached in the present chapter is that the distinction between unsegmented and segmental organizational type successfully differentiates comparatively warless and warlike foragers, and that each of these organizational designs also modulates the effects of other variables on the frequency of war. This is entirely consistent with the fundamental concept that war and society coevolve. Moreover, the findings presented in this chapter lay the groundwork for the development of a model of the early coevolution of war and society that can be applied to the Upper Paleolithic and to archaeological data pertaining to lethal intergroup conflict during that period (35,000 to 10,000 B.P.) in chapter 4. Thus while variables measuring exogamy, sedentarism, food storage, and population density do not independently covary with the frequency of war in foraging societies, consideration of these variables nevertheless contributes to the development of a composite picture of unsegmented foraging societies. These societies manifest an organizational design in which (1) social groups are limited to the family, kindred, and local community, (2) marriage links an individual to his or her spouse's family, and (3) elementary forms of classificatory kinship adhere to the contours of the bilateral kindred. In addition, both marriage payments and kin group member liability to vengeance are absent. The frequency of local group exogamy is uniformly 40 percent or higher. Settlement pattern is either fully migratory or seminomadic with an absence of food storage (and of the potential for accumulation and economic inequality that food storage engenders). Population density is variable, ranging from less than 0.2 to as many as 5 persons per square mile, but is characteristically below 1 person per square mile. These features delineate the sociocultural milieu that shapes and is shaped by intergroup armed conflict in the initial coevolution of war and society.

CHAPTER 3

The Origin of War:
A Transitional Case

Warfare is not an endemic condition of human existence but an episodic feature of human history (and prehistory) observed at certain times and places but not others. Addressing the question of what accounts for differences between foraging societies in the prevalence of warfare has led to several important findings that orient further inquiry concerning the origination of war. First, we have seen that the distinctive feature of comparatively warless foraging societies is organizational: such societies are almost invariably of the unsegmented variety (i.e., of a particular structural type).[1] Second, these unsegmented societies uniformly lack certain patterns of vengeance that are conducive to the escalation of conflict. More specifically, unsegmented societies lack the concept of group responsibility for causing a death, and the concept of group liability to retribution that renders any member of a killer's collectivity (rather than the malefactor alone) a legitimate target for retaliation. Third, it is evident that violence is not a unitary phenomenon and that the development of war entails the institutionalization of practices governed by a distinctive social logic that renders the killing of a killer's consociate a socially meaningful, morally appropriate, and emotionally gratifying form of reciprocation. War thus originates as a transition from one form of retributive collective violence to another, that is, as a transition from capital punishment to blood feud, with these representing different patterns of vengeance (in the broad sense of this term) or different modalities of reciprocity in the realm of violence. The social logic that underwrites blood feud (and war) is integral to segmental societies as a structural type, while the more restrictive social logic of capital punishment is consistent with the characteristics of unsegmented societies. This is due to the fact that elaboration of the concept of social substitution (or the absence of such elaboration) has both morphological and ideological concomitants. A social logic and a social type thus go hand in hand.

Although comparatively warless foraging societies are almost invariably of the unsegmented type, a few unsegmented societies manifest a higher frequency of warfare. These cases are of theoretical importance in a number of respects. They serve to remind us that unsegmented societies are not incapable of war—they are not "peaceful" in the utopian sense—but rather have the lowest frequency of war compared to other foraging societies. This is largely attributable to the fact that revenge is not a potential cause of war in unsegmented societies, although it is an extremely common cause of war among stateless societies as a group. In other words, the absence of what is arguably the most prevalent cause of warfare within tribal societies (and between local groups of neighboring tribal societies) is conducive to a markedly reduced incidence of armed conflict, although such conflict may still occur for other reasons. But what reasons? This is one of the key questions we will seek to answer in this chapter by examining the warfare that does take place within and between unsegmented societies.

What differentiates those unsegmented foraging societies with more frequent warfare from their comparatively warless counterparts? This question is readily answerable by separating out the unsegmented societies from the larger sample of foraging societies considered in the last chapter. The two unsegmented societies with the highest frequency of warfare are the Slave and the Andaman Islanders. The Slave were raided annually by the warlike Cree, and the causes of this warfare consequently are not attributable to any internal characteristics of Slave society, but to the characteristics of the attacking Cree (a segmental society) and the milieu of eighteenth-century European expansion into the New World that shaped Cree history. From the Slave we thus learn only that unsegmented societies may manifest a high frequency of warfare when subject to relentless external attack.

The Andaman Islanders present a more complex and interesting case in that both internal and external war are reported to have occurred with some frequency under indigenous conditions.[2] This warfare is thus attributable to features of the Andaman Islanders' social existence rather than exogenous factors. Moreover, the Andaman Islanders are distinctive among the unsegmented societies as a group in that they are the only semi-nomadic society with a population density in excess of one person per square mile. Although the Copper Eskimo, Ingalik, Slave, and Andaman Islanders all utilize seasonal permanent quarters (and are thus "seminomadic"), these are winter quarters occupied during a time of minimal social contact between groups in the first three cases. In contrast, the seasonal quarters of the Andamanese are located in close proximity to rich aquatic resources and are occupied during the most favorable season for exploiting these resources and at a time of heightened intergroup interaction. Moreover, the tropical islands occupied by the Andamanese constitute a circumscribed environment while the territorial domains of all of the other unsegmented societies are located upon expansive continental land masses that afford a potential for migration into adjacent areas. Eskimo,

Ingalik, and Slave local groups that come into conflict with their neighbors—for whatever reason—can readily move apart and employ the dissociative mechanism of conflict resolution that is so frequently reported for foraging societies. In contrast, the Andamanese cannot create significant spatial separations between local groups during much of the year. These comparative data tentatively suggest that a higher frequency of warfare occurs among unsegmented societies under certain demographic and ecological conditions. However, the main point to be emphasized at this juncture is that the Andamanese are a particularly important case to examine in detail in order to further our inquiry into the origin of war. A comprehensive examination of this ethnographic case is thus the central focus of this chapter.

The Andaman Islands

The Andaman Islands are located in the Sea of Bengal 120 miles south of the southeast tip of Burma (Cape Negrais) and 340 miles north of the northern tip of Sumatra (see map 1). There are other islands between the Andamans and these coasts—the (uninhabited) Cocos Islands and the Preparis Islands in the north and the Nicobar Archipelago in the south—but there were no inhabited islands within 80 miles of the Andamans until the nineteenth century (Radcliffe-Brown 1964:1–2). The Andaman group consists of Great Andaman, Little Andaman, and about two hundred small islands and islets that together make up a land area of 2,580 square miles (Lal 1976:1). However, the three parts of Great Andaman Island—North Andaman, Middle Andaman (including Baratang Island), and South Andaman—account for 64 percent of this total (1,660 square miles). Great Andaman is roughly 160 miles long by 20 miles wide. Little Andaman, which is 30 miles to the south of Rutland Island (at the tip of South Andaman) is 238 square miles (and about 25 miles long by 16 wide) (see map 2).

The Andaman Islands were indigenously inhabited by thirteen named groups that each claimed a separate identity, possessed a distinctive language or dialect, and occupied a particular territory. These groups have been designated as "tribes" in the literature since the 1880s, and it is convenient to continue to employ this designation (while at the same time recognizing that the word *tribe* here refers to an ethnic or cultural group rather than a cohesive political entity). The relationships among the languages or dialects spoken by members of these thirteen tribes are shown in figure 1[3] while the territorial distribution of the tribes (circa 1880) is shown on map 2.[4] Generally speaking, the closest linguistic relationships are between neighboring tribes, such that the languages or dialects of the four

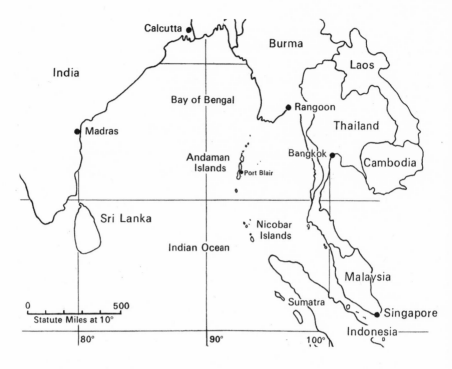

Map 1.   South Asia, showing the position of the Andaman Islands.
(Reproduced from Singh 1978, endsheets.)

tribes of North Andaman are more closely related to each other than to any of the four languages of Middle Andaman (including Baratang Island), and the same pattern is applicable to Middle Andaman as well. However, this covariation between propinquity and closeness of linguistic relationship breaks down in South Andaman in that the Jarawa language is quite distantly related to the language of the neighboring Bea, but closely related to the languages of Little Andaman Island (Onge) and of Sentinel Island.[5] This suggests that the Jarawa are intrusive. Radcliffe-Brown (1964:13) argues:

> There can be no doubt that the Jarawa are the descendants of emigrants who at some time in the past made their way across from the Little Andaman and thrust themselves upon the inhabitants of Rutland Island and the South Andaman, maintaining their footing in the new country by force of arms.

This armed conflict continued during the early decades of British colonial presence in the islands, and accounts of it will be examined in detail further along.

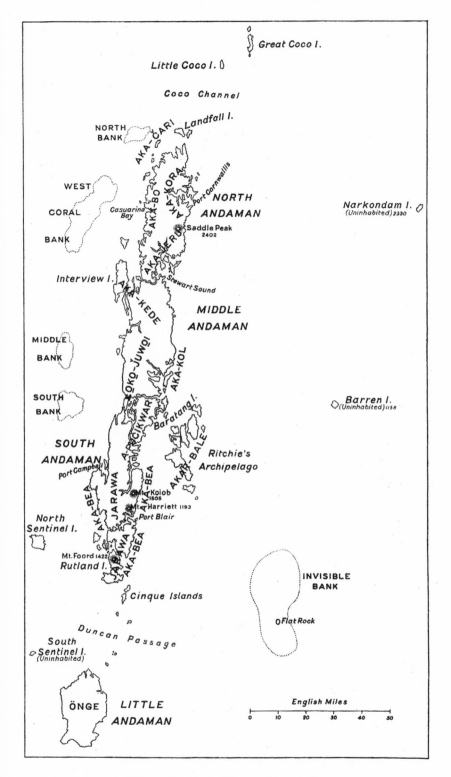

Map 2. The Andaman Islands, showing the distribution of tribes. (Reproduced from Radcliffe-Brown 1964 [1922], 10. Reprinted with the permission of Cambridge University Press.)

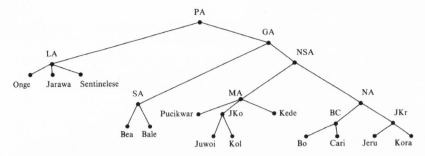

PA Proto-Andamanese; LA (Proto-)Little Andamanese; GA (Proto-)Great Andamanese; SA (Proto-)South Andamanese; NSA (Proto-)Non-South Andamanese; MA (Proto-)Middle Andamanese; NA (Proto-)North Andamanese; JKo (Proto-)Juwoi-Kol; BC (Proto-)Bo-Cari; JKr (Proto-)Jeru-Kora.

Fig. 1. The relationship between Andamanese dialects and languages. (Reproduced from Zide and Pandya 1989, 649. Courtesy of the *Journal of the American Oriental Society.*)

The archaeological data presently available indicate that the Andaman Islands have been inhabited for 2,200 years and that the material culture and subsistence-settlement patterns (revealed through the excavation of kitchen-middens) display substantial continuity throughout this period (Cipriani 1966; Dutta 1978; Cooper 1985, 1987, 1993a:398). The coastal topography of the Andamans includes raised beaches "on the Ritchie archipelago, north-east corner of Chatham Island and in the east coast of South Andaman" (Lal 1976:12) and thus affords an excellent opportunity to discover the coastal settlements of greatest antiquity, since at least some of these would be immune to submergence due to changing sea levels or subsidence (which may possibly have occurred at other locations). Cooper (1990b:99, 104) also indicates that the submergence of older coastal sites is unlikely, and this reduces the possibility that the date for initial occupation will be significantly pushed back by additional archaeological excavation.

Dutta (1978:56) cogently argues that the Andamanese are most likely derived from a physically similar Negrito population that inhabited the smaller islands of the Mergui Archipelago, located near the coast of Lower Burma. These postulated progenitors are a seafaring people,[6] and the migration could have occurred as the result of a canoe being swept out to sea by a tropical storm. This might well have occurred a number of times, inasmuch as historical records indicate that a number of European sailing ships were cast upon Andaman shores by storms during the eighteenth and nineteenth centuries. It is thus quite possible that Greater Andaman and Little Andaman were independently settled by different sets of migrants derived from the same general area of the Lower Burma coast and adjacent islands. If these two sets of migrants spoke related but somewhat different languages or dialects, that would account for a degree of linguistic difference that is difficult to accommodate within a time frame allowing for only 2,200 years of divergence from a common proto-language. However, the significant point for our purposes is that the Andaman Islands constitute a rich but circumscribed environment containing two sets of hunter-gatherers of the unsegmented organizational type that speak mutually unintelligible languages, irrespective of how that arose. Moreover, it is evident that the Andaman Islands present us with something akin to a natural laboratory in which the analogue of an experiment concerning the origin of war has been conducted.

Cultural History

Although the Andaman Islands are geographically isolated, they are located not far from sea-lanes that have been traversed by sailing ships for over 2,000 years, and they appear on second century A.D. Ptolemaic maps (Cooper 1989:134). However, the islands were avoided by travelers and traders (especially before the sixteenth century) due to the Andaman Islanders' reputation for hostility to outsiders, while considerable maritime traffic passed through the Nicobar Islands to the south (136–39). This hostility has been interpreted as a defensive response to slave raids by Malay and Burmese vessels (136–39), although it is also consistent with a more general pattern of response toward intruders discussed further along. In any event, shipwrecked mariners and the members of landing parties seeking to replenish water supplies were often killed by the Andamanese. The first attempt to establish a colony in the islands was in fact initiated in 1789 by the British East India Company in order to alleviate "the menace to shipping constituted by the islands and their inhabitants" (Radcliffe-Brown 1964:9) and to secure a harbor that might serve as a naval base if needed. This effort was abandoned after a few years due to heavy mortality from tropical diseases (e.g., malaria), and a permanent settlement was not established until more than sixty years later.

In 1858 a penal settlement was established at what had come to be known as Port Blair in South Andaman, a sheltered natural harbor that had also been selected as the site of the initial settlement in 1789 (but occupied only until 1792).[7] A large number of prisoners who had been convicted of participating in the Indian (Sepoy) Mutiny of 1857 were transported to the settlement and set to tasks of forest clearance and construction. This work was first begun on two small uninhabited islands at the mouth of the harbor that were secure from hostile encounters with the Andaman Islanders. However, in the first three and a half months 140 of 773 convicts escaped and eluded recapture (while 87 others were hanged for attempted escape) (Portman 1899:258). One man who had been part of a group of 21 escapees made his way back to the penal colony after the convicts were attacked by about 100 Andaman Islanders. He believed all his companions were killed, and it appears that the same fate probably befell nearly all of the unrecaptured escapees excepting those who drowned.

There was, however, one other survivor from among the early escapees who returned to the penal settlement after having lived for a little more than a year with the Andamanese (Portman 1899:279–86). Dudhnath Tewari escaped in the night with 90 others on makeshift rafts as part of a planned breakout. Another 40 convicts who had escaped at the same time from another island that formed part of the settlement joined this group several days later. This combined party of 130 moved into the dense tropical forest of Great Andaman Island believing it was connected by land to Burma, where they might find refuge. They moved slowly and circuitously through the forest for nearly two weeks without directly encountering the Andamanese, although they came upon their deserted huts. But then at midday of the fourteenth day they were attacked by about 100 bowmen. Tewari was wounded by arrows but took flight and managed to escape. He and two other convicts reached the west coast of South Andaman, about ten miles across the island from Port Blair. However, they were spotted on the beach the following morning and immediately attacked by the men of an Andamanese band of 60 persons. Tewari's two companions were killed, and he was wounded. He feigned death and then supplicated himself when the Andamanese approached to retrieve their arrows. He was shot yet again in the hip and wrist but again pleaded for mercy and this time was spared. He was taken in a canoe to a settlement on an offshore island and his wounds treated. Though initially regarded with suspicion, he was gradually incorporated into the band, being given a wife about four months after his capture. He eventually learned the language of his captors, of the Bea (or Aka-Bea) tribe, and this enabled him to understand that a large group of Andamanese were massing for an attack on the penal settlement in April 1859. He slipped away from the attacking force to warn the settlement shortly before what has become known as "The Battle of Aberdeen" on May 14, 1859, and was subsequently pardoned and allowed to return to India. I will take up the events of this battle shortly, after first recounting some of the encounters between the Andamanese and the military contingent of the penal settlement that had taken place in the intervening year between Tewari's escape and return.

One initial impact of the penal settlement upon the Andaman Islanders was their experience of encountering large groups of escaped convicts, who undoubtedly appeared as marauding bands of interlopers. However, they soon encountered the military contingent of the penal settlement as well. Shortly after the settlement's inception, a naval party was dispatched to the main island to collect thatching leaves at the head of a creek occupied by an Andamanese band. This provoked a conflict in which a naval officer was killed (Portman 1899:265), which inclined the settlement's armed forces to seek revenge. Another skirmish several months later provided occasion for the punitive destruction of forty Andamanese dwellings. Dr. J. P. Walker, the superintendent of the penal settlement, encouraged the troops under his authority to pursue an aggressive policy toward the Andamanese, although this was contrary to the instructions he had been given. Dr. Walker duly filed reports of those engagements, and these reports resulted in a sharp reprimand from his superiors. This may usefully be quoted as it provides an unvarnished internal critique of early colonial encounters with the Andamanese grounded in the time and milieu of that period.

You have already been made aware of the wishes of the Court of Directors in regard to the policy to be observed towards the natives of the Andamans, and in paragraph 13 of my letter No. 1079, dated 12th ultimo, you were requested to 'adhere strictly to the conciliating line of conduct which has hitherto been observed towards the aborigines', to 'absolutely prohibit any aggression upon them' and not to allow force on any account to be resorted to 'unless it be absolutely necessary to repel their attacks.'

8. These instructions are of date subsequent to the occurrence now reported, but Lieutenant Templer's proceedings appear to the President in Council to afford very proper opportunity for emphatically repeating them for your guidance, and for that of all the officers and men employed at the Settlement.

9. On this occasion, as it appears from the papers, our people were the assailants. Though the disposition of the natives at large is known to be hostile, there is no ground assigned for supposing that they appeared on the north side of the port and established a village there with any special intention of giving annoyance. The attack, therefore, was unprovoked and without justification. The native who was seen in a canoe very naturally tried to get away when he saw the armed boat approaching, but there was no reason for immediately giving chase and pursuing the man to within the reach of the arrows of his own countrymen.

10. The subsequent capture of the canoes and partial destruction of the village appear to have been ordered as [an] act of retaliation for the attack of the natives on the boat; but this

attack was provoked by Lieutenant Templer's pursuit of the man in the canoe, and the complete destruction of the village on a subsequent day was an unnecessary and deliberate act of revenge not calculated, any more than the original pursuit of the canoe, to induce the natives to abandon their hostility towards us.

11. The President in Council fully appreciates the difficulties of your position. But the aborigines of the Andamans are apparently unable to conceive the possibility of the two races co-existing on the islands, except on terms of internecine hostility. This idea is assuredly strengthened by every attack we make upon them, and can only be driven out of their minds by a course of persistent conciliation and forbearance on our part. The President in council would have been disposed to encourage the settlement of a village of these savages on the north side of the bay, where they could not at present interfere with the progress of the Settlement or give us any annoyance, and where they might gradually become familiar with our appearance and divest themselves of the fear which is obviously the moving cause of their present aversion. Every effort must be made to teach them that we desire to cultivate friendly relations, and have no intention of attacking them or doing them any injury, unless they compel us to act in self-defense. (Portman 1899:271–73)

Dr. Walker's response to these criticisms was to propose clearing fifty square miles of tropical forest stretching outward from Port Blair to straits and ocean that would provide natural barriers on three sides, while the fourth was to be secured by a military cordon of "entrenchments, fortlets or stockades" (Portman 1899:273). The intention was to keep the Andamanese at a distance. A less ambitious plan of forest clearance around Port Blair was eventually approved and the work begun with convict labor in early 1859. The Andamanese were understandably

alarmed and enraged at the manner in which their country was being cleared and appropriated on all sides, and the conflicts with the Naval Guard, in which the latter were the aggressors, only increased that alarm. (Portman 1899:289)

The Andamanese consequently began to endeavor to expel convict parties working on the main island. In early April, 200 bowmen drove off a work party, killing four convicts and wounding five others and appropriating tools, clothes, and cooking vessels left behind. The convicts were of course unarmed and also worked unguarded inasmuch as they were by now apprised of the probable fate of escapees. Those who had been troublesome worked in fetters, while the best behaved attained supervisory positions over their peers. All in all, they were not in a position to offer serious resistance to large parties of Andamanese bowmen, who thus readily achieved their objective of disrupting forest clearance, without suffering any casualties, and were rewarded with booty as well. This initial success undoubtedly encouraged others to participate, and a much larger force estimated to number 1,500 Andamanese attacked only eight days after the first offensive foray. But this "attack," as it has been described, was most curious in character.

> On the 14th April, at about noon, when the convicts of the two divisions were employed in cooking, they were suddenly attacked by a very large number of aborigines, estimated at about 1,500, armed with small axes and knives, in addition to bows and arrows. The convicts attempted to resist, but were quite unequal to the work, and after having three killed on the spot, and six severely wounded, they were obliged to retire into the sea under the protecting fire of the Naval guard boat moored off the landing place, while the savages remained in possession of the encampment, and carried off the working tools, clothing, and cooking vessels of the two divisions. Out of the 446 convicts present, 12 had fetters on, and these the savages selected, and having removed their fetters, carried them off into the jungle, and they have not been seen since.
>
> The convicts described the savages as showing no disposition to attack any one with a mark of imprisonment (such as the iron ring around the ankle), unless opposed, but as anxious to attack and murder the section gangsmen, the sub-division gangsmen, and the division gangsmen, who do not wear the ring, and are marked by wearing a red turban, badge, and coloured belt. They called upon the convicts to stand aside and let them go into the water and attack the naval Guard in the boat. During the two hours they had possession of the encampment they beckoned to the convicts to come and dance with them, and they, from fear, complied. Ludicrous groups of savages with a convict on each side, with arms entwined, were engaged in stamping motions which appeared intended for dancing. (Portman 1899:277)

This encounter contains many features of the Andamanese peacemaking ceremony later described by Radcliffe-Brown (1964:134), but unknown to the British administrators of the time or to Portman, a late-nineteenth-century administrator who provides this account (based on government reports from this earlier period). In the peacemaking ceremony, the "forgiving party" are the visitors, coming (by prior arrangement) to the camp of those who have committed acts of hostility against them. The visitors come armed, but set their weapons aside to dance with their hosts. The visitors first express their anger by shouting and making threatening gestures as they dance toward their passive hosts, but then each man of the forgiving party grasps the shoulders of a man of the offending party who is facing him and jumps "up and down to the time of the dance" (Radcliffe-Brown 1964:134–35). Although the Andamanese peacemaking ceremony contains other elements (especially including participation of the women and a conclusion in which the two sides sit down and weep together and later exchange gifts), the efforts of the Andamanese to dance with the convicts is unintelligible except as an attempt to resolve past hostilities. Moreover, the Andamanese clearly recognized that chained individuals were not clearing forest of their own free will. They were able to distinguish the oppressors from the oppressed, targeting the former and liberating the latter in full view of their fellow workers. This so-called attack on the convicts by the largest party of Andamanese ever to assemble was clearly not an attack at all, but an attempt to transcend past acts of hostility and make common cause with the convicts against the British.

The Battle of Aberdeen occurred a month later. "Owing to timely warning from two escaped convicts who had been traveling with the aborigines, the attack was provided for and the plunder of the tools on a large scale prevented" (Portman 1899:278). A party of the Naval Guard was landed and established forward positions atop Aberdeen hill (with the convict work party at their rear) so as to engage the Andamanese while their schooner was anchored where it could supply supporting fire. Despite these military preparations, made possible by advance warning, the Naval Guard was unable to hold their position against the Andamanese who attacked from the edge of the uncut forest. The Naval Guard retreated and took to their landing boats, from whence they were able to fire over the heads of the convicts, who had retreated into the water along the shore. The schooner's guns likewise fired on the Andamanese, who nevertheless held the convict station for more than half an hour "plundering everything worth carrying off" (Portman 1899:278–79).[8] The hill was then reportedly retaken by elements of the Naval Brigade, with support from some of the convicts. Nevertheless, none of the convicts were wounded (278–79), a point that is consistent with the interpretation that the Andamanese hoped to effect a mutually advantageous alliance with the convicts against their captors. Portman (294) reports that the Andamanese ceased their past practice of killing escaped convicts in the latter part of this year (1860), but only "took away their brass pots and the leg irons off their legs," which he interprets as "looting them of all the metal they had." However, he also notes:

Cases occurred of runaways actually being kept for a short time by the Andamanese, and being well fed by them on pork. The Andamanese may have had some idea of getting the convicts to make common cause with them against the Government. (1899: 294)

This provides the key to understanding the earlier Andamanese response to forest clearance carried out by convict work parties, a response in which only supervisory personnel were attacked.

One would imagine that the Battle of Aberdeen was a major disappointment to the Andamanese, in that they had a government military contingent between themselves and the convict work party so that the latter could have turned on their captors and attacked them with their axes to good effect. But the convicts did not avail themselves of this opportunity. The Andamanese also suffered betrayal at the hands of the convict Tewari, who had lived among them for a year.[9] The Battle of Aberdeen thus was indeed a victory for the government forces, and one that marked a turning point in their relations with the Andamanese.

A few days afterwards another attack was threatened, but though the Andamanese entered the place where the convicts were clearing the jungle, they did not follow them when they retreated to the station. (1899:294)

After this final unsuccessful effort to see if the convicts would join with them, the Andamanese no longer came together in large numbers to oppose the progress of the settlement. Conflict was limited to minor attacks on naval landing parties seeking water and to the pilfering of tools from work parties. Dr. Walker was replaced by a Captain Haughton who was intent on establishing friendly relations with the Andamanese (in accordance with government policy) and who also discontinued the noxious policy of forest clearance that had incited them to aggressive resistance.[10]

At the time of the first short-lived effort to establish a settlement on Chatham Island at the entry to Port Blair (in 1789–92), the Jarawa occupied the southern side of the harbor and the Bea tribe occupied the northern side. Sixty-six years later (in 1858), the Jarawa were many miles to the south of Port Blair and outside of the general area impacted by the establishment of the penal colony. The colonial administration was unaware of their existence until 1863, when friendly members of the Bea tribe who were guiding an exploratory patrol made every effort to dissuade the officer in charge from proceeding further southward by pantomiming the likelihood of being shot on sight (Portman 1899:435). The earliest accounts thus indicate that a state of war obtained between the Jarawa and Bea and that this warfare had resulted in territory changing hands.

From the Aka-Bea-da [Bea] I have learnt that in former times the Jarawas were more numerous and powerful than they are now, and they inhabited the southern part of the Harbor of Port Blair, the Western part, and much of the neighboring interior. Many 'Kitchen-Middens' on the shores of the Harbour have been pointed out to me as the sites of Jarawa villages, and the Aka-Bea-da further prove their contention by showing that these shell-heaps contain the refuse of articles which the Jarawas eat, but which the Aka-Bea-da will not touch. (Portman 1899:702)

The early accounts provided by Bea informants also indicate that traditionally the Bea and Jarawa fought whenever they encountered one another (704, 712).

The Andaman Islanders have suffered severe depopulation since the 1870s as a result of introduced diseases, most notably syphilis, measles, smallpox, mumps, and influenza (Portman 1899:607–15; Malhotra 1989: 119–22; Radcliffe-Brown 1964:17). Portman (1899:614) estimates that back-to-back measles and smallpox epidemics in 1877 killed half to two-thirds of the population of Great Andaman Island, excepting the Jarawa who were unaffected. Syphilis caused sterility and increased infant mortality. Radcliffe-Brown (1964:18) estimates the 1858 population of Great Andaman as 4,950 and that of Little Andaman and Sentinel Island as an additional 700. By 1901, the ten Great Andaman Tribes (excluding Jarawa) had decreased to 625 persons and the population subsequently fell steadily decade by decade to only 23 persons in 1951 (but then stabilized at about that level through 1981) (Malhotra 1989:20; Chakraborty 1990:14–17).

The Jarawa maintained their hostility to escaped convicts, their Bea neighbors, the government, and settlers who immigrated later, and they were consequently less affected by introduced diseases. This hostility to outsiders has continued up to the present (e.g., there were 89 recorded Jarawa raids between 1946 and 1963 and 28 recorded Jarawa attacks over the five-year period of 1983 to 1988; Sarkar 1990:47–48, 66–71). This has prevented any censuses from being conducted. However, the Jarawa are variously estimated to have numbered between 200 and 468 in 1901, to have declined to perhaps as few as 50 persons in the 1950s (after being bombed by the Japanese during World War II), and to number at least 106 (actually observed) persons in 1987 (Sarkar 1990:10). Large numbers of children seen in 1987 bode well for the continued viability of the Jarawa population.[11]

These data indicate that the population size and relative military strength of the Jarawa and Bea shifted over time. In 1858, Radcliffe-Brown (1964:25) estimates there were 1,000 Bea and only 200 Jarawa. Portman (1899:702) believes that the Jarawa had been more numerous in 1789, when they occupied a larger territory. He speculates that disease may have been introduced by the initial (1789–92) settlement that led to Jarawa decline but left the Bea relatively unaffected, facilitating the territorial expansion of the latter. There is no evidence that can be brought to bear on this speculation, pro or con. However, a reverse population shift in favor of the Jarawa is documented for the period from 1870 to 1901, inasmuch as the Bea had declined from 1,000 to only 37 persons by the latter date (Chakraborty 1990:14). As the Bea declined, the Jarawa appropriated the portion of Bea territory along the western side of South Andaman. By 1901 they had moved north into the interior section of the territory of the Puckiwar tribe on Baratang Island in Middle Andaman, and they continued northward into the vacated or sparsely inhabited territories of other depopulated Middle Andaman tribes in the ensuing decades (Lal 1976:51). After India gained independence from Britain (in 1947) the successor Indian administration of the Andamans set aside a 756-square-kilometer Jarawa Reserve along the west coast and interior of South and Middle Andaman where the Jarawa have since resided, while the small population of 23 Great Andamanese were relocated to Bluff Island and subsequently Strait Island.

It is important to carefully assess the effects of British colonial intrusion into the Andaman Islands upon the warfare we seek to examine, particularly the effects of the appropriation of territory around Port Blair and the effects of depopulation, both of which had the potential to alter the relationship of population to territory (and hence to food resources). It is possible that disease was differentially introduced in 1789 causing the Jarawa to decline in numbers while the Bea did not. However, this effect could only have been realized if there were no contacts between the two tribes so that disease was not passed from the Jarawa to the Bea. This condition would presuppose a prior and comprehensive state of hostilities between the local groups of these tribes, including an absence of intermarriage and the resultant relations of kinship that are invariably conducive to social interchange. In other words, an absence of disease transmission between neighboring local groups could occur if they were in a state of war with each other.

It is highly improbable that population decline would engender warfare where none previously existed, since a reduction in numbers produces surfeit rather than shortage: the resources that previously sustained a larger population of hunter-gatherers must necessarily be more than enough for a diminished population. Depopulation clearly provides no impetus to territorial expansion by the shrinking tribe. However, it may cause a territorial contraction. Inasmuch as hunter-gatherers are prone to move away from conflict, depopulation may engender disengagement along contested borders. If the Jarawa declined in numbers, they may have pulled back. And the Bea may have opportunistically occupied and exploited the vacated areas. The differential effects of the introduction of disease could therefore cause territory to change hands, but at the same time this would be expected to reduce the frequency of warfare by reducing the incidence of encounters between hostile groups.

An alternative hypothesis concerning the expansion of the Bea at the expense of the Jarawa between 1789 and 1858 can readily be proposed: namely, that the Bea outnumbered the Jarawa by more than 2 to 1 (i.e., 1,000 to 458, taking the highest estimate for the Jarawa). Under this scenario, there would be no differential depopulation (for which there is no evidence but Portman's hypothesizing), and territorial expansion would be accomplished in conjunction with armed conflict. In this case, neither the frequency of war nor the outcome would be attributable to the brief colonial presence of 1789 to 1792. Although we can not be certain which of these two alternative historical reconstructions is most accurate, we can readily conclude that in either case the state of war that existed in 1858 was not a product of this colonial intrusion. Moreover, the frequency of warfare between the Bea and Jarawa at this time would either be unaltered (if no differential depopulation had occurred) or reduced (if contraction engendered withdrawal).

The establishment of the penal settlement in 1858 entailed an appropriation of territory in the vicinity of Port Blair. Such territorial appropriation could potentially cause a displaced tribe to be pushed in on their neighbors, and so on outward in a ripple effect, causing pervasive conflict between neighboring tribes that formerly lived in peace. However, nothing of this sort occurred in this instance. Instead, the penal settlement simply expanded inland from uninhabited islands in Port Blair Harbor into the eastern part of Bea territory as the Bea declined from 1,000 to 37 persons between 1858 and 1901. The penal settlement did not cause a demographic compression that instigated warfare but instead engendered a decompression within a circumscribed environmental context that would be expected to alleviate resource competition.

It is of interest that the boundaries of the tribal territories of all eleven Great Andaman tribes changed between 1889 and 1901 (Lal 1976:51), even though each tribe was reduced in numbers. However, it was the more northern tribes, who suffered a lesser degree of depopulation, that expanded their territory. The Charier, Kede, and Kol tribes of North and Middle Andaman all drifted southward toward the most heavily depopulated region (while the Jarawa spread north, away from the colonial presence at Port Blair). The general tendency evident in these territorial shifts was toward a more even spacing of population over territory, so that tribes that declined significantly in size still enlarged their territory at the expense of neighbors who suffered even greater decreases. This was accomplished without noticeable conflict in the case of the ten Great Andaman tribes that form a continuous dialect chain from north to south. However, there were conflicts between members of some of these tribes and the Jarawa (whose language is not mutually intelligible with that of the other ten tribes).

The nature of one of the forms of conflict that indigenously took place between the Jarawa and Bea was very distinctive in character. According to Bea informants,

> The Aka-Bea and Jarawa were inveterate enemies. Whenever two parties of them met by any chance, or came into the neighborhood of one another, the larger party would attack the other. (Radcliffe-Brown 1964:86)

These encounters were occasioned by the food quest, or by resource exploitation more generally, and the conflict between these two unsegmented societies was thus grounded in resource competition between groups that jointly occupied the circumscribed environment of a tropical island. Thus when a party of collectors or hunters of one tribe arrived at a shellfish bed, honey tree, or hunting ground to find a party of hunters or gatherers of the other tribe already in place, a conflict ensued in which (according to Radcliffe-Brown's report) the larger group took possession of the contested resource by force of arms. In other words, the larger party attacked, and the smaller party was compelled to withdraw. However, an isolated individual caught unawares, or positioned so as to be unable to retreat, might readily be killed (86). Jarawa male attire anticipates this potentiality of ambush occurring in the course of daily subsistence activity.

> The Jarawa of both sexes, adult and children, do not cover their bodies. They remain completely naked [excepting body painting and the wearing of adornments]. However, a bark chest guard is used by the adult male. This may be considered specific to this tribe. A chest guard, identified by them as *kekar,* is prepared out of thick bark. It is round, with a double-fold and the two ends of the bark are fixed by a bark rope. This is worn by the male, not always, but whenever they go out of their habitats [*sic,* habitations] either for hunting or gathering. (Sarkar 1990:8)

The Jarawa chest guard is shown in plate 5.

Spontaneous attacks and opportunistic ambushes were not the only form of armed conflict between these two tribes. There were also at least some preplanned raids by the Jarawa on the Bea (and vice versa). However, the spontaneous impromptu fighting over access to resources embodied in the shoot-on-sight policy of each tribe toward the other is of especial interest because it is consistent with the historical data indicating that the Bea appropriated Jarawa territory between 1792 and 1858. In other words, we have two independent pieces of evidence showing (1) fighting over resources and (2) territory changing hands. When we also consider that the

Andaman Islands are a circumscribed environment, and that aboriginal population density was comparatively quite high for a hunter-gatherer population, there is little question as to the root cause of the state of war that obtained between the Jarawa and Bea. It is also clear that the basic conflict was indigenous rather than an artifact of colonial intrusion, although the latter had an effect upon raiding and counterraiding during the colonial era.

A mode of armed conflict entailing spontaneous shoot-on-sight attacks is also of especial interest because it does not require any military organization (unlike a raid or battle). The effective fighting force in engagements of this type is an economic group, shaped by the division of labor and settlement pattern, rather than a contingent of a political unit that has been recruited for, and functionally adapted to, the task of combat. In other words, the forces put into the field of potential combat are the combinations of coresident individuals who routinely hunt or gather together. The "battlefields" are dictated by the seasonal availability and spatial distribution of game and collectibles. The potential for engagement thus depends on the extent to which the antagonistic social groups occupy the same ecological niche. The Jarawa and Bea do not in fact occupy a single ecological niche, but rather partially overlapping niches whose principal orientations are to coastal and interior resource zones, respectively.

The Ecological Context of Resource Competition

The encampments of the coast dwellers (or *aryoto*) are typically situated at sheltered locations just back from a sandy beach, at a site selected for its proximity to a stream or other source of fresh water. The shallows offshore are exploited by the women, who "are able at low tide to catch fish in pools with their hand-nets, and to collect large quantities of shell-fish; while during the flood tides men enjoy exceptional facilities for shooting fish and harpooning turtles, etc." (Man 1885:39–40). Such sites are marked by extensive shell middens (Cooper 1985), and the coast dwellers move by dugout canoe from one such site to another every few months. At each location they inhabit a circle of family lean-tos (and one bachelors' lean-to) that face inward toward a shared communal space that serves as a dance ground (see fig. 2, based on Radcliffe-Brown 1964:34). Each of these local groups is composed of about forty to fifty persons (on average) who exploited a stretch of coast and hinterland encompassing a territory of about sixteen square miles (Radcliffe-Brown 1964:28).

Although the Andaman coast dwellers are oriented to the sea (from which they obtained fish, turtle, dugong, crabs, crayfish, prawns, and mollusks), detailed study of their diet indicates that a very substantial portion of their caloric intake is derived from the tropical forest behind the coastal

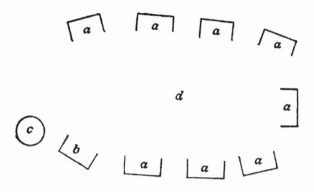

Fig. 2. Plan of Andamanese village (*a*, huts of married people; *b*, bachelors' hut; *c*, public cooking place; *d,* dancing ground). (Reproduced from Radcliffe-Brown 1964 [1922], 34. Reprinted with the permission of Cambridge University Press.)

strand (Erickson and Beckerman 1975; Bose 1964; Cooper 1992). The forest is a source of six wild tubers, including wild yams that are especially plentiful during the hot and dry season (March to mid-May) (Man 1885:122–33). Honey is available in sufficient quantity to constitute the principal food of the local group for several days at a time. Seeds of the jackfruit (*Artocarpus chaplasha*) are also collected in quantity during this season of abundance and buried in the ground for later consumption during the rainy season (mid-May to mid-November). The forest is also a source of many other edible fruits (including pandanus), as well as a variety of game animals. Pig hunting predominates during the rainy season, during which it makes an important contribution to the diet. Other less important terrestrial game animals include civet cats (*Paradoxurus tytleri*), monitor lizards, snakes, pigeons, waterfowl, and flying foxes, plus beetle larvae and wood grubs. The seasonal availability of the principal staples (including marine resources) is shown in table 11. This also brings out the complementarity of foods derived from the forest and the sea, respectively.

The gendered division of labor has a spatial dimension in that women's chores largely keep them in the vicinity of the encampment while men's pursuits take them further afield.

A man hunts and fishes, using the bow and arrow and the harpoon; he makes his own bows and arrows, his adze and knife, cuts canoes and makes rope for harpoon lines. A woman collects fruits and digs up roots with her digging stick; she catches prawns and crabs and small fish with her small fishing net; she provides the firewood and the water of the family and does the cooking (i.e., the family cooking, but not the common cooking, which is entirely done by men); she makes all such objects as baskets, nets of thread, and personal ornaments either for herself or her husband. (Radcliffe-Brown 1964:43–44)

Both men and women join in collecting honey, jackfruit seeds, and tubers during the hot and dry season (39). However, women and boys under the age of twelve take no part in pig-hunting expeditions carried out in the interior of the islands by groups of two to five men (Man 1885:137). The potential for encounters between the coast dwellers and the forest dwellers (including the Jarawa) occurs mainly in the context of these pig hunts (and possibly during honey collection as well). However, the seasonal cycles of resource exploitation of these two differentially adapted populations are conducive to mutual avoidance. In other words, the region of overlap between their respective ecological niches is exploited by the forest dwellers during the dry season and by the coast dwellers during the rains.

The forest dwellers (*eremtaga*) resided in large beehive-shaped communal huts that consisted of a cluster of family lean-tos drawn into a tight circle so as to make it possible to roof over the central communal space with palm-leaf mats. During the rains, the residents of a local group remained in the vicinity of this main camp, with the men focusing their efforts on hunting pigs that were readily taken close at hand during this time of year (when fruits, tubers, and honey were also less available) (Radcliffe-Brown 1964:36). Meanwhile, the coast dwellers took advantage of this same seasonal availability of wild pig to exploit the interior hinterland of their territories. During the following cool season (mid-November to mid-February) and the hot and dry season (mid-February to mid-May),

TABLE 11.   Seasonal Availability of the Staples of the Andamanese Diet

	Cool and Dry Season		Hot and Dry Season			Rainy (Monsoon) Season					
	Dec	Jan	Feb	Mar	Apr	May	June	July	Aug	Sept	Oct	Nov
Jack-fruit					+	+	+					
Root/tuber	+	+	+	+	+				+			+
Honey	+	+	+	+	+				+			+
Shellfish	+				+	+	+	+	+	+	+	+
Fish	+	+	+	+	+	+			+		+	+
Turtle	+	+	+	+	+				+			
Turtle egg					+	+						
Pig	+				+	+	+	+	+	+	+	+

Source: Dutta 1978:49, by permission of the Anthropological Survey of India.

the forest dwellers moved out from their base camp to temporary hunting camps dispersed over their territory, while the coast dwellers retired to their beach encampments and directed their efforts to turtle harpooning and shooting fish rather than hunting terrestrial game. The spatiotemporal ambits of *aryoto* and *eremtaga* hunting parties were thus potentially distinct. However, both groups heavily exploited honey, which became abundant in April.

Most of the ten Great Andaman tribes encompassed both coastal and forest-dwelling local groups. A pair of these groups would occasionally meld together for a few days during the hot and dry season and engage in joint hunting, feasting, dancing, and the exchange of gifts. This enabled forest dwellers to "obtain such things as shells, red paint made with turtle fat, and other objects with which they could not provide themselves in any other way" (Radcliffe-Brown 1964:83). However, the main purpose of these gatherings was to promote amicable relations between neighboring bands, as both the *aryoto* and *eremtaga* were economically self-sufficient with respect to the essentials of subsistence. Portman (1899:26) notes that fights sometimes occurred between coastal and forest-dwelling bands of the same tribe, despite intermarriage.

The Jarawa lacked canoes and did not occupy any encampments along the coast (in 1858), with the exception of an inaccessible cliff-top settlement at the southern tip of Rutland Island. Although their base camps were invariably located in the upland interior of Rutland and South Andaman Islands, they sometimes came down to the coast to shoot fish and collect shellfish in the shallows (Portman 1899:724, 743, 735, 758). In contrast, the Bea occupied the entire coastline of both these islands, as well as the offshore islets, except for the rocky southern end of Rutland Island and the eastern shore of Port Campbell. In addition, the Bea occupied the interior of south Andaman from Port Blair to the Middle Strait (Portman 1899:25). The Jarawa were thus exclusively forest dwellers, while the Bea included both forest-dweller and coastal divisions. However, the Bea forest dwellers occupied a ridgeline separated from the ridgeline occupied by the Jarawa, except at the point at which they form the tip of a V. The main zone of conflict may thus be characterized as the points of overlap between coastal and interior ecological niches that were partially but not entirely discrete. Both groups relied significantly upon wild yams and honey during the hot and dry season, and both hunted wild pigs in the rainy season (although in zones that tended to be spatially discrete).

The juncture between the territories of coastal and forest-dwelling bands of the Bea and Jarawa tribes (respectively) was not delineated by environmental discontinuities but by armed conflicts. Bea guides made it clear to the colonial parties initially exploring the interior that passage upstream beyond a certain point would provoke certain attack.

Jacko pointed to my heart and represented the act of a savage
aiming at me with his bow and arrow, of the arrow piercing my
heart and my falling wounded, closing my eyes and expiring.
Topsy also pathetically enacted the death scene, and both waved
their hands deprecatingly in the direction disapproved of, and
entreated me not to proceed further but to return [to base]. (Portman 1899:435)

It is evident from this account that an aggressively defended Jarawa territorial boundary was clearly recognized by the Bea in 1863, only a few years
after the founding of the penal colony.

Radcliffe-Brown emphasizes that the landowning or territorial unit
was the local group (or band), not the tribe, and that

A man might hunt over the country of his own [local] group at all
times, but he might not hunt over the country of another group
without the permission of the members of that group. (Radcliffe-
Brown 1964:29)

Prior to depopulation, hunting or fishing in the territory of another band
had the potential to generate "a serious quarrel" (29), even among bands
of the same tribe. Man (1885:46) reports that "sharp retribution . . . causing serious loss of life, and resulting in long-standing tribal feud" followed
violation of territorial rights by bands of different tribes, and by *aryoto*
and *eremtaga* local groups of the same tribe. This emphasis on territorial
claims is intelligible given the circumscribed environment the Andaman
Islanders occupied.

The Andaman Islands are of especial interest with respect to the question of the origin of war because they constitute a *regional system* of unsegmented societies encompassing thirteen linguistically distinct tribes,
including two sets of tribes that speak mutually unintelligible languages.
Although unsegmented foraging societies as a group are characterized by
a comparatively lower frequency of warfare than segmental foraging societies, both internal and external war occur regularly in the Andaman case,
that is, both war between the constituent communities of a single cultural
group and those of two different cultural groups (i.e., the Jarawa and the
Bea). The fact that the Andaman Islands contain a regional system of
unsegmented societies provides something of a natural laboratory for
examining interactions between such societies (to the extent that indigenous practices are discernible). We thus have an opportunity to address
important questions concerning the location(s) where warfare erupts, its
causes, and the manner in which it is conducted. What has emerged thus
far is that war occurs at those points where there is resource competition,
that it is a product of this competition, and that it is conducted in a manner consistent with the maintenance of exclusive access to the resources of

a bounded territory. However, conflict between local groups that speak the same language, or mutually intelligible dialects of the same language, is subject to resolution (through the peacemaking ceremony) while external war is endemic and unremitting. Hence the Bea and Jarawa fight whenever they encounter one another and have no other form of interaction. These points remain to be fleshed out, but it is nonetheless useful to highlight the broad outlines of the overall picture that is taking shape as we examine the ethnographic data.

External War

The character of the external warfare between the Bea and Jarawa is exemplified by the conflicts that occurred between 1880 and 1896. A comprehensive account of these is supplied by Portman (1899:729–63), who was the officer responsible for dealing with such matters during this period. The Bea, who were by then on friendly terms with the government, reported thirteen incidents in which they were subject to attack by the Jarawa. This included eleven instances in which Bea parties engaging in subsistence activities that intruded into Jarawa domains were attacked, one instance in which Bea were shot in close proximity to their own settlement by members of a Jarawa raiding party, and one additional instance in which the location of the armed conflict is not reported. The following incidents are typical of the engagements that occurred in the interior of the island.

> On the 16th of August, 1893, 'Rima,' an Andamanese man from Homfray Strait, brought in the news to me that, about a month before, while four other Andamanese were pig hunting in the jungle south of the eastern entrance to the Strait, two Jarawas were seen, who had been attracted by the noise of the dogs.
>
> These Jarawas at once fired on our people, killing an old man named 'Lipaia,' and wounding another man of the same name in the back (who subsequently died from the effects of the wound). Rima fired one arrow in return, wounding a Jarawa in the left shoulder, and then our people ran away. The dead men were buried on a small island at the entrance to the Strait. (Portman 1899:751)

> On the 15th of September, 1893, when Lokala and Total, two Andamanese men, were out pig hunting near Amit-la-boicho in Baratan Island, they came upon a party of Jarawas who fired on them. Total escaped, but was so frightened that he lost his way in the jungle, and it was two days before he returned to his village

of Lekera-lunta, bringing with him Lokala, who had been badly wounded in the right shoulder and in the lower part of the spine. They then came in to report to me, and Lokala was treated in Haddo Hospital by Dr. Gupta. He died on the 26th from his wounds.

The large iron head of one arrow was stuck in three of his vertebrae, and considerable force had to be used before it could be extracted. (Portman 1899:752)

In all, there were five instances in which Bea pig hunters were targeted, one incident involving a Bea honey collector, and one in which a Bea party traveling through the interior was attacked. Three Bea hunters were killed and three individuals wounded in these encounters, with one of the latter being a woman accompanying a pig hunting party on their return to camp. Two Jarawa were reportedly wounded.[12]

There were four instances in which Bea were attacked while encamped on the beach, or traveling by canoe, including the following.

On the 25th [of August 1893], an Andamanese man, named 'Ria Chana,' reported to me that, as he was coming through the Middle Straits in his canoe four days before, a single Jarawa, who was shooting fish on the west bank opposite Retin, fired at him, missing him. Ria Chana fired three arrows in return, missing the Jarawa, who then decamped. (Portman 1899:751)

On the 10th of September, 1889, at about 6 A.M., a party of Jarawas attacked some of the Port Mouat Andamanese, who had gone out to hunt turtle with a Convict Petty Officer, and having been up all night, were asleep in camp on the shore at Lekera about ten miles north of the outer harbour of Port Mouat.

The Jarawas were first seen by one of our Andamanese, who instinctively took up his bow and arrows; on this the former fired, hitting an Andamanese man named Ira Terra in the thigh as he was lying down, the arrow completely penetrating the thigh and entering the stomach. A general fight seems to have ensued, both parties retiring in the end. There appears to have been no other motive for this attack than the mutual dislike and dread these tribes have for each other. (Portman 1899:746)

On the 22nd of August, 1894, I received a report from a party of Andamanese who had been turtle hunting on the west coast, that on the 19th they were in camp in Port Campbell, and while they were cooking a pig in their hut just inside the jungle on the sea-coast, one of their number, Wologa Jerra-bud, had gone out on the beach to pluck some leaves, when he met a single adult male Jarawa, who at once shot him through the right lung with a pig-arrow. Wologa screamed, staggered back to the hut, and fell dead. The Jarawa ran away, and nothing more has been seen of him or his tribe.

This murder was entirely unprovoked, as Wologa was unarmed at the time, and it can only be attributed to the inveterate hostility of the Jarawas to all strangers, a hostility caused by ignorance and timidity. On the 24th I sent a party of 16 convicts and 38 Andamanese with instructions to follow the Jarawa tracks, and, if possible, catch some. They tracked from the place where Wologa was murdered, and on the side of a hill in the interior found a large hut resembling those in the Little Andaman. (Portman 1899:757)

It is evident that the Bea turtle-hunting party involved in the third incident had recently established a beach encampment that was in relatively close proximity to a Jarawa base camp, and that the Bea had engaged in pig hunting in the hinterland behind their settlement as well as exploitation of marine resources. The Jarawa attack appears to have been designed to induce the Bea to move elsewhere so that their hunting parties would not impinge on Jarawa territory or discover the location of the Jarawa base camp (subsequently found by the government party sent out by Portman). The second incident cited above may also have been a preemptive attack motivated by the same concerns. Both instances have something of the character of a "raid" in that the Jarawa came into Bea encampments on the coast to carry out an attack. However, the description suggests that these may well have been impromptu rather than preplanned engagements, carried out by Jarawa hunters who had just discovered Bea newly arrived in the area and sought to avail themselves of the earliest advantageous opportunity to attack and expel the intruders.

The only incident that conforms to the prototypical concept of a raid occurred in the vicinity of the colonial settlement, far from the Jarawa domain.

On the 1st of February, 1893, an Andamanese girl named 'Bira,' one of a party of eleven women living in the Brigade Creek Home, and engaged in collecting *pan* leaves in the adjacent jungle, got separated from the others, and in the evening was missed. A search was made for her, and on the 2nd, at about 11 A.M. her body transfixed by a Jarawa arrow was found a few hundred yards from the Home.

Another similar arrow was sticking in a tree close to the body.

A party of Andamanese was sent on the evening of the 2nd in

search of the Jarawas, but after remaining seven days in the jungle, and having tracked the Jarawas up the centre of the South Andaman to a point between Kyd Island and Port Campbell, they returned without having seen them. They stated that the jungle, since the cyclone, was almost impassable, and several of them were wounded by thorns, etc., in the search.

There appears to have been no reason for this murder. The Jarawas thus come at intervals on the outskirts of the Settlement, murder in this manner any one they meet, and then retreat into their own jungle, where it is almost impossible to find them. (Portman 1899:751)

This attack may possibly have been retaliatory. However, the other eleven incidents are all readily interpretable as spontaneous attacks prompted by infringement of the Jarawa territorial domain rather than revenge.

Although Radcliffe-Brown's (1964:86) characterization of armed conflict between the Bea and Jarawa is accurate with regard to the point that they fought whenever they encountered one another by chance, his depiction of a group-to-group confrontation in which the larger party initiated the fight is not borne out by the colonial record. What these data show instead is that a Jarawa hunting party of only two men did not hesitate to attack a party of four Bea pig hunters when they possessed the advantage of surprise. Similarly, even a single Jarawa might follow the Bea back to their beach camp in order to wait for a favorable opportunity to shoot an individual and then flee. Opportunistic ambush (rather than confrontation) was typical (although confrontations of the type Radcliffe-Brown describes undoubtedly occurred as well). When the nature of the wounds inflicted is described, it is clear that the victim was generally unaware of the presence of the Jarawa when the arrow was released. Those Bea who were killed were often shot in the back. In all, there were six Bea killed and five wounded in these thirteen incidents. Only two Jarawa were reportedly wounded by return fire (with left shoulder wounds consistent with the fact that they were deploying their bows at the time). The casualty rate the Jarawa inflicted in these encounters was substantial, with an average of nearly one per attack, and a very high six to five ratio of fatalities to nonfatal woundings.[13] In contrast, the Jarawa only incurred wounds from which they were very likely to recover. Because these engagements were predominantly encounters between hunting parties, women comprise only a small fraction of the casualties on both sides (i.e., two of thirteen). One Bea woman was wounded traveling in the interior with hunters, and one was killed near her settlement in a raid. Comparative study of tribal warfare in segmental societies indicates that women and children typically account for half or more than half the casualties when raiding is the principal form of combat. The distinctive mode of Bea-Jarawa warfare thus has demographic consequences that are quite different from those associated with raiding. Moreover, this distinctive mode of warfare is associated with resource competition rather than revenge, whose purposes can be satisfied by killing a woman or child (in social substitution for the perpetrator of a prior killing). Jarawa attacks targeted the perpetrators of a crime of trespass in all but one instance. Indeed, the interpretation that capital punishment was the Jarawa penalty for trespass and the "theft" of game from Jarawa territory is consistent with the ethnographic data contained in the colonial records reviewed here.

Most of the conflicts in the interior occurred during the rainy season (mid-May to mid-November) and the early part of the following cool season (up to December) when the Bea hunted pigs in the hinterland back from their coastal encampments and the Jarawa hunted pigs in the vicinity of their base camp (see table 11). If the Bea happened to move along the coast to a beach site directly below a Jarawa upland base camp during this season, the potentiality for both groups to hunt in different parts of the interior would not be realized and a clash would be likely to occur. The Jarawa practice of hunting almost daily enabled them to continually patrol their territory and to intercept intruders before the latter discovered the location of the Jarawa base camp, which was typically secluded. Under precontact conditions this would have made it difficult for the Bea to retaliate. Reconnaissance would be a prerequisite. During the colonial period under consideration (1880–96) Portman organized very large parties including police, up to 30 convicts, and as many as 140 Bea and other friendly Andamanese to comb the interior for weeks in search of the Jarawa responsible for these killings, but with very little success. The Jarawa split into small groups of only two or three persons that moved very rapidly and never reoccupied a camp that had been discovered (Portman 1899:750). Typically, Portman's expeditions yielded only an elderly woman or two and sometimes small children (both of whom were detained for a period and then released with presents as a gesture of the government's desire to establish amicable relations with the Jarawa). The Jarawa have sustained themselves up to the present by these stratagems. The capacity of the Jarawa to establish and maintain occupation of Great Andaman despite the fact that they were significantly outnumbered by the Bea is also intelligible in light of these features of their adaptation to endemic warfare.

Internal War

Both Man (1885:46) and Radcliffe-Brown (1964:29) report that violation of territorial claims also led to armed conflict between local groups of the other ten Great Andaman tribes (apart from that between the Bea and Jarawa). However, among and between bands of these tribes there were also other potential sources of conflict that arose out of social interaction (absent in the Jarawa-Bea case). Internal war differed from external war in that it sometimes appeared to be instigated by factors other than resource competition and also in that it contained the possibility for achieving conflict resolution by peaceful means.

The Andaman Islanders are similar to Fabbro's Peaceful Societies discussed in chapter 1 in that homicide occurs frequently. In Portman's (1899:33) characterization, Andamanese men "are gentle and pleasant to each other, and kind to children, but having no legal or other restraint on their passions, are easily roused to anger, when they commit murder." Women also fight each other, sometimes employing sticks, although no female homicides are reported (Man 1885:43; Radcliffe-Brown 1964:50).[14] Usually, a homicide engenders no sequel. Although the perpetrator may occasionally be killed by a friend or relative of the victim, there is no stipulated obligation to avenge a murder (Man 1885:42). Redress of wrongs is governed by the principle of self-help, with no explicit kin group responsibility or liability (see table 5, chap. 2). As Radcliffe-Brown (1964:48) puts it, "There does not appear to have been in the Andamans any such thing as the punishment of crime," there being no social group charged with the redress of injurious or antisocial actions on the part of an individual. "If one person injured another it was left to the injured one to seek vengeance if he wished and if he dared" (52).

The wrongs that might prompt such individual retaliation included wounding, theft, adultery (also regarded as a form of theft), and sickness-sending (i.e., the shamanic induction of illness through manipulation of certain spirits). Man (1885:44) reports that adultery was rare indigenously (and that abduction, rape, and seduction were entirely unknown). In contrast, Radcliffe-Brown (1964:70–71) notes that there was "great laxity" with respect to marital fidelity at the time of his fieldwork and that "very often the husband seems to condone the adultery of his wife." (Premarital sexual relations were also condoned and constituted a prelude to marriage.) Thus Man's reconstruction proposes that adultery rarely led to conflict during the precolonial era because adultery rarely occurred, while Radcliffe-Brown's data suggest that a lack of spousal concern with frequent infidelity during the colonial period produced the same net result, namely, very little male conflict over sexual access to women. Radcliffe-Brown (50) also reports that theft was rare. The overall impression one gains from the ethnographic sources (including Portman) is that fighting between men (and between women) occurred with some frequency in the course of social life within the local group, but that minor slights and irritants rather than serious wrongdoing instigated the altercations (see Man

1885:27, 42–43) (the pattern appears similar to that among the Mbuti discussed earlier). Reliance on the principle of individualistic self-help often tends to be associated with a "don't tread on me" response to slights in unsegmented societies, and female fighting (which is typically reported) is indicative of the fact that women act on their own behalf in the same manner as men (rather than behaving as the wards of men in situations of interpersonal conflict).

The concept of individual (rather than group) responsibility for the redress of wrongs is embodied in Andamanese customs that impose protective tabus and purification rites upon a man who has slain another, in order that he may avoid retaliation by the spirit of the deceased.

> If a man kills another in a fight between two villages, or in a private quarrel, he leaves his village and goes to live by himself in the jungle, where he must stay for some weeks, or even months. His wife, and one or two of his friends may live with him or visit him and attend to his wants. For some weeks the homicide must observe a rigorous tabu. He must not handle a bow or arrow. He must not feed himself or touch any food with his hands, but must be fed by his wife or a friend. He must keep his neck and upper lip covered with red paint, and must wear plumes of shredded *Tetranthera* wood (*celmo*) in his belt before and behind, and in his necklace at the back of his neck. If he breaks any of these rules it is supposed that the spirit of the man he has killed will cause him to be ill. At the end of a few weeks the homicide undergoes a sort of purification ceremony. His hands are first rubbed with white clay (*tol-odu*) and then with red paint. After this he may wash his hands and may then feed himself with his hands and may handle bows and arrows. He retains the plumes of shredded wood for a year or so. (Radcliffe-Brown 1964:133)

Although homicide eliminates the very person responsible for redress under a regime of self-help (i.e., the victim), this does not mean that a man can kill with impunity. Vengeance is still a possibility at the spirit level. But by the same token there is no real need for the murder victim's bereaved kin and friends to assume responsibility for blood vengeance. This is why murder typically engenders no sequel. It is also evident that a belief in retaliation by the spirit of the deceased would inhibit the development of group-level vengeance obligations.

As in other unsegmented societies examined earlier, the concept of achieving redress through self-help markedly reduced the potentiality for individual conflict to escalate to the group level or for revenge to underwrite reciprocating acts of violence between social groups. However, group-level conflict *could* occur when the parties to a transgression were themselves groups, as in the case of one hunting party trespassing on the territory of another. Inasmuch as bands claimed exclusive rights to a territorial domain, the "injured party" was also a social group. And it is evident that the "crime" of trespass and theft of game was in fact "punished" (contra Radcliffe-Brown's generalization noted above). These concepts of crime and punishment are analytically appropriate in that malefactors were specifically targeted as a consequence of violations of norms of moral behavior.

The joint gathering of two local groups also provided an occasion for the generation of group-level conflict.

> Quarrels were more likely to occur at the meetings of different local groups that took place in the fine weather, and such quarrels might occasionally end in the murder of some one. In such a case the quarrel would be taken up by the group of the murdered man, and a feud would be set up between them and the local group to which the murderer belonged. Such was one of the common causes of origin of the petty warfare that formerly existed in the Andamans. (Radcliffe-Brown 1964:50)

In these contexts involving a joint gathering of two bands, an offense "such as an assault or theft" was regarded as a premeditated provocation (Man 1885:44) and therefore essentially an insult to the group (either the hosts or the guests). This interpretation on the part of the Andamanese suggests that they themselves believed there was an underlying cause of the interpersonal conflicts that arose in this context, such that these conflicts were not to be taken at face value. Inasmuch as conflict over women was reportedly infrequent, there appears to be only one plausible candidate for this underlying cause, namely, resource competition. These meetings were sometimes undertaken as a means of ending past quarrels (Radcliffe-Brown 1964:84), and this also suggests that territorial infringement may have been the source of the residual ill feelings that erupted in fighting. If this was indeed the case, then the fighting that took place at the meetings of local groups that shared a boundary between their territories may also be seen as a display of strength between competitors. Radcliffe-Brown (1964:84) describes the general atmosphere of these gatherings as one of "amiable rivalry," where each man and woman among the hosts and guests tried to "outdo the others in generosity" in the exchange of gifts (including bows, arrows, adzes, baskets, nets, red ochre, white clay, shells, and pieces of iron from shipwrecks that were worked into arrowheads). In short, these were occasions for the exchange of gifts and blows between rivalrous neighbors.

When all went well, the two groups joined together in hunting and fishing expeditions, as well as in feasting, dancing, and the exchange of gifts. The joint hunting and fishing would have entailed the exploitation of resources along the borders between territories that might otherwise have been contested, and thus only utilized under peril of attack. This utilization of border areas would have facilitated the maintenance of high population densities in a circumscribed environment in which there were "occasional times of scarcity" (Radcliffe-Brown 1964:401). In contrast, the endemic warfare between the Bea and Jarawa entailed wider spacing that resulted in a lower overall population density in South Andaman than in the other parts of the island (19).

Although the Andamanese lacked either group-based or kin-based vengeance obligations, members of a local group shared rights in a common territorial domain. Conflict arising out of infringement of these rights thus mobilized the men of a local group in joint retaliatory action. Although the principle of achieving redress through self-help curtailed the escalation of individual conflict into group conflict, as in other unsegmented societies, warfare might nevertheless occur. As in the capital punishment characteristic of unsegmented societies, the perpetrators of a criminal act were targeted. This held true not only when trespassers were ambushed on the spot but also when a raid was carried out against a neighboring group as the result of a "quarrel" or a murder (which, I have argued, were most probably underwritten by past conflicts over resources). In such a raid, an effort was made to shoot the men of the community, although women and children might also be killed in the confusion of a predawn attack (Radcliffe-Brown 1964:85). (This vulnerability of bystanders is not unlike the situation among the !Kung described in chapter 2.) Thus while the social substitution that underwrites taking vengeance against any member of a perpetrator's social group is absent, armed conflict between groups is not. What the transitional Andamanese case reveals is the specific circumstances under which warfare arises between local groups in an unsegmented foraging society that lacks the concepts of group responsibility for, and group liability to, vengeance, namely, a state of resource competition between territorial local groups in a circumscribed environment where maximum population density has been attained (as evidenced by periodic food shortages). The character of this warfare is behaviorally similar to that which occurs in segmental societies (insofar as it involved raid and counterraid between communities) except in that women and children were not targeted and that peace was relatively easily established due to the absence of vengeance obligations. Moreover, women were able to initiate the cessation of armed conflict because they were recognized as individuals distinct from the perpetrator (or perpetrators) of trespass or homicide whose death might be sought in punishment or retribution. Thus Andamanese women could walk into a settlement their menfolk had recently raided in order to seek to arrange a peace, a practice that would be unimaginable in many segmental societies where vengeance is applicable to all group members (and also in those in which abduction was practiced).

Radcliffe-Brown (1964:85–86) provides a concise description of Andamanese warfare that exemplifies these characteristics.

> It does not seem that there was ever such a thing as a stand-up fight between two parties. The whole art of fighting was to come upon your enemies by surprise, kill one or two of them and then retreat. A local group that had some grievance against another would decide to make an attack. They might seek and obtain the aid of friends from other local groups. The men who were to take part in the expedition would paint themselves and put on various ornaments and join in a dance. They would then set out, either by land or by sea, in the direction of the encampment they meant to attack. Their weapons consisted of bows and arrows, and they carried no shields or other defensive weapons. They would not venture to attack the enemy's camp unless they were certain of taking it by surprise. For this reason such attacks were generally made either in the evening when the camp would be busy with the preparation of the evening meal, or at early dawn, when every one would be asleep. The attacking party would rush the camp and shoot as many men as they could. If they met with any serious resistance or lost one of their own number they would immediately retire. Those attacked, if they were really taken by surprise, were generally compelled to save themselves by flight. Though the aim of the attacking party was to kill the men, it often happened that women or children were killed. The whole fight would last only a few minutes ending either with the retirement of the attackers before resistance, or the flight of those attacked into the jungle. A wounded enemy would be killed if found.
>
> Such attacks and counter-attacks might be continued for some years, thus establishing a feud between two neighboring local groups. More usually, however, after one or two such fights peace would be made. In the tribes of the North Andaman there was a special peace-making ceremony. . . . All peace negotiations were conducted through the women. One or two of the women of the one group would be sent to interview the women of the other group to see if they were willing to forget the past and make friends. It seems that it was largely the rancor of the women over their slain relatives that kept the feud alive, the men of the two parties being willing to make friends much more readily than the women.

The dance that took place prior to a raid served the purpose of welding the participants into an operational group and engendering a transitory military organization suited to the task at hand. The dance provided an occasion for anger to be shared and intensified so as to generate a consensus of collective emotion as well as a sense of shared injustice that facilitated the unified pursuit of a common cause of retaliation (see Radcliffe-Brown 1964:252–53). Plumes of *Tetranthera* wood made from the shaft of the arrows used in fighting and pig hunting were "carried in a dance preceding a fight, and at such times the natives used to rub their bows with the shredded wood in order to ensure success in battle" (261). *Tetranthera* plumes were also worn by an individual who was in seclusion following a homicide, in order to avoid vengeance at the hands of the spirit of the man he had killed (133). In both cases, the plumes are employed to ward off spirits of the dead that are believed to be the cause of illness (and death from illness). The spirits of enemies, and of territory other than one's own country, are especially dangerous (182, 301).

The ceremonial war dance thus provides a venue for both organizing and legitimating war-making. The participants are unified and reassured of their invulnerability to hostile spirits by ritual employment of the talismanic *Tetranthera* plumes. They also bask in the adulatory encouragement of their womenfolk, who clap to mark time as they dance, and on whose behalf (as well as their own) the warriors prosecute the feud and seek retribution. It is noteworthy that all the elements that enter into the definition of war outlined in the Introduction are clearly manifested in the war dance that precedes an Andamanese raid on a neighboring local group of the same tribe (or a tribe speaking a closely related language). In contrast, many of these elements are tacit and unelaborated in the spontaneous armed conflict between Bea and Jarawa hunting parties that constitutes the main form of external war.

In the peacemaking ceremony, the "forgiving party" comes to the settlement of the local group responsible for the last raid or other act of hostility. The dance ground of the hosts is prepared by suspending a ritually potent shredded palm leaf (*koro*) from lengths of cane tied to posts. The cane is associated with and symbolically represents the rainbow, which is believed to be a bridge to the world of the spirits of the dead. The *koro* fiber forms part of the women's pubic covering and connotes tabu, the regenerative birthing powers of the female genitals, and also a critical link to the spirit world (as will be elucidated further along). The men of the host group stand with their backs to the "rainbow" and their arms outstretched sideways along the top of it. Although unarmed, they essentially occupy a spirit-guaranteed sanctuary and are immune from attack. The visitors enter the camp dancing, while the host women, seated along one side of the dance ground behind their menfolk, mark time by clapping their hands on their thighs (see plate 4).

The visitors dance forward in front of the men standing at the *koro-cop,* and then, still dancing all the time, pass backwards and forwards between the standing men, bending their heads as they pass beneath the suspended cane. The dancers make threatening gestures at the men standing at the *koro-cop,* and every now and then break into a shrill shout. The men at the *koro* stand silent and motionless, and are expected to show no sign of fear.

After they have been dancing thus for a little time, the leader of the dancers approaches the man at one end of the *koro* and, taking him by the shoulders from the front, leaps vigorously up and down to the time of the dance, thus giving the man he holds a good shaking. The leader then passes on to the next man in the row while another of the dancers goes through the same performance with the first man. This is continued until each of the dancers has "shaken" each of the standing men. The dancers then pass under the *koro* and shake their enemies in the same manner from the back. After a little more dancing the dancers retire, and the women of the visiting group come forward and dance in much the same way that the men have done, each woman giving each of the men of the other group a good shaking.

When the men have been through their dance the two parties of men and women sit down and weep together.

The two groups remain camped together for a few days, spending the time in hunting and dancing together. Presents are exchanged, as at the ordinary meetings of different groups. The men of the two groups exchange bows with one another. (Radcliffe-Brown 1964:134–35)

It is noteworthy that each individual man and woman of the forgiving party must enact a reconciliation with every man of the erstwhile enemy group so that peace is grounded in a consensus in which everyone participates. Peace requires a dissolution of rancor on the part of the women as well as the men, and this substantiates Radcliffe-Brown's observation that the women are equally involved in the moral legitimation of war-making through which male participation in lethal violence is collectively sanctioned and rendered laudable and prestige-enhancing (prowess in war being esteemed; see Radcliffe-Brown 1964:45). The peacemaking dance thus reverses the collective anger generated by the war dance and supplants it with an equally collective forgiveness and reconciliation. The Andamanese thus *make* war and *make* peace as social constructions. Neither state transpires by happenstance. Moreover, these are created social conditions in which there is ritual entailment of the spirits of the dead, including the potentially vengeful spirits of those individuals whose deaths

Plate 1.   A man of the *Akar-Bale* tribe with South Andaman bow and arrows, wearing belt and necklace of netting and *Dentalium* shells (height 1,494 mm, 4 feet 9 inches). (Reproduced from A. R. Radcliffe-Brown, *The Andaman Islanders* (Cambridge: Cambridge University Press, 1933 [1922]), opposite page 30.)

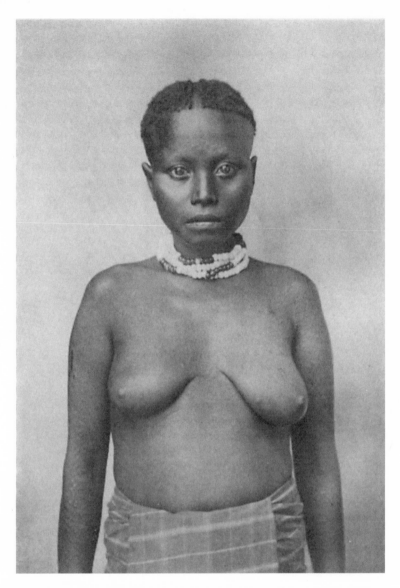

Plate 2.   A young married woman. (Reproduced from A. R. Radcliffe-Brown, *The Andaman Islanders* (Cambridge: Cambridge University Press, 1933 [1922], opposite page 27.)

Plate 3. An Andaman Islander shooting fish with bow and arrow on the reefs at Port Blair. (Reproduced from A. R. Radcliffe-Brown, *The Andaman Islanders* (Cambridge: Cambridge University Press, 1933 [1922], frontispiece.)

Plate 4. The peacemaking dance of the North Andaman. (Reproduced from A. R. Radcliffe-Brown, *The Andaman Islanders* (Cambridge: Cambridge University Press, 1933 [1922], opposite page 134.)

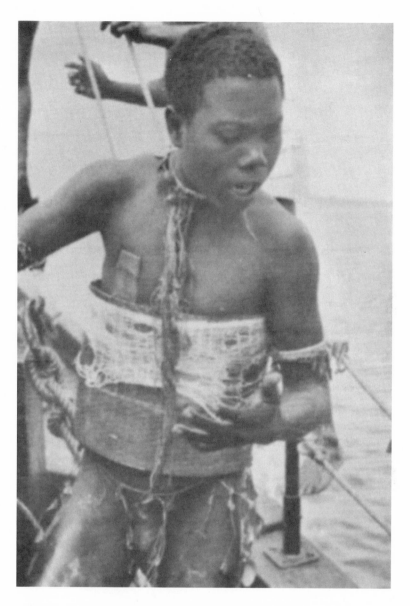

Plate 5.   A Jarawa comes aboard. (Originally published in Singh 1978.
Reproduced by permission of Vikas Publishing House.)

Plate 6.   Shooting fish in Tidal Creek near Port Blair. (Reproduced from Man 1885, plate IX.)

Plate 7. A turtle-hunt. (Reproduced from Man 1885, plate XI.)

played a role in the recourse to raiding (and who are the principal injured parties). As noted earlier, peace is rendered much more readily attainable by the absence of stipulated vengeance obligations on the part of the living next of kin and fellow countrymen of those slain in an altercation or raid. Past acts of hostility can thus be erased by the dissipation of individual ill-feeling, by the shared emotional release of joint weeping, and by the enactment of goodwill through gift-giving and coparticipation in feasting, dancing, and hunting. Those who stood divided and opposed are thus made one and united in friendship (Radcliffe-Brown 1964:242).

The symbolism of the *koro* remains to be addressed. The *koro* is made from the leaflets of the young unopened leaves of a species of palm. A tassel made from this fiber adorns the outer part of the leaf apron that women wear (or historically wore) as a covering over the pudenda (Radcliffe-Brown 1964:454, 479). A *koro* tassel is also "suspended near the grave of a dead person and at the entrance of the village at which the death took place" (454). When an individual dies, he (or she) is initiated into the world of the dead at a ceremony very similar to the peacemaking ceremony. The initiate sits on *koro* fiber, which is also placed in his armpits and over his belly. Then, as in the peacemaking ceremony, he stands "against a suspended cane from which depend bunches of this same *koro,* so in the initiation into the spirit world the initiate has to stand against the rainbow while the dancing spirits shake it and him" (290). Spirits of the dead are responsible for illness and illness-caused deaths, and in this respect a state of hostility obtains between the living and the dead. The peacemaking ceremony is thus appropriate to induction into the spirit world. The rainbow is the point of connection between these worlds.

Radcliffe-Brown (1964:291) interprets the *koro* fiber "as a sign that the spot where it is placed is tabu, or, in more precise terms, that the spot must be avoided because of the presence there of a force or power that makes things dangerous." He argues that this dangerous force is present at the fresh gravesite and at the tension-filled peacekeeping ceremony when former antagonists meet but are enjoined from attack by tabu.

How then does this belief in the fibre as a mark of tabu come about? The fibre is worn by the women of the Little Andaman to cover their pudenda, and it was formerly worn in this way by the women of the North Andaman. We may conclude that this was an old element in the Andaman culture dating back to the remote period when the inhabitants of the Little Andaman became separated from those of the Great Andaman. Now in a very special sense the sexual organs of women are tabu, and, without discussing the matter in detail, we may suppose that the Andaman Islanders regard the genitals of women as a spot in which resides the same sort of force or power that makes the spirits, or the body of a dead man, dangerous. One point may be mentioned as throwing light on this subject, and helping forward the argument, namely that the natives of the North Andaman often use the expression *Lau-buku* (meaning literally "spirit-woman" or "female spirits") to denote women collectively instead of the phrase that might be expected—*n'e-buku*. It would seem that by reason of their sex and the special ideas that are associated with it, women are regarded as having a very special relation with the world of spirits. We may conclude that the *koro* fiber, being a convenient material for the purpose, was first used as a covering for the women, and in this way came to be used as a sign of tabu in general, or else that for some unknown reason the fibre was selected as a suitable material to mark any kind of tabu, and so came to be used both as a covering for women and also as a sign of warning at the grave and the village that has been visited by death. (Radcliffe-Brown 1964:291–92)

Additional ethnographic data provided in Radcliffe-Brown's account make it possible to present a revised interpretation of *koro* and of women's role in peacemaking more generally. The point of departure for this reinterpretation begins with a consideration of the *oko-jumu,* the Andamanese spirit-medium that Radcliffe-Brown labels a "medicine-man" or "dreamer." An individual becomes an *oko-jumu* by "dying and coming back to life" (through recovery from loss of consciousness), by being spirited away and residing among the spirits (and apart from the community) for a time, and "by having intercourse with the spirits in his dreams" (300–301). A spirit medium is essentially an individual whose dream persona (or spirit double) is able to enter the spirit world, who has established relations with the spirits of the dead and who is thus able to enlist their cooperation to bring about both the alleviation of illness (which spirits cause) and sickness-sending. It is evident from Radcliffe-Brown's account that an *oko-jumu* establishes relations with the spirits by having sexual intercourse with a spirit-woman and thereby acquiring a spirit "wife" (and thus also spirit in-laws). An *oko-jumu* thus returns from a sojourn among the spirits decorated with *koro* fiber (301). Man (1885:136) reports that a successful hunter brings back a pig's tail as confirmatory evidence of his accomplishment (and to elicit assistance in carrying in the carcass), and the *koro* fiber is an analogous trophy, evidence of a tryst in the spirit world and thus confirmation of an intimate relationship with powerful spirits who can induce or cure illness. The term *spirit-woman* thus designates the male spirit-mediums' links to the spirit world, their collective spirit-wives (as the grammatical construction indicates) and not living women. It would consequently be more accurate to say that men who are *oko-jumu* have a special relation to the world of the spirits through these spirit-women than that living women themselves possess such a relation. However, the critical spirits that are accessible to the living and whose assistance can cure illness (or direct it) are female spirits, and a spirit medium has no powers at all apart from his capacity to enlist his spirit-wife's efforts on his behalf.[15]

The *koro* fiber is thus significant because it is the pubic covering of the spirit-woman (and not because it was historically worn by living North Andamanese women in the distant past as Radcliffe-Brown [1964:291] speculates). *Koro* is then as much symbolic of a point of connection and of access to the spirit world as is the rainbow. It follows that the men who stand grasping these symbols in their outstretched arms at the peacemaking ceremony are under the protection of the spirit-women. Peace is thus brought about both by the real wives of the men who stand in a relation of enmity to each other and by the spirit-women (or spirit-wives of the mediums) of the two groups. The former negotiate the peace and make arrangements for holding the peacemaking ceremony, while the latter guarantee the sanctuary-space in which reconciliation is achieved in the course of that ceremony. Moreover, the spirit-women are liaison to the spirits of those killed in the conflict and are in a position to effect reconciliation in the relation of these vengeful spirits to the living, so as to render the participants in peacemaking immune from illness caused by the spirits of the slain. The *koro* thus marks the presence and involvement of the (unseen) spirit-women in all the contexts in which it is manifested, and this is the "force or power" whose existence is deduced by Radcliffe-Brown (and analytically labeled "tabu").

Symbolically, peace may perhaps also be interpreted as a female-generated rebirth in the sense that the end of war is life-giving and provides a fresh start in social relations between groups. Neighboring local groups were often linked by intermarriage and the widespread adoption of children, who were given to friends of another band to rear although regularly visited by their parents (Radcliffe-Brown 1964:77).[16] These practices would be conducive to the maintenance of peace between groups so linked. One would certainly be unlikely to raid a settlement in which one's own adopted-out children resided.

The Andaman Islanders provide us with a model of the origin of war among and between the local groups of a regional system of unsegmented hunting and gathering societies—societies that are characterized by only those social groups that are culturally universal (i.e., the family, bilateral kindred, local group, and ethnic/linguistic "tribe"). The applicability of this model to the Upper Paleolithic is explored in the next chapter.

It is exceptionally interesting that peacemaking evolved in tandem with the development of internal war, although peace was unattainable in external war (between cultural groups that speak mutually unintelligible languages). While external war is unremitting and constitutes a condition of existence that defines the boundaries of the niches exploited by two populations, internal war originates as an alternation of war and peace, that is, as a war/peace system. In light of this, the origin of (internal) war is also at the same time the origin of peace (as a socially constructed condition). The Andamanese display a striking propensity to seek the resolution of conflict. Early in the colonial encounter when the Andamanese were able to raise a force of 1,500 men, they sought to conduct a peace dance with the convicts who were trespassing upon and despoiling their lands when they might as readily have utilized their numerical advantage to annihilate them. There is thus a sense in which the Andamanese could be characterized as peace-seeking even though they manifest a comparatively high frequency of warfare.

CHAPTER 4

The Early Coevolution of
War and Society

The origin of war is a question of enduring interest because the conclusions reached are of central relevance to our conceptions of human nature, and such conceptions inform the political philosophies that shape and legitimize our social institutions. The origin of war is thus much more than a matter of antiquarian curiosity.

The earliest modern formulation of the trinity of interrelationship between human nature, war, and the constitution of society was put forward by Thomas Hobbes, in the *Leviathan,* published in 1651. In very brief, Hobbes argued that the "nature of man" was the source of a general societal condition of war (or propensity to war) that gave rise to the need for an overarching state form of government in order to guarantee the peace, and that such government was achievable by the application of Reason. While the condition whereby "every man is enemy to every man" is initially posited by Hobbes (1958:107) on the basis of logical deduction (from his observations that men are by nature equal and lack a natural system of domination), Hobbes ultimately turns to ethnographic observation to substantiate this deduction.

> It may peradventure be thought there was never such a time nor condition of war as this, and I believe it was never generally so over all the world; but there are many places where they live so now. For the savage people in many places of America, except the government of small families, the concord whereof depends on natural lust, have no government at all and live at this day in the brutish manner as I said before [in continual fear and danger of violent death]. (Hobbes 1958:108)

Hobbes thus not only broaches the important question of the nexus of interrelationship between human nature, war, and society, but also implicitly proposes that this question is susceptible to empirical investigation through consideration of the ethnography of contemporary prestate societies. While little was known concerning such societies in 1651 (when *Leviathan* was published), it is fair to say that the relevant ethnographic data are now largely in hand. What remains is the task of analysis and interpretation, and of evaluating divergent interpretations.

The definition of war an analyst adopts can have a significant effect on the conclusions that are reached concerning the prevalence, frequency, and antiquity of warfare. For example, one could take the position that the killing of a member of one local group by a member of a neighboring group is intrinsically a political act, insofar as it impinges on intergroup relations, and therefore should be considered an act of war. One could then conclude that "war" (defined as lethal violence between spatially distinct groups) occurs in every known ethnographic case, as well as among our genetically closest primate relatives, the chimpanzees, and that war is consequently a primordial, universal and pervasive feature of human society.

The difficulty with this definitional approach is that quite disparate phenomena are included within the same category. Although the Peloponnesian War (of 431–404 B.C.) and the Franco-Prussian War (of A.D. 1870–71) share a range of attributes in common, the members of the postulated category of "war" (as defined above) have only a single attribute in common. Analogously, one could include monarch butterflies and robins in the same category (flying life-forms with distinctive orange markings) based on a single similarity. The question that then arises is whether one learns anything significant about the phenomena under consideration by definitionally constructing such a category (or whether inquiry is instead channeled in unproductive directions).

At issue here are the criteria for establishing a definition of war as a unitary phenomenon both cross-culturally and over time. A heuristically useful definition should not only encompass similar phenomena but also exclude dissimilar and divergent phenomena; in other words it should make conceptually pertinent *distinctions* as well as grouping together instances or cases that can be considered versions, renditions, or permutations of a unitary phenomenon. A definition that includes a number of attributes automatically tells us more about the phenomenon than a single-attribute definition. A definition that encompasses the distinctive features of the phenomenon is even more informative. Ideally, these distinctive features should pinpoint what is central to the constitution of the phenomenon under consideration. The category "vascular plants" (defined as those with conductive tissue in organs distinguished as roots, stems, and leaves) is thus a heuristically useful category while "flying life-forms with distinctive orange markings" is not.

It is not the case that one definition of war is as good as another. Rather, there are explicit logical criteria for establishing a superior definition. Moreover, I would argue that the definition outlined in the Introduction fully meets these criteria. It includes multiple attributes (seven in all) and highlights the distinctive, constituting feature of war, namely, that one group member is socially substitutable for another in the context of intergroup armed conflict so that any member of a collectivity (or any class of members such as adult males) can be a legitimate target for retaliatory vengeance. It also makes a critical distinction between capital punishment and war, while at the same time facilitating the grouping together of instances of armed conflict that have occurred at widely different times and places (historically and cross-culturally). Moreover, this distinction is heuristically useful in another way in that it also provides a framework for considering the evolution of lethal conflict. The adoption of a definition that glosses over distinctions not only forwards a primordialist view of war (implicitly or explicitly) but also impedes analysis of transformations in the modalities of lethal violence that have occurred in the course of human history and prehistory.

From this vantage point, pongicide (or conspecific lethal violence among the great apes), capital punishment, and war are distinct phenomena rather than members of a unitary category. Pongicide is an analogue of homicide, and both are undoubtedly ancient. However, chimpanzees lack both capital punishment and war.[1] While capital punishment is a cultural universal found in all known human societies (Otterbein 1986), war is clearly not universal. All cross-cultural surveys of the incidence of warfare have identified a number of sociocultural systems in which war (as defined by the particular author) is considered to be rare or nonexistent. In Ross's (1983) coding of ninety societies in the Standard Cross-Cultural Sample, twelve (or 13.3 percent) were so classified. Ember (1978) likewise found that warfare was rare or absent among three (or 9.7 percent) of a worldwide sample of thirty-one hunter-gatherer societies (with zero reliance on agriculture and herding). Moreover, the percentage of societies that lack war would increase if the distinction between war and capital punishment developed in the present study were rigorously utilized in coding the societies in such cross-cultural samples. Ember (1978:447) does not make this distinction at all in that she defines warfare as "fighting between two or more territorial units (at the community level and up) as long as there is a group of fighters on at least one side." The high frequency of warfare she reports for hunter-gatherers is inflated by this definition.

Although Ross's (1983) codes involve more fine-grained distinctions, there are nevertheless some instances in which capital punishment is coded as internal war. For example, the !Kung are coded as manifesting internal war once a generation (code 3) while the extended discussion of the !Kung lethal violence in earlier chapters made it clear that individuals other than the perpetrator of a prior homicide are never the explicit target of attempted retaliation. The !Kung thus should be coded as a society where both internal and external war are rare to nonexistent, and the Yahgan code should likewise be revised for the same reasons. This would increase the proportion of warless societies in Ross's sample to 15.6 percent (14/90). Moreover, it would change the proportion of warless foraging societies to 20 percent (5/25) (with every instance being an unsegmented society). There are also yet other foraging societies, such as the Slave, who are subject to frequent external attacks by their (segmental) neighbors, but who never respond in kind. This is to say that warless societies—and those that would lack war if they were not beset by warlike neighbors—are quite well represented in the ethnographic record (and constitute 24 percent—6/25—of Ross's representative sample of foraging societies). War is thus neither universal nor pervasive. Moreover, it is most likely to be rare to nonexistent among unsegmented foraging societies (with little or no dependence on agriculture), and that suggests an earlier prehistory characterized by much more extensive zones of warlessness than the period covered by recorded history.

This brings us once again to the central point that warfare is an episodic feature of human history and prehistory observed at certain times and places but not others. Moreover, the vast majority of societies in which warfare does occur are characterized by the alternation of war and peace; there are relatively few societies—only about 6 percent—in which warfare is continual and peace almost unknown.[2] It is only in this relatively small percentage of cases that something approximating a Hobbesian social condition of pervasive and unending warfare can be found. It might thus be said that it is "the nature of man" (or of humankind) to conclude episodes of armed conflict between neighboring social groups by breaking off hostilities, by truce, and/or by reestablishing peaceful relations. This is particularly applicable to unstratified societies (lacking state or chiefdom forms of organization) where warfare is rarely terminated by a decisive military victory (such that a conclusion to warfare is established by successful conquest or domination).

Hobbes's central argument is entirely undercut by the fact that the Andaman Islanders terminate warfare by making peace. Clearly, the Leviathan (i.e., the state) is not the sine qua non of peace, nor is "government" essential to its establishment. Hobbes thus glosses over the most prominent feature of warfare in stateless societies, namely, the fact that it is episodic and typically alternates with periods of peace. Although Hobbes acknowledges that actual armed conflict is intermittent, he argues that a "state of war" exists at all times. But if neighboring Andamanese local groups annually camped together in order to engage in the peacemaking practices of feasting, dancing, and the exchange of gifts, then it would be more accurate to characterize the prevailing condition as one of positive peace (i.e., as a state of peace rather than a state of war). Such peace is actively fostered, being neither "natural" nor merely an absence of war. Moreover, festive joint gatherings intended to promote peace and goodwill are commonplace among hunter-gatherers. In the literature these are variously referred to as corroboree (among the Australian Aboriginees) and as fairs and Messenger Feasts (in the North American Arctic) (see Elkin 1938; Burch 1984:305–6).

If war is not a primordial feature of human society then it must have originated at some point in the human past (rather than being a carryover from our prehuman ancestors). This raises the question of the conditions under which warfare is initiated in a sociocultural context (or regional system) where it did not previously exist. The typicality of war/peace alternation prompts a similar concern with the initiation of armed conflict in a context of prevailing peace. Both comparison of warless and warlike foraging societies and consideration of the natural experiment represented by the Andamanese case provide important insights with respect to this issue of origination. To what extent can these insights be projected back in time in order to elucidate the preagricultural Upper Paleolithic period of human prehistory? The question of the prevalence of prehistoric warfare has been pointedly raised by Keeley's (1996) recent survey of a substantial body of relevant ethnographic and archaeological data and by his denunciation of what he sees as "the pacification of the past," the tendency to discount archaeological evidence of lethal violence.

We have seen that warfare is typically rare to nonexistent within and between unsegmented foraging societies, although it may occur with greater frequency under specific conditions manifested in the Andamanese case. If it can furthermore be established that the societal type represented by unsegmented societies was widely distributed during the Upper Paleolithic (35,000–10,000 B.P.) then we would have a basis for constructing a model of the frequency, extent, and distribution of warfare during that period.

The social organization of the societies that existed during the earlier part of the Upper Paleolithic is considered by Gamble (1982) and Whallon (1989). Whallon argues that the expansion of human populations into Australia and Siberia during the early part of this period allows us to make deductions concerning the human capabilities, communication systems, and organizations that would be required to exploit environments characterized by low resource density, diversity, and predictability (e.g., the Arctic gateway to the New World and the deserts of Australia). In such environments, unpredictable year-to-year fluctuations in resource availability at any given location produce situations of localized shortage (and abundance) that render cooperation between local groups highly adaptive. The extensive traveling, visiting, and intercommunity ceremonial gatherings that are well-developed among ethnographically known hunter-gatherers in desert and arctic environments facilitate a flow of information concerning the disposition of resources in other areas beyond those directly known (1989:437). In order to ensure requisite access to mates and resources in those neighboring areas, Whallon also posits the presence of kinship systems, inasmuch as "they constitute the only reliable mechanism for the extension of relationships beyond the range of regular face-to-face contacts" (438). Networks of kin relations would then provide the basis for a rudimentary regional integration. Kinship systems also readily facilitate the seasonal aggregation of dispersed clusters of families into intermediate-sized local groups and the merger of these into still larger gatherings during the relatively brief seasonal periods when concentrations of resources permit this. Egalitarian social organization is also critical inasmuch as it is difficult to mesh two or more separate hierarchies without conflict, including the eruption of fighting for position. The dominance hierarchies found in great ape social groups pose empirically documented difficulties in this respect (438; see also Knauft 1991: 395–97).

The organizational characteristics deduced to be present during the early Upper Paleolithic are fully compatible with the characteristics of unsegmented societies. These organizational characteristics include the family and local group. The presence of the family also implies the regulation of sexual relations by incest prohibitions and the collaboration of married couples in provisioning their children by pooling resources gleaned through a sexual division of labor (see Gough 1976:205–6). Although unsegmented societies lack any formal organization beyond the level of the local group, such groups are not socially isolated but are linked to neighboring local groups by some combination of intermarriage, adoption of the children of living parents by siblings and cousins, kin ties arising from intermarriage, visiting, gift exchange, and collective social gatherings entailing joint feasting, singing, and dancing. Unsegmented foraging societies are also typically egalitarian.[3]

The question arises as to whether early Upper Paleolithic societies might have manifested forms of kinship organization other than those characteristic of unsegmented societies. The answer to this question is that the sequence of transformations in kinship organization is well-known and that Eskimo and Hawaiian kinship terminology and bilateral kindreds are the point of departure for subsequent developments (see Murdock 1949:184–261). The earliest kinship systems can only have been very much like those characteristic of unsegmented societies. Thus if classificatory kinship and the networks of social relations predicated upon it first arose at the time of the expansion of human populations into environments characterized by sparse and unpredictable resources, the initial development would necessarily entail the emergence of these bilateral forms of kinship-based organization. However, the date at which this occurred could have been somewhat earlier than the 35,000 B.P. which has conventionally been taken as the inception of the Upper Paleolithic, since human populations reached Australia before that date.[4]

It is important to note that the category "unsegmented societies" is an organizational type, not an economic type (although many unsegmented societies are also foraging societies). Many of the difficulties that may arise from employing ethnographic analogies based on modern hunter-gatherer societies in interpreting prehistory are therefore moot. This can be illustrated by consideration of Dickson's very useful summary of the "limitations to the uncritical use of the basic model [of hunting and gathering society] in the interpretation of Paleolithic period culture" (1990:116). Many of these limitations stem from transposing the characteristics of an economy adapted to one environment, such as the Arctic, to a considerably different environment, such as late Pleistocene Europe, where subsistence was based on the hunting of now-extinct animals. In contrast, we have seen that unsegmented societies occur in a wide variety of environments (arctic, tropical, desert, coastal, etc.), and therefore this organizational type is clearly not a specialized adaptation to any specific set of environmental conditions. Indeed, it is a type of organization well-suited to human populations engaged in the colonization of previously uninhabited environmental zones. Moreover, there is no intrinsic difficulty in applying the model of unsegmented societies to interpretation of the prehistory of the wide variety of environments for which its occurrence is documented. It is noteworthy in this respect that Dickson (1990:186) proposes that the Lapps (Saami) possessed "an ethnographic subsistence and settlement system that may parallel those of the [European] Upper Paleolithic period." Coincidentally, the Lapps are one of the 32 unsegmented societies in Murdock's (1981) world ethnographic sample of 563 societies.[5]

The organizational type "unsegmented societies" also contrasts with the "basic model of hunting and gathering society" outlined by Dickson (1990:186) in a number of other respects. This type of organization is not limited to pedestrian hunter-gatherers but also occurs among those who rely on marine or riverine resources (as exemplified by the Bea and the Jarawa of the Andaman Islands, respectively). It encompasses seminomadic foragers who occupy seasonal permanent quarters as well as fully mobile foragers (see chap. 2, table 8). Unsegmented foraging societies may attain comparatively high population densities (see chap. 2, table 10). These points respond to Dickson's concern that reconstructions of prehistoric societies "must not assume uniformity among food-collecting societies."

Dickson (1990:178) also notes that modern hunter-gatherers typically occupy marginal environments unsuited to agriculture and herding rather than the prime environments they occupied during the Paleolithic. While this is certainly an accurate generalization, the Andaman Islands—which constitutes the central case to be utilized as an ethnographic analogy in the present study—is an exception. The Andaman Islands are very much a prime environment. The Andaman Islands are also an exception with respect to Dickson's (179) concern that "the majority of hunter-gatherers known to science have (or had) established symbiotic ties, trading arrangements, or patron/client relations with agricultural peoples by the time their cultures were studied." The Andaman Islanders were quite isolated from relations with agriculturalists. Although they were subject to depopulation as a result of colonization, Man (1885) provides an account of their traditional society and economy based on observations during the period from 1869 to 1880 and thus largely predating the severe epidemics of 1877 and thereafter. While the Andaman Islands were certainly not pristine and untouched by civilization in the 1870s, the effects of contact can be taken into account in evaluating the data relevant to the questions under consideration (as discussed in chap. 3).

Dickson (1990:179) also questions "the assumption that modern hunting and gathering peoples retain the institutions and behavior patterns of the Paleolithic period." This is another area in which concerns that are appropriate with respect to the "basic model of hunter-gatherer societies" do not pose like problems for the construct "unsegmented societies." The applicability of this construct to the Paleolithic can be argued on the grounds that the characteristics of unsegmented societies match those that Whallon (1989) and others have deduced from the geographic expansion of human populations during that period. Moreover, the fact that unsegmented societies manifest only those social groups that are cultural universals—the family, local community, and bilateral kindred—provides an additional ground for application of this organizational model to prehistoric societies. Unsegmented societies likewise manifest the forms of kinship systems from which other types of kinship systems are known to develop. In other words, "unsegmented societies" is a construct which we have multiple reasons to believe to be applicable to earlier prehistory. It is not based on unreflective ethnographic analogy. In point of fact it is derived from a theoretically based insight that warfare entails concepts of social substitution that are absent in certain societies, and the empirical validation of a working hypothesis that societies which lacked social forms embodying the concept of social substitution would also tend to have the lowest reported frequencies of warfare. The construct is thus a model for which ethnographic cases can be found, including cases in both rich and sparse environments.

It is important to recall that the morphological characteristics of unsegmented societies have ideological concomitants. This organizational type exhibits a distinctive social logic, very different from the social logic of segmental societies (which is grounded in social substitution). This relation between organizational type and social logic provides an avenue for positing additional cultural aspects of early societies, such as the presence of capital punishment (also another cultural universal) and the absence of classic blood feud. It is consequently unnecessary to assume that contemporary hunter-gatherers retain Paleolithic behavior patterns. What is assumed instead is that an empirically documented relation between an organizational type and a social logic is invariant over time. (This same assumption is often made with respect to state forms of organization.) The structural type "unsegmented societies" thus encompasses potentialities for extrapolation that go beyond those of the subsistence type "hunter-gatherers."

The status of the Andaman Islands case as a natural experiment is also relevant to the issue of assuming the retention of Paleolithic traits. I assume that the Andaman Islanders manifest the characteristics of an unsegmented society because they are derived from the proto-Selung, or a similar sociocultural system of seafaring people of the south Asian coastal waters as Dutta (1978:56) argues. The various features of an unsegmented society are suited to the lifeways of these Sea Gypsies and are present because they are adaptive in that context. It would not matter if the antecedents of the Sea Gypsies had possessed segmental forms of organization at an earlier point in time (say 8000 B.P.) provided that these had been superseded by unsegmented forms as a result of their maritime adaptation. There is thus no presumption that the Andaman Islanders retain forms of organization that have remained unchanged for some 35,000 years, and that they are "unevolved." Rather, the ancestors of the Andaman Islanders who reached those islands about 2,200 years ago manifested an unsegmented organization as a result of their particular culture history. It was also a form of organization suited to the colonization of an uninhabited territory and thus initially remained unchanged for that reason. The amount of time that has elapsed since the Andaman Islands population approached the carrying capacity of the environment (evidenced by reports of periodic food shortages in the late 1800s) could not have been great in evolutionary terms so that the absence of an evolutionary transformation of social organization is not surprising.

It is in these respects that the Andaman Islands case represents a natural experiment. Suppose that one were able to place a form of social organization comparable to that prevalent 35,000 years ago on an isolated, uninhabited tropical island rich in resources and were then able to return to it 2,200 years later to assess the development of resource competition and social conflict in a circumscribed environment under these experimental conditions. Suppose warfare to be initially absent—since it is characteristically rare to nonexistent among unsegmented societies of this type—but present 2,200 years later. We would then have an ideal case in which to examine the critical question of the conditions under which warfare is initiated in a sociocultural context where it did not previously exist. The Andaman Islands case is also ideal in that the islands supported a regional system of thirteen unsegmented societies, making it possible to examine the specific locales where armed conflict usually took place (as well as those where it was infrequent) and to isolate precipitating factors and the characteristics of the forms of combat that occurred. Moreover, one may address the question of whether warfare is contagious and thus spreads outward like the ripples on a pond from the initial zone of conflict into adjacent areas. In short, the Andaman case provides an excellent basis for consideration of the origin of war and for constructing a model of the frequency, extent, and distribution of warfare in the early Upper Paleolithic. Because the Andaman case has the character of an experiment, it is a case from which one may confidently generalize. In other words, the case provides a basis for employing inductive logic to reason from the particular to the general. It is also important to recall that the Andaman case has been selected from a representative sample of the world's five thousand or more ethnographically described societies because it manifests a specific combination of characteristics (as an unsegmented society isolated from agriculturalists with a high frequency of warfare that is not attributable to attacks by segmental neighbors). Moreover, this representative sample has been constructed so as to provide a principled basis for generalization. There are thus several clear grounds for generalizing from this highly selected case.

The construct "unsegmented societies" differs most notably from the basic model of hunting and gathering societies with respect to the issue of armed conflict. According to this basic model, "hunter-gatherers tend to act out their hostility in raids and ambushes motivated by revenge" (Dickson 1990:166). They are said to be characterized by feud rather than "true warfare," entailing battles between armies of military specialists. However, we have seen that unsegmented societies lack the defining characteristic of feud, namely, that "blood revenge is often taken by a small group of men who lie in ambush and kill an unsuspecting relative of the man whose act of homicide is being avenged" (Otterbein 1968:279). On the contrary, it is only the killer himself who is the target of retribution. While feud may well precede "true warfare" in the evolution of armed conflict (as Dickson supposes), capital punishment also precedes feud.

Dickson's recapitulation of received wisdom with respect to the character of armed conflict among hunter-gatherers is based on a number of earlier studies of the evolution of war. A succession of authors have argued that centralized political systems (i.e., chiefdoms and states) engage in war for distinctly different reasons than uncentralized political systems (i.e., bands and tribes)[6] (Malinowski 1941; Wright 1942; Newcomb 1960; Naroll 1966; Otterbein 1970). All these authors agree that states and chiefdoms go to war for the purpose of achieving political control; they seek conquest and domination of a territorial domain whose inhabitants are subjugated, and from whom tribute or taxes are subsequently exacted. In contrast, bands and tribes do not make war to attain political control but for some combination of purposes potentially including revenge, defense, land, plunder (i.e., booty), and prestige (including trophies and honors). The central point is that there is a relationship between the organizational characteristics of a society, on one hand, and the motives and objectives that prompt engagement in warfare, on the other hand. It follows that there is very clear evidence for a coevolution of war and society. The present study strongly confirms both these general points and explores their implication for the origin of war, namely, that early war would be expected to be distinctive in character.

Quincy Wright (1942:560–61) argued on the basis of extensive comparative data that the motives for war were cumulative: societies that made war to secure political control also made war for economic reasons (land and plunder), social reasons (prestige), and defense. Likewise, societies that made war for economic reasons did so for social and defensive purposes as well, while those who warred for social reasons also did so for defense. The order of motives, from most inclusive to least, was thus (1) political control, (2) economic gain, (3) social status, and (4) defense. Naroll (n.d.) and Otterbein (1970) concur regarding the cumulative nature of war objectives but differ concerning the rank order of social and economic purposes. They found, based on representative cross-cultural samples, that "prestige is a more advanced cause of war than plunder, in the sense that whenever reasons of prestige are found, so are economic reasons, but where economic reasons are found, prestige reasons need not be present" (Otterbein 1970:66). Economic motives are thus the least inclusive, excepting defense. All three authors agreed that any society that fought wars for any purpose would engage in warfare for defense. Naroll (n.d.) and Otterbein (1970) both included revenge as well as defense in this first-order category.

These cross-cultural findings concerning (1) the cumulative character of war objectives and (2) the general relationship between political organization and war objectives (or motives) are illustrated in table 12. This table is reproduced from a popular text (Bodley 1985:205) in order to show how cross-cultural studies of war have been represented as established knowledge. The table is a simplification of Otterbein's (1970) data (on which it is based) presented to illustrate the main points. Bodley (1985:206) also includes a table not reproduced here showing the specific percentage of bands, tribes, chiefdoms, and states in Otterbein's sample that engaged in warfare for each of these objectives. These findings imply that warfare originates among uncentralized societies as a result of some group taking revenge for a homicide, and due to defense against revenge-motivated attacks by neighbors. Table 12 suggests that those band societies that are not peaceful (or warless) make war only for those reasons (as exemplified by the Tiwi). These understandings of Otterbein's work are the likeliest source of the general expectation that hunter-gatherers are characterized by feud, that is, by small-scale, revenge-motivated attacks. There is also an implicit assumption that Otterbein's conclusions, which are framed in terms of organizational type (band societies), are equally applicable to an economic type (hunter-gatherers), since most hunter-gatherers exhibit this form of organization. Dickson (1990:163) includes band organization as part of the "basic model of hunting and gathering society."

In his 1970 study, Otterbein was concerned with the evolution of war and did not focus on the specific characteristics of hunter-gatherer warfare or the question of the origin of war (as opposed to its progressive modification).[7] However, the coded data for the 10 hunter-gatherer societies in Otterbein's representative sample can be separated out. These data show (table 13) that warfare is rare to nonexistent among 30 percent (3/10) of hunter-gatherers, but that six of the remaining seven societies that do engage in war do so for economic reasons ("plunder," including land and booty) as well as defense/revenge, while four of these six make war for prestige as well. These data indicate that it is rare for hunter-gatherers to fight *only* for defense and revenge (contra Dickson's generalization). They tend either to be warless or to engage in war for multiple reasons, most notably economic reasons plus defense and revenge. This suggests a very different picture of the origin of war: that it originates from resource com-

TABLE 12.   An Illustration of the Relationship between Political Organization and War Motives

	Defense	Plunder	Prestige	Control
Uncentralized				
Bands				
Copper Eskimo	0	0	0	0
Tiwi	+	0	0	0
Tribes				
Somali	+	+	0	0
Wondi	+	+	+	0
Centralized				
Chiefdoms				
Sema	+	+	+	0
Mutair	+	+	+	0
States				
Thai	+	+	+	+
Aztec	+	+	+	+

Source: Bodley 1985:205, reproduced by permission of Mayfield Publishing Company.

petition and defense against (or retaliation for) economically motivated attacks by neighbors.

Having established that the organizational characteristics deduced for early Upper Paleolithic society are essentially the characteristics of unsegmented foraging societies, and that the problems attendant upon the use of unreflective ethnographic analogy are not applicable to the construct "unsegmented foraging societies," we may proceed with the task of constructing a model of the character, frequency, extent, and distribution of warfare circa 35,000 years ago.

Warfare is typically rare to nonexistent within and between unsegmented foraging societies inhabiting environments characterized by low resource density, diversity, and predictability at densities below 0.2 persons per square mile. Moreover, it is reasonable to assume that this was equally true 35,000 years ago. The absence or near absence of war under these conditions is a product of the critical importance of cooperation (emphasized by Whallon [1989]) rather than an absence of resource competition. Conditions favoring resource competition are in fact quite likely to be present when there are fluctuations in resource availability at any given location from year to year. In the Australian desert, game clusters where sporadic rainfall stimulates thicker vegetation, while in the Arctic, migratory caribou herds periodically elect alternate routes. In either case, a local group (or a regional band consisting of a number of associated local groups) may experience food shortages while their neighbors enjoy plenty. The ingredients for seizure, by force of arms, of vital subsistence resources necessary to survival are clearly in place. But so too are the ingredients for sharing resources so as to establish a reciprocal entitlement to share in the future

TABLE 13.   The Motives for War among Hunter-Gatherer Societies

Society	Trait		
	Defense	Plunder	Prestige
Copper Eskimo	0	0	0
Dorobo	0	0	0
Monachi	0	0	0
Tiwi	+	0	0
Andamanese	+	+	0
Tehuelche	+	+	0
Abipon	+	+	+
Comox	+	+	+
Plains Cree	+	+	+
Wishram	+	+	+

Source: Data from Otterbein 1970:66–67, 148–49.

should the need arise. What then determines one outcome rather than the other? I would argue that the distinctive character of external warfare between unsegmented societies is decisive. If the neighboring groups in this example adopted the shoot-on-sight mode of conflict over resources that obtained between the Bea and Jarawa—and that represents the form of resource-based warfare manifested by unsegmented foragers—survival chances would be significantly impaired. Local groups or regional bands denied access to critical resources during periods of severe shortage would experience famine-related patterns of mortality that particularly increase infant and child deaths. Under these conditions it would be difficult for the overall population to attain the growth levels necessary for expansion beyond the margins of such environments.

This raises a more general question (and one students often ask). Why don't warlike societies die out as a consequence of the impact of warfare-related mortality on long-term survival? The answer to this query is that male warfare deaths typically have virtually no effect on the number of children born to the female component of the population (as a result of polygyny and widow remarriage) so that the next generation can readily be as large or larger than the last despite endemic war. A society such as the Mae Enga of New Guinea in which 25 percent of male deaths are due to warfare, and mortality from war is 0.32 percent per annum, may nonetheless double its population every twenty-five years and expand its territorial domain (see Meggitt 1965; Meggitt 1977:110–12; Wiessner and Tumu 1998; Keeley 1996:195–96). A warlike society may thus grow and expand rather than dying out.

However, this result is contingent upon forms of warfare characteristic of segmental societies. The kind of warfare that occurs between unsegmented societies is quite different because it intrinsically entails denial of access to resources during periods of scarcity. Individuals venturing outside their territory in order to exploit resources further afield are subject to fatal ambush. Female collectors of vegetable foods would be especially vulnerable. The demographic consequences of the resultant inability to alleviate periodic but acute short-term famine conditions are quite different from those involving high male mortality. Child deaths and reduced births due to adult female mortality decrease the size of the population for two generations, because fewer females attain reproductive age fifteen years after the event. In the meantime, the surviving adult males of the group subject to the added mortality among their offspring will still have the remainder of their natural lifetimes to inflict commensurate damage upon their neighbors, when the latter experience a similar situation of food shortage. In this type of environment societies that engage in continuous hostile relations with their neighbors characterized by a shoot-on-sight policy effectively reduce both their own and their neighbors' chances of survival over the long term. It is consequently likely that warlike societies *were* selected against during the early Upper Paleolithic and, more importantly, that they were unable to colonize environments characterized by low resource density, diversity, and predictability. The societies that initially spread to all corners of the globe—and passed through the Arctic gateway to the New World—were thus those that achieved a degree of regional integration through some combination of intermarriage, visiting, gift exchange, joint feasting, and festive intercommunity gatherings entailing singing and dancing. Such practices fostered a state of positive peace that provided a basis for sharing and cooperation. In other words, it was not merely the absence of war but the presence of a positive peace that facilitated Upper Paleolithic migrations.

Paradoxically, it is not a paucity of resources that provides conditions favorable to the origination of war but rather reliability and abundance. It is under these latter circumstances that a society can afford to have enemies for neighbors. The comparative reliability of agriculture as a mode of subsistence thus transforms the character, frequency, extent, and distribution of warfare within regional systems. Prior to the development of agriculture, conditions compatible with the origination of warfare would be found only at particularly favorable locations within a few regional systems of unsegmented societies (although such conditions could have been present at an early date). This in turn has implications for modeling the frequency and distribution of war during the early Upper Paleolithic. However, the character of early warfare needs to be more fully examined before exploring these questions of frequency and distribution.

Every prior comparative study of war has documented a strong covariation between type of society and type of warfare. War and society clearly coevolve. This implies that war in the early Upper Paleolithic would differ from the warfare of most modern hunter-gatherers, especially those that are themselves segmental societies or are subject to attack by segmental neighbors (and that analogies based on such societies would lead to misinterpretation).

This same general principle of typological covariation between war and society suggests that the forms of collective armed conflict that occur within and between unsegmented societies would be distinctive in character. The ethnography clearly bears this out. It is important to fully describe and summarize the characteristics that have emerged from consideration of ethnographic cases because the character of armed conflict prefigures its frequency and distribution (as we have just seen with respect to environments in which food resources are unreliable from year to year). It is the chain of causality that extends from type of society to type of armed conflict (or war) to the frequency and distribution of armed conflict in specifiable environmental regimes that makes reconstruction of conditions 35,000 years ago a feasible enterprise.

Spontaneous conflicts over access to resources occur both within and between unsegmented foraging societies in environments that are rich in naturally occurring subsistence resources, that are characterized by high resource density, diversity, and reliability, and that support population densities in excess of 0.2 persons per square mile. The incidence and severity of conflict is amplified by higher population densities and/or environmental circumscription (cf. Carneiro 1988). This spontaneous conflict—which may entail lethal violence—differs from what has been described in the ethnographic literature on tribal warfare as "raiding" (and from the definition of war presented in the Introduction) in that it is *not* deliberate or preplanned, it entails no military organization recruited for the explicit purpose of carrying out an armed incursion into foreign territory, and it is triggered by an unsought chance encounter (that contains the possibility of ambush). The principal objective of the parties to these spontaneous conflicts is to secure subsistence resources without sharing them with others. If this monopolistic appropriation is contested, the members of the local group seeking it are prepared to fight. However, recourse to armed conflict is only a means to an economic end, whereas causing deaths as payback for prior casualties inflicted upon one's own group is the primary purpose of the prototypical raid. The contending forces in these spontaneous conflicts are the combinations of coresidents who routinely hunt or gather together, the weapons employed are the implements they normally carry with them for food procurement, and the sites of conflict are the outer margins of the areas they habitually exploit. In all these respects, this is a distinctive form of conflict, different from capital punishment, feud, and war. It is also characteristic of a particular type of society and is manifested in a specifiable environmental context.

The general proposition stated above (in italics) is applicable not only to the Andaman Islanders, but also to other unsegmented societies in our sample, that is, the Yahgan and Mbuti. Yahgan families relied on shellfish as a dietary staple and moved along the beach from one shellfish bed to another every few days. "If . . . a family attempted to exploit a site already occupied by another family, a fight ensued" (Steward and Faron 1959:402). Lothrop (1928:164) reports that the weaker group usually withdrew from contested sites when trouble arose, but that fighting sometimes occurred. Fights that began between individuals expanded as relatives and friends on both sides became involved "probably in an endeavor to stop the encounter but sometimes to aid their man. Clubs [i.e., four-foot staves], paddles, spears, slings and stones were the weapons used" (164). Injuries were inflicted and fatalities sometimes occurred (accounting for much of the high reported homicide rate; see note 12, chap. 2). Lothrop also notes that "the land was thickly settled in relation to its food supply" (1928:15) and that this accounted for the occasional slaughter of shipwrecked sailors guilty of trespass and the taking of food resources to which they had no rights. "The Indians resented any trespassing . . . , dealing a similar fate to one another under the same provocation" (15). What was typically manifested internally as a brawl or a melee over contested resources was thus manifested externally by the outright killing of trespassers.

Among the Mbuti each band claimed exclusive rights to a hunting territory bounded by natural features. A band could request permission to exploit a portion of a neighboring band's territory if their own was currently unproductive. But hunting without permission constituted trespass, except when engaged in a hot pursuit of quarry that originated in one's own territory, in which case a portion of the game procured should be sent to the owners of the territory where the chase concluded (Turnbull 1965:220). Under any other circumstances trespass was understood as entailing the theft of game or honey and could potentially lead to conflict. Turnbull did not observe any instances of armed conflict, but the prospect of this was broached when incidents of trespass occurred during his fieldwork (1965:220; 1961:287–88). He considered talk of spearing intruders "a figure of speech to indicate extreme anger" (1965:220). However, one of his informants provides a concise account of the conditions under which trespass could lead to fighting.

> Every year those Pygmies come into our land and we go into theirs. There is plenty of food; so long as we do not meet there is no fighting. If we do meet, then those who are not in their own land run away and leave behind whatever they have stolen. (Turnbull 1961:288)

Conflicts over resources among the Mbuti, Yahgan, and Andamanese display a common underlying pattern modulated by the relative scarcity or abundance of food resources. Among the Mbuti, where "there is plenty of food," chance encounters between territory owners and trespassers trigger immediate withdrawal by the latter, so there is "no fighting." However, the Mbuti informant's elucidation of the relevant variables makes it clear that the situation would unfold differently if food were not plentiful. This is the situation that obtains among the Yahgan, where population density is greater relative to resources. Under these conditions, rival claimants to a shellfish bed sometimes fight for possession of it. Alternatively, the weaker party may withdraw. In either case the issue is not decided by the relative merits of each party's claim (as with the Mbuti owners and trespassers), but by fighting strength, either demonstrated or assessed. Lethal weapons—fish spears and clubs used for killing seals—were employed and there was a risk of fatal injury.

This pattern whereby the stronger party takes possession of contested resources is identical to that reported for the Andamanese (Radcliffe-Brown 1964:86). However, the Jarawa have made two adaptations to the potentiality for such conflict. First, Jarawa men wear body armor at all times while engaged in hunting and gathering, and second, they attack immediately whenever they have the advantage of surprise (irrespective of numerical strength). A "display" phase in which relative strength is assessed and the weaker party has an opportunity to withdraw without conflict taking place is thus deleted. In its place there is a shoot-on-sight policy. This in turn precludes any other types of interactions between the Jarawa and Bea (such as visiting, exchange, and intermarriage). These conditions thus constitute a comprehensive "state of war" (in the Hobbesian sense) punctuated by episodic hostile encounters. In these engagements casualties are inflicted, and when a party of hunters is taken unawares the wounds suffered are fatal more often than not (as documented in chap. 3).

This set of three cases of unsegmented foraging societies in environments rich in resources provides a clear composite picture of progressive intensification of resource-based conflict eventuating in the origination of war. The conflicts over trespass that take place between Mbuti bands do not fulfill the criteria of a definition of war (but rather constitute peaceful dispute settlement). On the other hand, one would not hesitate to characterize the Jarawa-Bea conflict as war. When the men of a Jarawa hunting party don their body armor, collect their bows and arrows, and go forth from the settlement to hunt they are also engaged in patrolling their territory and carrying out a "search and destroy" mission with respect to intruders. This conforms to the definitional criteria that war entails collective armed conflict in which the deaths of other persons are envisioned in advance, and this envisioning is encoded in the purposeful act of taking up lethal weapons (and, in this case, body armor as well). Although we lack exegesis by the Jarawa, it is evident that they regard trespass as a criminal act of theft of game and collectibles, as do the Yahgan and Mbuti, who explicitly express this view. It follows that the killing of trespassers by the Jarawa constitutes an act that they see as morally justified, laudable, and worthy of esteem. If this were the full extent of Jarawa-Bea armed conflict, it would constitute a capital punishment modality, rather than fulfilling all the attributes of war, since only malefactors (i.e., thieving trespassers) are killed. However, the beginnings of social substitution are evident in the Jarawa shooting of a Bea woman who was traveling with a group of pig hunters on their return to camp and in the one instance (discussed in chap. 3) in which a Bea woman was killed while gathering leaves in close proximity to her own settlement. This incident also qualifies as a raid, entailing a preplanned foray into enemy territory for the purpose of killing an unsuspecting individual (rather than representing an unanticipated clash between two groups of leaf gatherers).

The Jarawa thus manifest precisely the features one would expect in the early phases of the development of war. The majority of incidents of armed conflict are spontaneous conflicts over resources, but adaptation to the prospect of this has led to a policy of attacking whenever a Jarawa hunting party has the advantage of surprise. When conditions for an immediate attack are unfavorable, the Jarawa may follow the Bea back to their encampment and wait for an opportunity to shoot one of the Bea intruders while the latter make preparations to feast on the game they have (from the Jarawa perspective) stolen. The central motif continues to be capital punishment of thieving trespassers, and the attack is directly consequent upon such theft, but the locale has now shifted from the scene of the crime to the perpetrators' encampment. The objective is to shoot one of the perpetrators if possible, but the particular Bea individual who enters the tropical forest behind the beach (looking for leaves to be used for the repast) may potentially be any member of the community (as in the incident of August 22, 1894, described in chap. 3). The strategic requirement of surprise necessitates social substitution in this context, and the resultant fatality is encompassed in an event that fulfills the criteria of our definition of war. Moreover, an effort on the part of the Bea to exact capital punishment by killing the Jarawa perpetrator of this ambush would confront a problem of being unable to identify the specific individual responsible, further promoting recourse to social substitution. The ingredients for a transition from capital punishment to war are thus in place. But at the same time the elements of a logic of capital punishment are still very much in evidence, indicating a social transformation in progress. In other words, the Jarawa and the Bea provide an in-process illustration of the origination of war in a context of resource competition.

The Yahgan are on the brink of the same transition from capital punishment and spontaneous conflict over resources to war, just shy of manifesting the conditions that fully constitute warfare. Disputes over access to resources lead to fights between individuals that escalate into brawls involving supporters on both sides. Lethal weapons that are at hand are also employed, so that collective armed conflict resulting in fatalities obtains. Collective kin group responsibility for vengeance devolves upon the close relations of the person slain. There is subsequently a coordinated and preplanned effort to fulfill the vengeance obligation. Sources differ concerning the target of this vengeance. Bridges (1886, 1893) states that only the malefactor is subject to retribution, and that the murderer's family and relatives concede the legitimacy of this and make no effort to defend him (Lothrop 1928:165). Gusinde (1931:885) concurs in this view in one statement but in another says, "if they cannot get the murderer, they get someone else, which often leads to pitched battles between families" (901). Lothrop (1928:165) reports:

> Organized warfare, during which any member of one group would kill on sight any member of another group, as among the [neighboring] Ona, was unknown to the Yahgan, but blood revenge was sometimes executed on the relative of a murderer.

All in all, this suggests that an effort was made to take vengeance on the murderer if possible, but that a relative of the malefactor could be substituted if direct vengeance was unachievable.[8] Thus kin group responsibility for vengeance is recognized while full kin group liability is not, inasmuch as the malefactor—rather than any member of his kin group—is very much the preferred target. Social substitution is conditional rather than automatic and only "sometimes" occurs. Nonetheless, this is the endpoint and furthest possible development of capital punishment, and the penultimate step prior to the emergence of classic blood feud (which constitutes a form of war). Thus, while the Yahgan manifest spontaneous conflict over access to resources, war is appropriately coded as nonexistent. They are nevertheless an informative case with regard to the process leading to the origin of war.

Capital punishment and spontaneous conflict over access to resources thus constitute two modes of intergroup armed conflict that are both clearly distinguishable from war and antecedent to it. Capital punishment differs from spontaneous conflict over resources in that it entails an organized, planned, and premeditated attack. However, these two modes of collective violence otherwise manifest the same attributes detailed in table 1 of the Introduction, that is, (1) collective armed conflict, (2) collectively sanctioned, (3) morally justified, (4) with participation esteemed by group members, and (5) directed to instrumental objectives. These five attributes are also characteristic of war and feud. However, capital punishment and spontaneous conflict over resources differ from war and feud, and are similar to each other, in that malefactors are the individuals explicitly targeted for lethal violence (i.e., murderers and thieving trespassers). Social substitution, the hallmark of war, is absent. But at the same time the pathway leading to the development of social substitution is readily apparent via a progression to the intermediate "malefactor if possible" form of retaliation. Thus the origination of war in a sociocultural context where it did not previously exist entails a transition from one modality of collective violence to another (rather than a transition from peaceful nonviolence to lethal armed conflict). Moreover, these antecedent forms of collective violence are characteristic of a particular type of society—unsegmented foraging societies—as the well-established general concept of a coevolution of war and society would suggest.

The eight unsegmented foraging societies that comprise our represen-

tative sample substantially conform to the two italicized general propositions formulated and elucidated in the preceding discussion. The !Kung
and Copper Eskimo inhabit environments characterized by low resource
density, diversity, and predictability at densities below 0.2 persons per
square mile. In both cases war is rare to nonexistent, and spontaneous
conflict over access to resources is absent or insignificant.[9] The Slave
inhabit an environmental zone characterized by an absence of year-to-year
reliability of subsistence resources (Rogers and Smith 1981:130) at a
significantly higher density (0.2 to 1.0 persons per square mile; see chap. 2,
table 10). The Slave were subject to intensive raiding by the segmental
Cree that was amplified by colonial fur-trade influences in the late 1700s.
This had several important effects. The Slave were to some degree displaced from their aboriginal territory and compressed into a more
restricted domain.[10] Regional bands were pushed in on each other leading
to territorial rearrangements and bringing groups that were strangers to
each other into contact (Mason 1946:36). The consequences of compression (which is analogous to environmental circumscription) combined
with an increased incidence of trespass by unknown (nonneighboring)
bands were exactly what the argument developed in this chapter would
lead one to expect.

> Every stranger was [regarded as] a 'bad Indian' endeavoring to
> work evil [witchcraft], and as such [was] to be slain from ambush
> before he could do any harm. When two unacquainted hunters
> approached, unless they greeted each other from beyond arrow
> range, they endeavored to kill each other. (36)

In other words, the Slave adopted a shoot-on-sight policy toward
strangers during this period.

The Semang, Mbuti, Yahgan, and Andamanese inhabit environments rich in naturally occurring subsistence resources that are reliably
available (seasonally) from year to year. The Semang have the lowest population density (less than 0.2 per square mile; see chap. 2, table 10), and
conflicts over access to resources are not reported (cf. Dentan 1968:80).
Mbuti and Yahgan population densities are in the 0.2 to 1.0 per square
mile range (chap. 2, table 10) while the Andamanese density prior to
depopulation averaged 2.25 persons per square mile (Radcliffe-Brown
1964:18). These four cases conform to the proposition that the incidence
and severity of spontaneous conflicts over access to resources are corre-
lated with the degree to which the availability of resources (relative to population) is restricted, as shown in table 14. Although the frequency of war
does not covary with population density, as noted in chapter 2 (table 10),
the frequency and severity of *spontaneous conflicts over resources* do
covary with resource availability. This finding also illustrates the heuristic
value of making more fine-grained distinctions between forms of collective

violence and between types of societies, rather than employing an encompassing definition of war and an undifferentiated category of foragers that
makes covariation difficult to discover. It is these distinctions that make it
possible to transcend Keeley's (1996:118) dictum "that absolutely no correlation exists between the frequency of warfare and the density of human
population."

The Ingalik case remains to be discussed in order to complete our
consideration of the eight unsegmented foraging societies in the representative sample. The Ingalik aboriginally occupied a portion of the Yukon
and Kuskokwim river basins in Alaska where they subsisted upon fish
(including salmon) and a wide variety of game and migratory birds. They
have been described as living in an environment "rich in resources" at the
time of initial exploration in 1843–44 (Snow 1981:603). They suffered
depopulation due to introduced diseases that reduced their numbers from
1,500 to less than 500 persons by 1880 (614). The population density of less
than 0.2 persons per square mile given by Murdock and Wilson (1972:270,
289) (and utilized in chap. 2, table 10) is for the year 1885, subsequent to
this depopulation. No warfare occurred during the seventy-five-year
period from 1883 to 1958 (Osgood 1958:271). During this period a low
population density (due to depopulation) was thus associated with an
absence of warfare. However, warfare is reported for the initial contact
period, prior to depopulation.[11] The traditional enemies of the Ingalik
were two neighboring segmental societies, the Koyukon and Kolchan,
while no significant conflicts occurred between the Ingalik and their unsegmented Kuskowagamuit Eskimo neighbors (Snow 1981:603; Oswalt

TABLE 14.   The Relation between Conflict and Resource Availability
among Unsegmented Foraging Societies in Environments Rich in Resources

Incidence and Severity of Spontaneous Conflicts Over Access to Resources	Availability of Resources Relative to Population		
	Plentiful	Restricted	Subject to Periodic Scarcity
Absent	Semang		
Occasional, peacefully resolved	Mbuti		
Frequent brawls, some fatalities		Yahgan	
Shoot-on-sight policy			Jarawa and Bea

1962:11). The Ingalik repaid raids upon their settlements in kind. When they attacked a Koyukon or Kolchan village they endeavored to block the doors of the dwellings and to shoot the men trapped inside through the smoke hole. When successful in dispatching their enemies in this manner, caches were looted and captured women and children also appropriated. The frequency of such raids is not clear from Osgood's (1958:63–65) account, based on an informant's recollection of stories from an earlier era, though he notes that "a number of years might elapse" between an initial conflict and a subsequent retaliatory raid.

The Ingalik case is thus consistent with the pattern of covariation shown in table 14. When resources were plentiful relative to population (after 1883), conflict over resources was absent. When resources were more restricted (in the 1840s), the Ingalik were subject to raids and engaged in counterraiding. Internal war was absent, and external war was a consequence of attacks by segmental neighbors.

The comparative analysis of warless societies carried out in chapter 1 suggests that the origin of war entails a transition from one form of collective violence to another, rather than a transition from peaceful nonviolence to lethal armed conflict. The engine of this transformation is now apparent: restricted resource availability relative to population in environments rich in subsistence resources. Such restricted resource availability may occur when population growth or subsistence resource depletion takes place within a circumscribed environment such as the Andaman Islands. In open continental environments unsegmented foragers tend to move away from conflict so that an encounter between two groups of hunters seeking to exploit the same area is likely to engender wider spacing between their respective bands in the future. It is only when there is no opportunity to withdraw that such incidents become frequent enough to lead to adaptive modification on the part of the groups involved. Actual fighting replaces a display of strength that eventuates in withdrawal of the weaker party. Open confrontation gives way to ambush of trespassers. The identity of the specific individual responsible for a death is obscured, and retaliation thus necessarily entails social substitution. A form of collective violence predicated on targeting perpetrators of trespass, game theft, and homicide thus gives way to retaliatory violence against the compatriots of such malefactors.

Once this transition from capital punishment (and spontaneous conflict over access to resources) to war is effected, resource availability is further constricted by avoidance of border areas that become too dangerous to exploit. In effect, a no-man's-land is established between groups. In the Andamanese case this unutilized zone confined the population density of South Andaman—inhabited by the Bea and Jarawa—to only 2.0 persons per square mile while the four tribes of North Andaman attained a density of 2.75 persons per square mile and those of Middle Andaman 2.5 persons per square mile. Radcliffe-Brown (1964:18–19) explicitly attributes this disparity to warfare alone (while attributing the difference between Great Andaman and Little Andaman densities to environmental variation). The peace-promoting joint gatherings discussed earlier specifically entail mutual exploitation of border areas between band territories and thus facilitate the attainment of higher population density. The origination of war between the local groups of neighboring unsegmented foraging societies is thus maladaptive in the first instance in that it compounds the problem of restricted resource availability. But at the same time this reinforces and augments the severity of the conditions that stimulate armed conflict. Peace holds significant advantages yet it is more difficult to reestablish. There is also the potentiality that mutual avoidance will solidify a state of enmity.

It has long been recognized that hunter-gatherers tend to move away from conflict. This practice is regarded as an effective conflict resolution mechanism. It also alleviates population pressure that is often the presumed underlying source of conflict, and withdrawal is thus regarded as adaptive in this respect as well. In systems theory terms, an increase in the variable *population density,* beyond a range of viability, generates conflict; the withdrawal response that engenders wider spacing leads to a return of the variable *population density* to a value within the range of viability and also results in the cessation of conflict. This negative feedback loop is considered adaptive in the strict sense of the term. Although conflict occurs, it is integral to a series of interrelationships that obviates the source of conflict. In short, conflict is part of the solution. This has been the received wisdom with regard to hunter-gatherers. However, what the Andamanese case shows is that this negative feedback loop turns into a positive feedback loop in a circumscribed environment. An increase in population density engenders conflict between social groups that then move farther apart, as in the standard model. But in this context moving apart entails compression into a pair of reduced territories separated by a largely unutilized zone. Population density within the two exploitable domains is pushed further outside a range of viability. Conflict is further stimulated and becomes chronic. But conflict is no longer part of a set of relationships that obviates its underlying cause. On the contrary it amplifies population pressure by restricting access and is part of the problem, not part of the solution. Collective armed conflict is thus maladaptive in the strict (systems theory) sense of the term.

There is also a question of the eventual consequences of this maladaptive response. Will population density decline due to increased mortality in order to return values to viable levels? Will war spread from its point of origin throughout the (circumscribed) regional system as one group pushes into another? These divergent potential outcomes remain to be explored.

The outcome of compression in the Andamanese case is dictated by the specific character of the warfare that occurs between the local groups of these unsegmented foraging societies. This is essentially a war of attrition. Each side is able to inflict not only casualties but also hardship on the other, by impairing their access to needed subsistence resources, but neither side is able to achieve dramatic territorial gains (in uncontested access) at the other's expense through a decisive victory. In other words, the outcome of the war of attrition is a stalemate. Moreover, the rate of attrition is very low. Quincy Wright (1942:569) has calculated mortality from warfare among the Andamanese as 0.02 percent per annum. The data presented in chapter 3 suggest a rate of 0.04 percent for the Bea, who were most heavily affected, with 83.3 percent (5/6) of this mortality being among males. The demographic consequences of such attrition thus would be negligible. Nevertheless, it is evident that population density declined, since South Andaman density was less than that of Middle and North Andaman (at the time of contact). If the Bea had pushed against their northern neighbors, and the latter had pushed against theirs in turn, the south-to-north gradient of increasing population density would disappear. The presence of the gradient thus betokens Bea population decline through downward adjustment in births and/or increased mortality (including infant mortality).[12]

At the level of organization represented by unsegmented societies, war generally does not hold forth the prospect of achieving a significant long-term payoff after incurring short-term hardship. It only holds the prospect of continuing long-term disadvantage (compared to peace) and is maladaptive in this respect as well. However, one might readily imagine unusual circumstances under which war would be preferable to the alternative. For example, a forest fire ignited by lightning might render a vast area uninhabitable, forcing the inhabitants to move into the territory of strangers and precipitating warfare that was adaptive for the intruders in such a context. The inconclusive character of warfare between unsegmented societies also makes an intrusive group difficult to dislodge. This same feature of prospective stalemate cuts both ways, in that decisive conquest is unattainable but an encroaching group also does not risk annihilation. The intrusive Jarawa were thus able to secure a foothold on Great Andaman Island despite their small numbers (compared to the Bea). This was also facilitated by their infiltration into an underutilized upland ecological zone. We do not know why the Jarawa moved into—rather than away from—conflict and took up an existence in which it was necessary to wear body armor while engaged in routine subsistence activity. However, it is plausible that they were prompted by a significant (but probably not permanent) deterioration in the conditions of their existence in Little Andaman at some time in the relatively recent past.

The Andamanese case indicates that war between the local groups of a pair of unsegmented foraging societies is highly localized, confined to a specific ecological zone, and not contagious. The principal zone of conflict between the predominantly coastal Bea and the interior-dwelling Jarawa was the area of seasonal overlap between their respective ecological niches. Although resource competition is the source of these conflicts, this condition of restricted resources relative to population does not engender a spread of warfare to other borders between groups. Neighboring Bea local groups maintained relations of positive peace with each other, and warfare also did not spread to the northern borders between the Bea and the neighboring Pucikwar tribe of Middle Andaman. This is attributable to the fact that positive peace between neighboring bands expands resource availability by facilitating exploitation of border areas. There is thus a strong impetus toward peaceful relations.

A capacity to maintain or reestablish peaceful relations is critical to group survival because armed conflict would otherwise be cumulatively additive and irreversible, ultimately leading to an all-fronts war with neighbors on every quarter and corresponding resource-base contraction. In other words, a band that responds to conflict along one border by initiating conflict along another places itself at an increased risk of group decline and extinction. The intrinsic disadvantages of this response to conflict work against the development of a pattern of contagion whereby war spreads from band to band like wildfire from a single point of origination within a regional system. Within unsegmented societies lethal armed conflict does not in itself engender further conflict but only occurs when and where the precipitating conditions (of resource scarcity) are present. This contrasts markedly with segmental societies where vengeance requirements ensure that one death leads to another and organizational features engender the alliance of clusters of local communities that both externalize armed conflict and augment the scale of the units involved in it. Simultaneous attacks by two allied groups upon a common neighbor can result in a rout, pushing refugees into other local groups further afield and spreading conflict. Military alliance provides a means by which numerical superiority can be attained, and this in turn creates the possibility of a decisive outcome (i.e., routing). In contrast, a war of attrition does not entail decisive outcomes and does not intrinsically tend to spread.

The general propositions that specify the incidence and character of warfare (and of spontaneous armed conflict) within and between local groups of unsegmented societies provide a basis for modeling the frequency and distribution of warfare circa 35,000 to 10,000 years ago. One would expect warfare to develop in rich environments in which compara- tively high population densities were sustained over extended periods of time and the local groups were also unable to move away from each other when conflicts over resources occurred. The Yahgan case indicates that the threshold for the transition from spontaneous lethal conflict over resources (followed by capital punishment) to warfare is quite high, because the Yahgan partially meet these conditions yet have not devel- oped warfare. The Yahgan inhabit the coastal zone of the Chilean archi- pelago, consisting of hundreds of islands, fjords, and rocky headlands. Their habitat is thus to a considerable extent environmentally circum- scribed, although extensive. However, the Yahgan differed from the Andaman Islanders in that their reliance on plant foods and land game was very slight. Fish were also unimportant. The main foods were shellfish, sea mammals, and birds procured along the beach (Steward and Faron 1959:399). The resources of any given area were depleted in a rela- tively short period of time, necessitating regular movement. There was thus little scope for staking and defending claims to a fixed territory. This suggests that war does not develop in circumscribed environments unless plant resources comprise a significant component of the diet.

We have seen that war (as defined in this study) is rare to nonexistent in 20 percent (5/25) of a representative world sample of foraging societies and that all these instances of comparatively warless societies are of the unsegmented type. However, not all unsegmented societies are warless. War is manifested among the Andamanese and also occurs when unseg- mented societies are subject to attack by segmental neighbors (i.e., the Slave and the Ingalik during the nineteenth century).[13] If all the societies of the early Upper Paleolithic were unsegmented, one would expect war to be limited to circumscribed environments such as the Andaman Islands. Such environments appear to be of very limited distribution and were in many cases uninhabited in 35,000 B.P. (due in part to a lack of watercraft). For example, the island of Crete in the Mediterranean Sea is a circumscribed environment of approximately the same dimensions as Great Andaman Island, but there is no evidence of human occupation until the Neolithic (after 10,000 B.P.). If circumscribed environments such as this were largely unoccupied during the Upper Paleolithic, then one would expect that nearly all early Upper Paleolithic societies were warless. This conclusion is further reinforced by the fact that war cannot readily spread from circum- scribed environments by virtue of the very features that render them cir- cumscribed. One would thus expect only isolated pockets of warfare in a world system consisting entirely of unsegmented societies (before circa 35,000 B.P.). This means that in nearly all regions of the world there was a relatively recent origin of war, in the sense of a transition from a prior state in which lethal conflict was limited to homicide, capital punishment, and spontaneous fighting over resources (and in which social substitution was absent).

The prevalence of warlessness at the inception of the Upper Paleolithic (in 35,000 B.P.) is contingent upon an absence of segmental foragers at that time in prehistory, since there are no segmental foraging societies in our representative sample (of seventeen) in which warfare is rare to nonexistent and only one society (the Warrau) where it is as infrequent as once a generation (see chap. 2, table 4). More than half (9/17) of the segmental foragers experience annual warfare. The development of segmental forms of organization at a later point in time would thus entail a significant transformation in the frequency, distribution, and character of war. Revenge-based raiding (characteristic of segmental societies) may arise from an initial homicide stemming from a commonplace interpersonal conflict. It therefore is not intrinsically linked to resource scarcity and may consequently occur in a wide variety of environmental contexts and at any population density (as evident from chap. 2, table 10). Warfare that is both frequent and widely distributed would be expected to be manifested in the archaeological record in the form of skeletal evidence of violent death, the relocation of habitations to defensive sites, changes in weapons technology, and the like. In other words, it is an empirical question as to whether the archaeological record supports an interpretation of the frequency and distribution of warfare during the Upper Paleolithic as limited to isolated pockets, on one hand, or widely prevalent, on the other.

The earliest conclusive archaeological evidence of warfare dates from 12,000 to 14,000 B.P. and is derived from a cemetery near the present-day town of Jebel Sahaba in the Sudan. This Nubian cemetery (site 117) is located atop a knoll about a kilometer from the Nile River. It contains remains of 59 individuals, of whom 24, or 40.7 percent, show evidence of violent death (Wendorf 1968:993). This evidence consists of stone projectile points and barbs embedded in the skeleton or resting within its compass. In all, 110 chipped stone artifacts were found in direct association with the burials, "almost all in positions which indicate they had penetrated the body either as points or barbs on projectiles or spears" (Wendorf 1968:959). Most of the individuals show evidence of multiple wounds (discussed further below).

There are a number of instances in which two or more individuals were buried in the same grave and thus presumed to have died at the same time. The age and sex distribution of these burial groups, and of the single burials that involve individuals found with projectile points believed to have caused their death, are shown in table 15 (based on data in Wendorf 1968:978, 992–93).

In the burial groups including several individuals who died at the same time, those killed included five males, seven females, and six children.

Three of the children show no direct evidence of violent death but all were buried in a common grave with adults who do. They were quite possibly killed by a spear withdrawn for reuse in the course of an ongoing attack. These instances of multiple deaths that occurred at the same time were probably a result of raids upon encampments or settlements where family members were gathered together, rather than being a result of hostile encounters that occurred in the course of subsistence activity organized by a gendered division of labor. A distribution of casualties in which more women and children than men are killed is indicative of raids upon habitations and is also a direct product of group member liability to vengeance. Six of eight adult females and six of seven children (of those who died a violent death) were buried with another individual. In contrast, seven of ten adult males who died of wounds were buried alone (five) or with another adult male (one double burial). Although some of these may have been killed during attacks on encampments, the higher incidence of single burials for males suggest that a number of them were probably killed in ambushes or confrontations that took place away from habitations, while the men were engaged in hunting or collecting.

The pattern of multiple wounds indicates that the individuals who inflicted them were motivated by vengeance and that the concepts of kin

TABLE 15.   The Age/Sex Distribution of Violent Deaths at Jebel Sahaba by Burial Groups

Burial Groups Identified by Burial Numbers	Adult Males	Adult Females	Children
25, 28, 34, 37	1	3	
100, 101, 102, 103		2	2**
26, 27, 29, 31	2	1	1*
13, 14			2
23, 24		1	1
20, 21	2		
47			1
44		1	
45		1	
17	1		
33	1		
38	1		
42	1		
106	1		
Totals	10	9	7

Note: This table omits Burials 30, 32, 35, and 36, which may have been disturbed by the interment of the group 25, 28, 34, and 37 (Wendorf 1968:992). Burial 36, an adult female, may have been contemporary with the first group. Burials 30, 32, and 35 are adults of unknown gender.

*All burials include projectile points presumed to be the cause of death except those marked with an asterisk. Each asterisk represents one child buried in a common grave with adults who show evidence of violent death.

group responsibility and liability guided their actions. A reconstruction of the probable sequence of events leading to death in several cases will show this. One middle-aged adult male (Burial 21) includes nineteen chipped stone artifacts attributable to at least nine different projectiles. He was wounded in the right forearm and right calf while facing an antagonist with whom he was most likely engaged in combat. He was probably brought down by several wounds received in the lower abdomen in the pelvic region. Then, lying on the ground, he received five to seven wounds to the left side of his ribs, chest, back, and left hip, and to the base of his neck and his head (see Wendorf 1968:966 for the list of projectile point locations on which this reconstruction is based). One young adult female (Burial 44) shows evidence of at least eleven or twelve wounds (based on twenty-one associated stone chips and flakes). She was probably disabled by a wound to the knee and then subsequently suffered nine or ten separate wounds to the torso and one to the cheek area of the face, with most of these wounds inflicted after she had fallen (see Wendorf 1968:978). These multiple wounds entail overkill that takes the form of pincushioning the torso and head of a fallen enemy who is already dead or fatally wounded.[14] This act reflects collective kin group responsibility on the part of the vengeance party, each of whom—acting in concert and in unison—delivers the coup de grâce with his own arrow or spear. This act of solidarity, which is meaningful to those who carry it out, is at the same time a communication to the enemy of unified group strength and resolve. The arrows and/or spears are also left in place. Even after 12,000 years, and across the gulf of cultural difference encompassed by that time span, one readily grasps the message that this is payback.

The liability of any group member to vengeance is evident from the killing of children. We know (from ethnographic analogy) that children do not commit homicide and are not killed as malefactors responsible for past deaths. However, children are killed as members of a group responsible for past deaths, in accordance with the principle of social substitution, in classic blood feud and in war.

Wendorf (1968:993) suggests that resource scarcity may have been responsible for the lethal armed conflict evident from these burials.

> Population pressures may have become too great with the deterioration of Late Pleistocene climate and the effects which this had on the herds of large savanna-type animals which were the primary source of food at this time. With this situation, the few localities which were particularly favorable for fishing would have been repeatedly fought over as sources of food became increasingly scarce.

The marsh along the Nile was also a source of sedge bulbs and rush bulbs, that is, of plant resources that comprised a significant portion of the diet

(Flannery, personal communication). The environmental context is thus similar to that found in the Andamanese case in that there are marine resources, plant resources, and game resources in three contiguous ecological zones (river, marsh, and savanna). Extrapolation from the Andamanese case thus suggests that this conflict may have been between one population that relied predominantly on savanna-based food resources and another that relied primarily on the riverine-marsh margins, with a zone of partial overlap between these ecological niches. Environmental circumscription was present in that the area located further back from the floodplain was arid and subject to seasonal drought. Either population increase or a period of reduced rainfall (typical of this region) may thus have pushed the savanna-dwellers into the zone of the marsh-edge dwellers, leading to an intensification of spontaneous lethal conflicts over resources that culminated in the development of war. Although this reconstruction is not the only possible interpretation, it is striking that the earliest archaeological site that provides conclusive evidence of war has all the characteristics postulated (on the basis of ethnographic comparison) as being instrumental to the origin of war. In short, this case readily fits the model.

The cemetery at Jebel Sahaba provides clear evidence of raids upon encampments (determinable from the age/sex distribution of multiple burials), of collective responsibility for vengeance (indicated by pincushioning), and of group liability (indicated by the killing of children). Moreover, these data also illustrate the point that it is not necessarily difficult to distinguish archaeologically between homicide, capital punishment, and war. Homicide and capital punishment both result in one death at a time, so that multiple burials would be absent. Those killed are predominantly adult males, although a substantial proportion of capital punishment executions may be adult females when death is believed to be due to sickness-sending in the form of sorcery or witchcraft. Adult females may be killed as bystanders in attempted capital punishment executions, as illustrated by the !Kung (discussed in chap. 1), but !Kung children are never killed in this way. Child deaths as a result of violence are thus almost invariably indicative of war and feud.[15] Pincushioning may occasionally be employed in the case of capital punishment, but as a routine practice it is clearly associated with vengeance killing in feud and war. Multiple wounds invariably indicate collective armed conflict, grounded in group responsibility to avenge a death. The size of the raiding party is generally equal to the number of arrows delivered in the coup de grâce volley, this being about five to eight in the case of Jebel Sahaba.

It can be argued that the burial of an individual subjected to pincushioning would invariably show clear evidence of violent death from multiple wounds. If stone-tipped projectiles form part of the lithic industry of the time period, then one would expect them to be employed in armed conflict. With a large number of arrows being fired, at least some projectile points would be expected to be embedded in bone, to nick bone surfaces, or to fragment, leaving stone chips in place even if shafts were removed before burial. Lambert (1997:93) estimates that 25 to 44 percent of projectile wounds leave scars on bone surfaces that are archaeologically identifiable (while the rest engender wounds that leave no skeletal evidence, although stone chips may be found within the compass of the skeleton). Pincushioning would thus be extremely unlikely to escape archaeological detection if it occurred.

It is important to recall that *collective* armed conflict (and collective responsibility for vengeance) are generally reflected in *multiple* wounds in the case of societies at this level of military organization. In classic blood feud and revenge-based warfare an unsuspecting individual is ambushed by a small group of men (Otterbein 1968:279). This invariably results in multiple projectile wounds because an incapacitated victim is repeatedly shot or speared. In other words, a wounded individual is dispatched. This also occurs in dawn raids upon habitations. It is only in battles between two lines of combatants that wounded individuals are able to withdraw to the rear in safety. Single projectile wounds that ultimately prove fatal do occur under these circumstances (and a proportion of burials of individuals who died in warfare would thus manifest no skeletal evidence of this). However, the warfare conducted by unsegmented (and most segmental) foragers takes the form of ambushes and raids, as opposed to battles. The wounded are dispatched, and this results in multiple projectile wounds or projectile wounds plus club or axe wounds to the head that are archaeologically detectable. In contrast, homicide tends to involve limited wounds. All of the murder cases examined by Steenhoven (1959:46) among the central Eskimo involved attacks from behind. As Balikci (1970:180) notes, "murderers were evidently careful to avoid a struggle." The forensic signatures of violent death from war and homicide respectively are thus likely to be quite different.

The preceding discussion provides a basis for evaluation of the archaeological record with respect to the question of the origin of war, that is, the transition from a social condition encompassing homicide, capital punishment, and spontaneous lethal conflict over resources to a social condition encompassing classic blood feud and war (entailing social substitution). We may begin by considering the cave wall art of the Upper Paleolithic and Mesolithic of Europe. The cave at Cougnac in France, dated to the Early Magdalenian, prior to Magdalenian III (circa 15,500 B.P.), contains a depiction that includes "three megaceros deer (two males and one female) . . . surrounding and partly superimposed over them are four unfinished figures: mammoth, ibex, stag, and a man run through [*sic,*

Fig. 3. Panel V at Cougnac. (Reproduced from Giedion 1962, 463. Reprinted with the permission of the National Gallery of Art.)

pierced] by spears" (Leroi-Gourhan 1968:324). The portion of this painting including the man is reproduced in figure 3.[16]

This scene may readily be interpreted as a portrayal of spontaneous conflict over resources. The man is a stranger whose face and identity are not known and therefore not represented. He has been encountered by a hunting party of three men (or more) and ambushed from behind. He appears to be running from his attackers, leaving them in command of the hunting domain where he has trespassed. Further along in the main gallery there is a similar depiction of a speared individual contained within the outline of a mammoth (fig. 4). In both paintings one gets a sense of a sequence of events in which the game animal has moved into the foreground of an area that the observers have taken possession of by expelling or slaying a trespasser. The two scenes thus memorialize spontaneous confrontations over game resources in which the social group of the painters

Fig. 4.　A section of Panel VIII at Cougnac. (Reproduced from Giedion 1962, 464. Reprinted with the permission of the National Gallery of Art.)

prevailed. Although other interpretations are possible, the one presented here shows that these depictions are readily intelligible in terms of the framework developed in this study. The archaeological data fit the model.

The fifth cavity of the cave at Remigia, Castellón, Spain, dated to circa 5000 to 3000 B.P. (Anzar 1954:317), contains a painting that has come to be called the "execution group," reproduced in figure 5. This clearly depicts an episode of pincushioning, showing ten archers with their bows raised—in unison and in jubilation—while an unarmed victim of vengeance lies dead or dying, pierced with ten arrows. This same scene is reproduced at a number of different caves in Spain dating to the

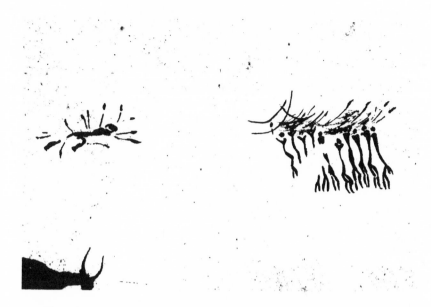

Fig. 5. The "Execution Group": A section of the fifth cavity at Remigia. (Redrawn from Sandars 1985:162.)

Mesolithic time period (Sandars 1985:164). Battle scenes involving two groups of archers are also depicted (161–63). However, the execution group is of particular interest because it so vividly portrays collective responsibility for vengeance encoded in the practice of pincushioning. The correspondence between this scene and the reconstruction of what transpired at Jebel Sahaba is also noteworthy.

The contrast between Cougnac (circa 15,500 B.P.) and Castellón (circa 5000 to 3000 B.P.) illustrates the transition that encompasses the origin of war. The execution scene clearly conveys a sense of vengeance, represented by overkill and jubilation, as well as the presence of a cohesive military organization acting in unison (also evident in battle scenes). Depictions of a fighting force are absent in European cave art prior to the Mesolithic.[17]

The archaeological record indicates that the Upper Paleolithic (35,000 to 10,000 B.P.) was a period of general warlessness, with the exception of a few isolated pockets in which environmental conditions of a very limited distribution favored the origin of war. Jebel Sahaba (14,000 to 12,000 B.P.) represents the prime example. There is only one other Upper Paleolithic burial that provides evidence of pincushioning (defined by multiple projectile wounds) indicative of collective responsibility for vengeance. This is also from the Nile Valley, several hundred miles downstream from Jebel Sahaba.[18] There is only one instance of the death of a child attributed to a projectile wound, indicative of group liability. This is noted by Keeley (1996:37) for the Italian site of Grimaldi dated to 34,000 to 24,000 B.P. Fatal cranial injuries (without accompanying projectile wounds) are evident in the archaeological record for this period, but these are likely to be due to homicide, capital punishment, or spontaneous fighting over resources (as exemplified by the Yahgan, who employ the clubs they carry to kill seals). Bows and arrows and/or spears are the weapons of choice when attempting to ambush an unsuspecting individual in classic blood feud. The same weapons are favored in dawn raids on settlements, because those being attacked possess such weapons, able to kill at a distance. A man armed only with a club might find himself a spear's length away from an antagonist.

Multiple burials—which are potentially indicative of raids upon encampments or habitations, as opposed to spontaneous conflicts over game—are not at all uncommon in the Upper Paleolithic and require some discussion. Harrold (1980:195–211) has compared thirty-six Middle Paleolithic and ninety-six Upper Paleolithic burials from Eurasian sites extending from Spain to the former Soviet Union. This comparison reveals, "Forty of the 91 Upper Paleolithic subjects for which data were available were found in multiple interments, as against only six of thirty-six Mousterian [Middle Paleolithic] subjects" (206). Moreover, females are overrepresented in these multiple burials (202) although the exact tally is not given.

This numerical comparison is heavily influenced by inclusion of the site of Predmosti in Czechoslovakia, where twenty individuals were interred in a common grave. If this site were separated out, then the figure for the remaining Upper Paleolithic multiple burials would be twenty of seventy-one subjects (from forty-two separate sites). The proportion of subjects in multiple burials would consequently be 16.7 and 28.4 percent for the Middle and Upper Paleolithic, respectively. This more accurately reflects the degree of change (as would a calculation of multiple burials as a percentage of all burials, a figure that cannot be derived from the data Harrold [1980] provides). A change of this moderate degree of magnitude might simply be due to an increase in the size of local groups (which increases the chances that two group members may die of disease within a few days of each other and be buried together).

The conditions of existence among hunter-gatherers are such that contagious disease readily spreads to all those who coreside. Food is widely shared among group members, who gather together daily at close quarters for communal dining, and there is ample opportunity for disease transmission in this context. When communicable disease is introduced into a population, deaths tend to occur over a short time span and to be very unevenly distributed among local groups, with some suffering substantial mortality, and others none at all (as visiting between groups is curtailed). For example, the Etoro of Papua New Guinea (whom I studied) suffered an influenza epidemic in January 1969 in which twenty-two individuals died (representing 5.7 percent of the Etoro population), with most of these deaths occurring in a single week (Kelly 1977:30). Twelve deaths took place in two neighboring communities (with a combined population of sixty-five persons) (Kelly 1993:228, 245–46). The corpses of the deceased were exposed on platforms and subsequently given secondary burial in family groups.

Starvation also produces multiple deaths within a short period of time. For example, Gillespie (1981b:330–31) reports that the Mountain Indians of the Canadian Northwest Territory (neighbors of the Slave) repeatedly suffered episodes of famine during the nineteenth century, with "most of" one group of 150 persons perishing during the severe winter of 1851–52.

Frayer (1997:183) notes that there are

> a number of double and multiple interments [in the Upper Paleolithic and Mesolithic] which are likely the result of homicides. While none preserves evidence of perimortem trauma, the fact that the corpses were buried simultaneously is suspicious since it is unlikely that two or three people would die of natural causes at the same time.

Keeley (1996:37) also argues that mass burials, such as the one at Predmosti, are evidence of lethal conflict given "the improbability of alternative explanations." However, communicable disease and starvation provide highly plausible alternative explanations for multiple burials and even mass graves. In winter there is no inducement to prompt burial, especially during a time of general illness and famine (and the first may conspire to produce the second). Multiple burials thus should not be interpreted as evidence of war *unless* skeletal indications of trauma or proximate projectile points support this, as they do at Jebel Sahaba. A multiple burial also effectively doubles the chances that a projectile would leave skeletal evidence, yet such evidence is lacking for Upper Paleolithic multiple burials (as Frayer attests).

In summarizing the findings of a recent volume concerned with examining the extent to which human skeletal remains provide evidence of prehistoric violence, Ferguson (1997:332) concludes that "the most significant finding is that violence and war [readily] leave recoverable traces." Violent death is generally detectable, although the question of whether it was a result of individual or collective action is less readily determined. It is consequently improbable that war would leave no trace of violent death in the archaeological record, and an absence (or paucity) of such evidence can be taken as accurately reflecting an absence (or paucity) of war (332). There are a number of surveys of this evidence, for different world regions, and they consistently indicate a low incidence of violent death during the Upper Paleolithic (Keeley 1996:37, Frayer 1997:182–83, and Ferguson 1997:332–34 summarize many of these surveys while Roper 1969 continues to be a standard reference on the subject). Moreover, indications of deaths attributable to war per se are scarcer still (i.e., pincushioning and the violent death of a child, reviewed above).

The general picture conveyed by this entire body of evidence for the Upper Paleolithic dovetails nicely with the model presented in this study. Spontaneous lethal conflicts over resources result in only very low mortality, and this would leave little or no trace in the archaeological record. The figure of 0.02 percent mortality per annum for the Andamanese (calculated by Wright [1942:569]) provides a benchmark, since nearly all of this was a result of spontaneous conflict rather than planned raids on encampments. This rate entails one death per year for the 4,950 person population of Great Andaman Island circa 1858 (Radcliffe-Brown 1964:18). If one assumes that half the population would die (of all causes) over a period of 25 years under natural conditions (i.e., in the absence of introduced disease), then only one of a hundred deaths (25/2,475) deaths would be due to spontaneous lethal conflicts. In other words, one of a hundred burials would show a projectile wound (or wounds). I assume a trespasser who was killed would have suffered multiple wounds (as in the Cougnac cave paintings), so that at least one of these would mark bone. However, the body of a slain trespasser might not be recovered and buried by his compatriots. If the odds of burial were less for the slain trespasser than for individuals who died of natural causes, more total burials would need to be subject to archaeological examination to provide a single instance of spontaneous lethal conflict in the archaeological record. Moreover, this numerical model is for a circumscribed environment in which spontaneous conflict over resources was chronic and had progressed to the shoot-on-sight stage. In a context such as Europe during the Upper Paleolithic, where population density was low and circumscription absent, a much lower incidence of conflict and fatalities would be expected.

Spontaneous conflicts over resources were also chronic among the Yahgan and resulted in a high rate of fatalities and subsequent retaliatory homicides (i.e., capital punishment). The overall homicide rate is the highest of all reported rates for the unsegmented societies considered in this study, totaling 178 per 100,000 per annum (see note 12, chap. 2). However, this would result in only about 9 (8.8) homicides out of every 100 deaths (again calculating that half the Yahgan population would die of natural causes over twenty-five years as in the Andamanese case). Burials would be expected to show extensive cranial trauma due to the use of clubs, so that no violent deaths would go undetected. Among the Andamanese, Man (1885:13) reports deaths from violence and accidents combined amount to "four or five percent" of total deaths. Among the !Kung San, violent deaths (from homicide, capital punishment, and accidental killings of bystanders)[19] would only constitute about 2 out of every 100 deaths from all causes, and these would probably be nondetectable due to use of small poisoned arrows. Thus, even though homicide rates in unsegmented foraging societies are high by cross-cultural comparative standards, they still constitute only a small fraction of all deaths. In environments that were *not* circumscribed, one might expect that something on the order of 2 out of 100 burials would show evidence of violent death (most probably in the form of cranial trauma).[20] Again, this is consistent with the available archaeological evidence for the Upper Paleolithic. These data thus support the conclusion that a social condition that encompassed homicide, capital punishment, and spontaneous lethal conflict over resources (but not feud and war) characterized this era, with the exception of isolated pockets (e.g., Jebel Sahaba).

The general proposition that war and society coevolve is well established. However, the implications of this for the origin of war have not previously been explored, namely, that prewar societies would be expected to be of a distinctive organizational type. The present study substantiates this expectation and also shows that this distinctive organizational type— unsegmented societies—evidences specific associated forms of lethal armed conflict that differ from war. This too is consistent with the coevolutionary view. Moreover, the data presented in this study make it possible not only to specify the characteristics of pre-warfare social formations but also to identify the conditions that generate the origination of war. In short, a general model for the initial evolution of war has been presented.

Fitting this general model to a chronology is a separate issue and one that has not been fully considered. In order to adequately address the question of *when* warfare originated, it would be necessary to survey the archaeological record worldwide, region by region. This is beyond the scope of the present work, and I have been content to present evidence showing that the archaeological record supports the conclusion that this transition occurred after 10,000 B.P. everywhere except the Nile Valley. This is sufficient to make the point that war is not primordial but has a definite origin in the relatively recent past.[21] At the same time it is instructive to note the companion point that homicide, the killing of a killer (capital punishment), and spontaneous, potentially lethal conflict over resources do appear to go well back into human prehistory.[22] However, these were rare events from an actor's point of view, in that lethal violence would be likely to occur within one's own local group only about once every hundred years (or once every twenty years in a regional band of five neighboring local groups).[23] The "nightmare past" that Hobbes envisioned in which individuals lived in continual fear of violent death clearly never existed. On the other hand, an effort to locate ethnographic instances of societies in which conflict is absent and utopia concretely exemplified invites disappointment.

However, unsegmented societies do display a very marked tendency toward the resolution of conflict and the restriction of lethal violence to isolated incidents widely spaced in time. Typically, a homicide engenders no sequel. The concept of individual responsibility for redress of wrongs tends to allocate retribution to the spirit of the deceased and this inhibits group-level vengeance obligations. When the family and kin of a homicide victim do take action they target the perpetrator so that a killer is killed and individuals prone to lethal violence are removed from society. A strong emphasis is placed on the reestablishment of a cooperative, communitarian ethic of sharing and goodwill (Knauft 1987, 1994). When a spontaneous conflict over resources takes place between neighboring local groups they tend to move apart, obviating the underlying cause of conflict. In the normal course of events continuous efforts are made to maintain relations of positive peace with neighboring groups through some combination of intermarriage, kin ties arising from marriage, adoption, visiting, gift exchange, and collective social gatherings entailing joint feasting, singing, and dancing. The prevailing condition of intergroup relations is one of positive peace (i.e., a state of peace rather than a Hobbesian state of war). Moreover, in circumscribed environments—in which conditions were conducive to the origination of war (as an outgrowth of the intensification of spontaneous lethal conflict over resources)—peacemaking practices coevolved and were elaborated. This was evident among the Yahgan who were on the brink of the transition from capital punishment to war. Although there was group responsibility for vengeance that devolved upon the family of a homicide victim,

> the Yahgan seem to have felt antipathy rather than hatred, so vengeance might be deferred for several years during which time mutual friends might compose the quarrel. (Lothrop 1928:165)

Moreover, Gusinde (1931:885) reported that a vengeance party might stop short of killing a murderer, instead administering a beating and accepting gift payments over time. These features betoken the development of third-party mediation and the seeds of a concept of compensation in lieu of retaliatory vengeance. Peacemaking institutions thus emerged as the frequency of conflict intensified. Among the Andamanese, a highly elaborated peacemaking ceremony also developed in conjunction with the origination of war. Although unsegmented societies cannot be described as peaceful in the utopian sense of the term (emphasizing an absence of conflict), they can accurately be characterized as markedly prone to the reestablishment of peaceful relations following an episode of lethal violence between neighboring groups as well as within the local community.

We have seen that war and society coevolve. One central aspect of this coevolution is that the elaboration of peacemaking goes hand in hand with the origin and development of war. The hope of future peace therefore does not require a nostalgic longing for a return to the simpler times of the Upper Paleolithic and/or the simpler ways of unsegmented societies. The human propensity to peacemaking, so strikingly evident from the characteristic alternation of war and peace, is central to the nexus of interrelationships between human nature, war, and society—and this bodes well for the future.

Notes

Introduction

1. My purpose here is merely to sketch the outlines of a widely shared view of the archaeological evidence pertaining to the origin of war. For a more extensive consideration of this question, and a sampling of some of the divergent interpretations, see *World Archaeology* (1986); Vencl, Sl. (1984); Gabriel (1990); Redmond (1994:57–116); and Keeley (1996); in addition to the article by Roper (1975) cited in the main text. The archaeological evidence is also reconsidered in the concluding chapter.

2. Ember (1978:443) attributes the "myth" that hunter-gatherers are relatively peaceful to Service (1966:60), Steward (1968:334), and the influential Lee and DeVore (1968) volume *Man the Hunter*. She does not mention the archaeological derivation of this view that I emphasize. This dates back at least to Childe (1941) and perhaps earlier. Ember also does not explicitly seek to make the point that semisedentary hunter-gatherers with a heavy reliance on fishing are neither more nor less warlike than mobile hunter-gatherers. She notes the relevant data (which I cite) in the context of discussing differences between her sample and the surveys of others, e.g., Lee (1968).

3. Otterbein (1986:9–13) provides an informative discussion of the definitional differences between capital punishment, homicide, political assassination, feuding, warfare, and human sacrifice (all these being forms of killing). I emphasize somewhat different points of differentiation between these (especially social substitutability discussed further along) but have benefited from Otterbein's consideration of definitions and also that of Boehm (1984:191–227). I am also indebted to Radcliffe-Brown's (1933) discussion of the concept of injury to the group among Australian Aborigines (also cited in Boehm 1984:195).

4. In societies that are classified by Otterbein as band societies (lacking forms of organization beyond the local group), the death penalty is typically applied to individuals who are thought to threaten the survival of the group (Otterbein 1986:108). The most widely recognized capital offense in these societies is witchcraft (including sorcery), and this encompasses causing death as well as illness by supernatural means (90). The principal objective of capital punishment is removal of a wrongdoer to preclude further harm to group members. The perpetrator of a supernaturally caused homicide may be either male or female.

5. Otterbein (1968:279–80) defines feud as blood revenge (following a homicide) occurring within a political community. If the same act involves members of two different political communities, it is classified as war. War and feud thus differ with respect to the structural level at which the armed conflict takes place, but are

otherwise similar in important respects. Both entail employment of the concept of social substitution. In my own usage, I thus tend to use the term *war* to subsume both unless the finer distinction between them is relevant to the issue at hand. See Boehm (1984:218–19) for a detailed definition of feud and discussion of the more limited, proportional retaliation that characterizes feud as opposed to all-out warfare.

The concept of social substitution is exemplified by customs such as the levirate and sororate in which a deceased spouse is replaced by a same-sex sibling (true or classificatory). One individual takes the place of, or substitutes for, another in a specific social context. Social substitution is discussed more extensively in chapter 2.

6. The fact that the participants in a capital punishment execution are persuaded of the moral appropriateness and legitimacy of their actions does not imply that there is invariably a comprehensive consensus on this score within their community. There may be differences of opinion within a context of broad-based support. This is equally true with respect to the exaction of blood vengeance in feud and the initiation of war in other societies. However, ethnographically reported disagreements commonly concern the advisability of joining an ally or attacking a neighboring community (given the intrinsic risks) rather than the issue of moral appropriateness. Likewise, the Gebusi may disagree among themselves as to whether the guilt of a particular alleged sorcerer has been established, but do not dispute the moral legitimacy of executing a guilty individual. At this more general level there is a society-wide moral consensus.

7. The Gebusi themselves cannot be classified as a warless society because they are subject to occasional lethal raids by their neighbors, the Bedamini (Knauft 1985:8–9, 118–21). However, they never counterraid the Bedamini. The Gebusi would thus be categorized as a society in which "external war" (war between different cultural/linguistic groups) occurred infrequently, while internal war (including feud) would be classified as "rare to nonexistent." In contrast, capital punishment is frequently employed.

Chapter 1

1. The Siriono were subject to raids by their neighbors to the south (the Yanaigua) and north (the wild Baure) according to the source Fabbro utilizes (Holmberg 1969:159). However, they responded by avoidance and withdrawal. Internal war between Siriono bands is also reported to be entirely absent (157).

2. Voltaire's novel *The Huron, or Pupil of Nature* is a satire of both Rousseau's concept of the "noble savage" and of a world that readily tolerates its own corruption while seeking to ennoble the Other. The novel likewise captures the difficulty of utopianizing real individuals, as opposed to the abstract representations of hypothetical persons that inhabit philosophical tracts. I mention Voltaire here because he provides an alternative mode of disagreement with Rousseau to that provided by Hobbes. In other words, I do not seek to play Hobbes to Fabbro's Rousseau, I seek a counterpoint more akin to that of Voltaire (1959).

3. The main modifications concern:

(1) a higher frequency of physical violence that produces no serious injury, i.e., what Holmberg (1969:159) terms "minor assault,"
(2) a more widespread incidence of violence between adult females, and
(3) homicide rates that are quite high by cross-cultural comparative standards.

4. The Siriono homicide rate is comparable to that of the !Kung, Mbuti, and Semai. Holmberg (1969:95, 131, 152) records one instance in which a man killed his wife during a drinking feast, this also being the context in which men pick fights with each other that take the form of wrestling matches. This occurred fifteen years before study in a study population that numbers 152 persons, yielding a homicide rate of 43.9 per 100,000 per annum. A second homicide (in which a man killed his sister) occurred within this study population "a number of years ago" (152), evidently predating the spousal homicide. Allowing twenty-five years for both cases yields a rate of 52.6. The Siriono case is thus similar to the Semai. Homicide is described as being "almost unknown" (152), although the rate is actually quite high due to the small size of the study population.

5. See Knauft (1987:458) for a discussion of comparative homicide rates and the difficulty comparison entails. For example, all Mbuti and nearly all Gebusi homicides are instances of capital punishment, while such homicides are excluded from the calculation of rates for the United States and other industrialized state societies. The U.S. homicide rate is on the order of 10 per 100,000 per annum.

6. It is important to keep in mind that band societies (or simple societies) lack the state forms of organization and world religions that impose and inculcate individual restraint. It would scarcely be surprising if harsh (as opposed to permissive) child socialization had divergent effects on levels of adult violence depending upon whether or not these institutions were present. Knauft (1987:473) makes a similar point. There may also be a cross-cultural pattern of covariation between a comparatively high frequency of warfare and secondary socialization practices (occurring in late childhood and adolescence) that inculcate cohesion, solidarity, a sense of shared projects and interests, and a group identity among males. In other words, secondary socialization may be much more closely related to the incidence of war than early childhood socialization (Knauft, personal communication).

7. The Netsilik are the eastern neighbors of the Copper Eskimo. Both were studied by Rasmussen (1931, 1932) as part of the Fifth Thule Expedition.

8. I noted earlier that it was counterintuitive that Siriono women strike each other but do not strike their children. This particular Netsilik conflict is useful in showing how "permissive" child rearing and female fighting can be combined in the same cultural system.

9. See Kelly (1993) for an extended treatment of different patterns of the gendered division of labor and their covarying effects on marriage, divorce, and male-female relations.

10. This contrasts with the role of fighting in establishing dominance among males of some other mammalian species.

11. Siriono society is the only society under consideration in which the local

community is composed of matrilocal (or, more precisely, uxorilocal) extended families. This suggests the hypothesis that spousal violence is more prevalent when few or none of a women's kin coreside with her in the same local group, as occurs under conditions of neolocal or patrilocal postmarital residence, and less prevalent when a woman's kinfolk are coresident (including her mother, father, sisters, and unmarried brothers).

Chapter 2

1. Lee (1979:393) provides a retrospective account of a conversation in which vengeance was discussed. An informant, whose father was killed when he came to the informant's aid in a fight with B, proposes to kill B "who started it all." However, his senior namesake, to whom he expresses this intention, emphatically disagrees, pointing out that it is "the one who has killed another" that should be killed in retaliation. The killer of the informant's father is thus targeted and subsequently executed.

2. Steenhoven's (1959) study provides the basis for Balikci's (1970:179–81) account of the seven recent homicides among the Netsilik.

3. The residential segregation of males and females is not uncommon in tribal societies generally. Men and adolescent boys occupy a central men's house while women, girls, and young children occupy separate dwellings. In these cases the family lacks a spatially distinct locus within the local community (although one may emerge in the context of production, distribution, and/or consumption). However, this residential arrangement is not found in unsegmented societies, but only in segmental societies (defined further along in the main body of the text).

4. See Collier and Rosaldo (1981), Collier (1988), and Kelly (1993) for a discussion of brideservice and the construct "brideservice societies."

5. Unsegmented societies are those societies that meet the following criteria in terms of Murdock's (1981:91–103) coding protocols (for predominant practices):

- Column 12, Mode of Marriage: 0 (no significant consideration), S (brideservice), T (token symbolic marriage payment), X (sister exchange)
- Column 14, Family Organization: any code except E (corporate extended families)
- Column 20, Patrilineal Kin Groups and Exogamy: 0 (absent)
- Column 22, Matrilineal Kin Groups and Exogamy: 0 (absent)
- Column 24, Cognatic Kin Groups: B (bilateral descent with kindreds unreported), K (bilateral descent with kindreds reported)
- Column 25, Cousin Marriage: N (first and second cousin marriage prohibited), O (first cousin marriage prohibited, no evidence reported for second cousin), S (first cousin marriage prohibited, second cousin marriage permitted but not preferred)
- Column 27, Kinship Terminology for Cousins: E (Eskimo), H (Hawaiian)
- Column 32, Jurisdictional Hierarchy: 20 ("the theoretical minimum, e.g.,

independent nuclear or polygynous families and autonomous bands or villages"; Murdock 1981, 99)

A society for which information is lacking on a particular point (such as cousin marriage) is included if it meets all other criteria.

6. The Siriono differ from the unsegmented societal design in that they possess corporate extended families (E) that constitute a segmentary level (jurisdictional hierarchy code 30). They also have preferred matrilateral cross-cousin marriage (Mm) and Crow terminology. They are thought to be a remnant of a more complex cultural group that moved into a remote forest region to escape Inca attacks centuries earlier (Holmberg 1969:11–14).

7. Honigmann describes wife-stealing and retaliatory raids between the Kaska and Beaver Indians and then extrapolates to the Slave on the grounds that the accounts of informants from neighboring tribes should be included "as probably illustrating the pattern of warfare in this general area" (1946:73). However, the Kaska and Beaver are not unsegmented societies, so that the use of such extrapolations to reconstruct Slave warfare is inappropriate with respect to the issues being investigated in this study.

8. Ideally, codes for warfare should carefully distinguish reciprocating collective armed conflict from one-sided attacks, since being subject to attack does not indicate any propensity to war. The only necessary correlate is warlike neighbors rather than internal features of the society. This is the difficulty with Ross's code for the Slave. Codes for external war should also take note of cases in which isolation makes this type of warfare improbable, as in the case of island societies. For example, the Tiwi of Melville and Bathurst Islands are coded as having annual internal war but no external war. This is potentially interpretable as due to the limitations of opportunity rather than inclination. However, an adjustment in the warfare frequency rating for the Tiwi would not affect the conclusions derived from table 4, since they already fall on the "frequent" side of the combined ratings. However, it might potentially be relevant to a correlation between other variables, such as population density and frequency of warfare.

9. Ericksen and Horton (1992) provide codes for all 186 societies in the standard cross-cultural sample. However, I have only utilized the codes for the societies in Ross's (1983) half-sample, since the pertinent codes pertaining to frequency of internal and external warfare are only available for the latter. However, the conclusions drawn from table 5 would not differ if all the foraging societies in the standard cross-cultural sample were considered.

10. There is one case in table 5, the Tiwi, in which "violent action by the kin group is punished or fined," code 5 (Ericksen and Horton 1992:62). The Tiwi are included with those societies characterized by self-redress (code 6), since they also lack *legitimated* kin group responsibility for vengeance. However, it is evident that kin group vengeance occurs among the Tiwi, otherwise there would be no need to punish it. This is to say that it is not group vengeance per se but the cultural formulation of its legitimacy that is absent in the Tiwi case.

11. Ericksen and Horton's code for the !Kung is evidently based on Marshall (1965) rather than Lee (1979); see Ericksen and Horton (1992:78). Lee's ethno-

graphic account, discussed in chapter 1, would suggest that the !Kung should be coded in the same category as the Copper Eskimo and Yahgan.

12. Bridges (1884:223–24) recorded 22 homicides between the years of 1871 to 1884 for a population of 949 persons (in 1883), yielding a homicide rate of 178 per 100,000 per annum. Homicide occurred frequently among the Slave as well, although no rate can be calculated. These data are consistent with the comparatively high homicide rates for Fabbro's Peaceful Societies and Knauft's Simple Societies discussed in chapter 1. Thus unsegmented societies (which largely overlap with these two other categorizations) are characterized by high homicide rates.

13. In unsegmented societies, and in uncentralized social systems without developed hierarchies, more generally, collective action is often instigated by one person who takes the initiative and begins a project in which others then join. A communal garden or dwelling may thus be initiated by a man who commences to fell some of the trees or to gather necessary materials for construction. The manner in which capital punishment becomes collective is thus consistent with the pattern that obtains in many other domains of social life.

14. Ericksen and Horton (1992:72) also found that there was no significant association between the presence of fraternal interest groups and the likelihood of classic blood feud, contrary to the early study of Otterbein and Otterbein (1965).

15. Kang (1979) has examined the degree of covariation between exogamy and an index of peaceful relations in a cross-cultural sample of fifty societies. She concludes that "peace and violence are equally likely between the social units regardless of the marriage rule" (94). The data presented in table 7 differ from those utilized in Kang's study in that she defines exogamy as "the cultural rule requiring marriage outside of a group" (87) whereas table 7 is concerned with the frequency of marriage outside of the group, so that empirical gradations of out-marriage are distinguished (as opposed to presence or absence of a cultural rule). Kang is also concerned with all types of societies, whereas table 7 is restricted to foraging societies. Such societies are also more relevant to the "early times" that were the focus of Tylor's theory.

Otterbein (1991:246) also points out that internal war is "present" in the case of 17 of 19 societies with exogamous patrilineal descent groups (and "absent" in the case of 4 of 14 societies in which patrilineal descent groups were not exogamous). However, a more fine-grained analysis that measured the frequency of internal war (vs. presence or absence) and the frequency of outmarriage (vs. presence or absence) might reveal a pattern of covariation similar to that manifested in table 7. In other words, extensive outmarriage may reduce rather than eliminate armed conflict, and this effect may be more pronounced among societies with little or no reliance on agriculture. Nevertheless, it is clear from Kang's and Otterbein's contributions that exogamy does not ensure peaceful relations between social groups.

16. The individual codes for internal and external war assigned by Ross (1983) to these 25 foraging societies are given below, with the internal warfare frequency code listed first, followed by a "+" and then the external warfare frequency code. Abipon 1+1, Ainu 1+1, Andamanese 2+2, Aweikoma 1+1, Bellacoola 3+2, C. Eskimo 4+4, Chiricahua 4+1, Comanche 4+1, Eyak 4+2, Gilyak 2+4, Gros

Venture 4+2, Ingalik 4+3, Klamath 1+1, !Kung 3+4, Mbuti 4+4, Nambicuara 2+2, Saulteaux 4+1, Semang 4+4, Shavante 1+1, Slave 2+1, Tiwi 1+4, Warrau 4+3, Yahgan 3+4, Yokuts 3+3, Yurok 3+3.

17. See Kelly (1985) for an exemplification of these points with respect to Nuer-Dinka warfare. The theft and/or destruction of fish caches is also reported in Indian-Eskimo conflicts; see, for example, De Laguna and McClellan (1981:642). This example is discussed further along in the text.

Chapter 3

1. I refer here to the findings presented in table 4, in which only one of seventeen segmental foraging societies (the Warrau) was found to have warfare (either internal or external) as infrequently as once a generation or less (code 7 or 8).

2. In terms of the codes developed by Ross (1983:182), the Andaman Islanders are classified as having external war at least once every five years (code 2) and internal war at least once every five years.

3. Zide and Pandya (1989:648) endorse the classification of Andaman languages and dialects developed by Manoharan (1983), and figure 1 reproduces their representation of this (1989:649). Zide and Pandya (1989) also provide a comprehensive annotated bibliography of sources on Andamanese linguistics. With respect to the question of the external relation of Andamanese languages to other languages of the world, Zide and Pandya (648, 656) are favorably disposed toward Greenberg's (1971) Indo-Pacific hypothesis

> that the Andamanese languages belong to a very large linguistic super-stock, the languages—language families—related to Andamanese being spoken in Oceania (largely in New Guinea, but also by some groups in Indonesia and Melanesia) and in aboriginal Tasmania.

In their view, this hypothesis is promising and merits substantial additional investigation.

4. Portman (1899), Man (1885), the Census of 1901, and Radcliffe-Brown (1964) all present somewhat different maps of Andamanese tribal areas. Lal (1976:51) provides maps that compare the territorial domains reported by Portman for the 1880s with those reported in the Census of 1901. These show that the Jarawa tribe was confined to the interior of Rutland Island and the southern half of South Andaman in the 1880s, but had moved into the interior of the northern half of South Andaman and the interior of Baratang Island in Middle Andaman by 1901. In this instance territory clearly changed hands. However, Radcliffe-Brown (1964:15) notes that boundaries between tribes are "difficult to discover," and some of the other differences may be due to changes in reportage rather than population movements. Map 2 follows the territorial distribution given by Radcliffe-Brown (1964:512).

5. Radcliffe-Brown (1964:11) reports that "of a vocabulary of several hundred words collected in Little Andaman there were less than a dozen in which the root or stem was clearly the same as that of words in the Great Andaman." Zide and Pandya (1989:650) suggest that lexical tabus present in the Andamans reduce

the number of cognates shared by related languages and distort glottochronological cal estimates of their date of divergence. However, the substantial degree of difference recorded suggests that the languages of Great Andaman and Little Andaman diverged at least several thousand years ago, even after one allows for extensive cognate reduction. The languages are grammatically similar, but not identical, and these grammatical differences would be unaffected by lexical tabus.

6. The negrito population that Dutta (1978:56) nominates as possible progenitors of the Andamanese are the "Selon" (better known as Selung) described by Lapicque (1894), who are Sea Gypsies who subsist by fishing and spend their entire lives on boats. It is of interest that the Selung are an unsegmented society, although such societies represent only 5.68 percent of the 563 societies in Murdock's (1981) representative world sample. This lends support to Dutta's hypothesis that the Andamanese and Selung are descendants of a common antecedent. However, their languages are unrelated, as the Selung now speak the Malayan languages of their neighbors (Murdock 1981:47).

7. In 1792 the settlement was relocated from a small offshore island at the entry to Port Blair to Port Cornwallis in the Northern Andamans. The settlement was disbanded in 1796 due to substantial illness and mortality at this second location (Singh 1978:28). The 1858 settlement returned to the Port Blair location, which had been more favorable in terms of the incidence of illness.

8. This obviously contradicts the above quoted statement by Portman that the plunder of tools "on a large scale" was prevented. Portman is evidently reluctant to admit that the Naval Guard beat a hasty retreat despite having the advantages of being forewarned and well-armed. One suspects that Aberdeen Hill was "retaken" after the Andamanese had begun to withdraw of their own volition, and that the whole event was not one of the finest moments for British arms. Portman (1899:442) is extremely critical of Reverend Corbyn for his "unjust ridicule" in describing the event as "a ludicrous skirmish known in the chronicles of the Settlement as the 'Battle of Aberdeen.'"

9. It is difficult to be certain of Tewari's intentions. He may have been unsuccessful in attempting to foment insurrection among the convicts, or he may have lacked an opportunity to do so. He may have feared that should he attempt this and be reported by a snitch he would be hanged. In any event, it is to his credit that he refused to assist the government in actions against the Andamanese. In the months after his return, he "had often been pressed to go out and head a party to capture Andamanese, but had refused to trust himself amongst them" (Portman 1899:298).

10. My account of the early colonial history of the Andaman Islands focuses only on those aspects that have a bearing on Andaman military and peacemaking capability, and on the effect of the penal settlement upon Bea-Jarawa conflict. For additional details see Portman (1899) and Singh (1978).

11. The Onge population declined from an estimated 672 in 1903 to 98 in 1983 (Pandya 1993:5). The Sentinelese, who inhabit North Sentinal Island, are hostile to outsiders and have never been censused. Their population is estimated to have remained stable at about 117 to 100 persons during the period from 1911 to 1990 based on counts of their dwellings (which they abandon to hide in the forest when government parties land on their island) (Pandit 1990:5, 12).

12. During this same period there were seven analogous incidents in which convicts who had settled in the islands on completion of their sentence were attacked by the Jarawa while hunting pigs in the interior. In all, nine of these convict-settlers were killed and four wounded (see Portman 1899:729–57). Three Jarawa also ambushed a large party of convicts and Andamanese sent out to find those responsible for one of these attacks. In this encounter two of the Jarawa were killed and the third wounded (748).

13. In the context of a discussion of depopulation, Man (1885:13) reports that "the proportion of deaths from violence and accident is believed to amount to four or five per cent." The six deaths noted here occurred over fifteen years within a Bea population that was in a process of rapid decline and numbered only thirty-seven persons in 1901.

14. Female verbal abuse that may constitute a prelude to fighting includes exclamations such as "May your face become hideous!" (Man 1885:43). This suggests that female fighting in this instance shares similarities with that reported among Fabbro's Peaceful Societies discussed in chapter 1. However, fighting between men and women is not reported, and it seems that a woman's male relatives would take her part in disagreements with her spouse to the extent that a man would need to consider their reaction should he seek to punish his wife for adultery (see Radcliffe-Brown 1964:50).

15. This complex of beliefs—in which male spirit mediums depend on powerful female spirits, on one hand, but, on the other hand, these powerful female spirits are also their wives and helpmates—is also found in Papua New Guinea. The Gebusi discussed in the introduction offer one well-described example of this type of belief system (see Knauft 1985, 1989), and the Etoro (whom I studied) provide another. See Kelly (1993:330–36) for an extended discussion of the manner in which relations between the genders are informed by this cosmological construction in which sexual intimacy and conjugality are the central organizing principles of relations with the supernatural. Conjugality is also widely employed as an organizing principle in other aspects of Andamanese cosmology. For example, the sun is conceptualized as wife of the moon (or, alternatively, the moon is wife of the sun), with the stars being their children. The powerful spirit Biliku, who is responsible for both violent storms and fine weather, is conceptualized as the wife of Taria, who is responsible for the rainy season (Radcliffe-Brown 1964:141, 150). Natural phenomena are generally personified (277–87), and moreover these personifications are often wedded to each other so that matrimony is central to the cosmological as well as social order.

16. Man (1885:57) reports that it was "rare" to find a child over seven years of age living with its parents, as most children were adopted. Adoption of the children of living parents as a general social practice is much more prevalent among unsegmented societies than among stateless societies in general. Adoption was widely practiced by the Copper Eskimo (Damas 1984:401), Slave (Asch 1981:344), and Mbuti (Turnbull 1965:116), as well as the Andamanese. The utilization of adoption should thus be added to the list of features characteristic of unsegmented foraging societies summarized at the end of chapter 2. It is of considerable significance demographically because outplacement is a functional alternative to infanticide for spacing children (among hunter-gatherers) that augments population growth.

Chapter 4

1. For discussion of collective conspecific lethal violence among chimpanzees, and its possible implications for human conflict, see Manson and Wrangham 1991, Knauft 1991, Goodale 1986, Power 1995, and Wrangham and Peterson 1996. See also note 22 below.

2. Otterbein (1968:280) classifies only three of fifty societies as manifesting "continual" internal and external war (both attacking and attacked). Five of the twenty-five foraging societies in Ross's sample experience yearly internal and external war (code 2 in table 4), although in many cases the instances of armed conflict are of very brief duration.

3. Three of the thirty-two unsegmented societies in Murdock's (1981) *Atlas of World Cultures* are coded as manifesting stratification based on wealth distinctions (column 67, code W), while one manifests a hereditary noble-commoner distinction (code D). The remainder lack class distinctions (code O). All of the eight unsegmented foraging societies in Ross's sample which are considered in this study are coded O. See also note 5 below.

For an extended treatment of the general issue of social inequality in simple societies see Kelly (1993). In the present context *egalitarian* conveys an absence of stratification based on wealth or hereditary distinction. However, unsegmented societies also manifest a comparatively minimal degree of gender inequality. The Andaman Islanders, in particular, have been considered by a number of authors to be the most gender egalitarian society known (Lowie 1924; Ortner 1990), and aspects of gender egalitarianism have been noted by the ethnographers of a number of other unsegmented societies as well.

4. Recent research indicates that human populations reached Australia about 50,000 years ago.

5. The Lapps are also one of the three unsegmented societies characterized by stratification based on wealth distinctions. This shows that social differentiation may develop in unsegmented societies and that the evolution of segmental organization is not a necessary prerequisite. Although unsegmented societies are characteristically egalitarian and unstratified, they are not invariably so. The Lapps are not a foraging society due to their substantial reliance on reindeer herding. However, the Nunamuit Eskimo are an example of a wealth-stratified unsegmented foraging society.

6. Bands are defined as politically autonomous local groups. Unsegmented societies are a form of band society in that they possess no political organization beyond the level of the local group, but unsegmented societies are defined in terms of a number of additional characteristics delineated in chapter 2 (see note 5, chap. 2). Tribes are segmental societies in which local groups are politically linked by one or more of a variety of organizational features (excluding political centralization).

7. In an instructive recent paper, Otterbein (n.d.) takes up the issue of the origin of war and reviews the archaeological record and primatological data.

8. The disagreement between sources presents a coding problem. Ericksen and Horton (1992:85) cite Gusinde (1931:885, 901, 904) as the basis for their coding and elect "malefactor only" (code 3) for the category "target of vengeance."

9. Damas (1984:392) characterizes Copper Eskimo and Netsilik subsistence as "marginal" compared to other Eskimo populations, with a seasonal period of "short rations" in the fall. Rainfall variability produces marked year-to-year fluctuations in the subsistence resources available to !Kung local groups (Lee 1979:352).

Balikci (1970:183–84) provides a very interesting account of a Netsilik revenge expedition that took place before 1830, in which a number of individuals other than the perpetrator of a prior homicide were killed. One could, on this basis, consider that war exists among the Netsilik, but the frequency would nevertheless be appropriately coded as "rare" (i.e., within the category "rare to nonexistent"). It is noteworthy that the dying headman of the group subject to retaliation (for the headman's son's act of homicide) said, "When we kill one man we don't kill any more, you people don't want to listen to us" (183). This suggests that normative retaliation for homicide was directed to the malefactor if possible, and that this was a very unusual incident.

10. Gillespie (1981a:161–68) provides a comprehensive review of the literature concerning territorial shifts resulting from Cree raids. Although the occurrence of these raids is well-documented, she questions the extent to which Cree raiding engendered displacement of other groups and argues for less extensive changes in exploitive range than earlier authors believed to be the case. However, she nevertheless concedes that the Cree displaced the inhabitants of the area along the Slave River which became a "war road" (167).

11. It is evident that the consequences of colonial intrusion may be either an increase or a decrease in the frequency of warfare, as exemplified by the Slave and the Ingalik cases respectively. Ferguson (1992) has drawn attention to the former outcome. Homicide rates may also change over time as a result of the imposition of jural institutions by colonial authorities. Homicide declined markedly among the Central Eskimo after 1920 (Balikci 1970:185), among the Andamanese after the late 1800s (Radcliffe-Brown 1964:49), and among the !Kung from 1955 through 1970 (Knauft 1987:458). See Kent (1989, 1990) and Knauft (1990) for an extended discussion of changes in the incidence of interpersonal violence and homicide among the !Kung over time.

12. Although the Andamanese have the highest population density of all eight unsegmented societies considered in this work, and the development of war is clearly related to this, it is noteworthy that the specific locale within the Andamanese regional system where warfare is most intense has the lowest population density on Great Andaman Island.

13. The larger population of San of which the !Kung are a part was also pressed by their segmental neighbors in earlier times and during the colonial era. These conflicts are reviewed by Keeley (1996:133–35).

14. Keeley (1996:102) discusses this practice under the heading of "mutilations." He is correct in recognizing it is communicative. The description of a victim "looking like a human pincushion" or porcupine recurs in the literature, and I have coined the term *pincushioning* as a shorthand for it.

15. Knauft (1985:118) reports that several Gebusi children were killed in conjunction with the sorcery execution of a parent. However, this occurs in less than 3

percent (3/107) of all internal sorcery executions (and the data are for a segmental society). There is thus a statistically slight chance that a multiple burial of an adult and a child could be due to capital punishment (sorcery execution) rather than war or feud. However, a single burial of a child showing evidence of violent death would be indicative of group liability to vengeance and thus of feud or war.

16. Figures 3 and 4 are copied from line drawings that reproduce the main features of the wall paintings. These are provided in Giedion (1962:463–64). He offers a quite different interpretation in which shamanic mystical experience rather than reality is being portrayed.

17. See Tacon and Chippendale (1994) for elucidation of a similar developmental sequence in Australia.

18. This burial, dated to 20,000 B.P., evidences three projectile point wounds. Wendorf and Schild (1986:62) posit that "the most logical explanation [of the cause of death] is that enemies speared this man [twice] from behind." He also had a partially healed wound (from a stone chip) in his left elbow, indicating that he had been involved in armed conflict a few days or weeks before his death. This suggests that his death may have been a vengeance killing, since he most probably prevailed in the earlier fight (or he would not in all likelihood have survived). In other words, he may well have been the perpetrator of an earlier homicide who was slain in retribution.

19. It should be noted that what has been included under the category of a "homicide rate" should ideally be partitioned so as to make the components identifiable. For example, the Gebusi have a very low incidence of simple homicide but an exceptionally high rate of capital punishment (sorcerer execution). The Yahgan have a high rate of spontaneous lethal violence over resources, etc.

20. One could argue that an incidence of violent deaths exceeding 9 percent of burials is indicative of war. The justification for this would be that the Yahgan, to whom this rate applies, are at the penultimate stage prior to the development of war (in that partial group liability to vengeance is in place). Moreover, there are no known cases I am aware of in which violent deaths exceed this rate in the absence of war (as defined in this study). The total frequency of violent deaths in a burial population thus provides another archaeological index of war.

21. It is important to note that an earlier origination of war—during the latter half of the Upper Paleolithic rather than the Neolithic, for example—would not alter my central conclusion that war has a definite origin late in the 2.9 million years that encompass the Paleolithic to present and that this event constitutes a major watershed in human history and prehistory because it triggers the transformative forces of a coevolution of war and society. The Upper Paleolithic spans 25,000 years and was a period of significant change in "technology, subsistence patterns, population density and distribution, trade, mortuary practices, and art" (Dickson 1990:85). Some of the preliminary elements of segmental organization may have also developed in certain regions during the latter part of the Upper Paleolithic. I do not seek to gloss over any of these important areas of documented or hypothesized change. I also do not seek to rule out an earlier origination of war, but rather to render this an empirical question to be addressed through a site-by-site analysis of the archaeological data for each region, a task best left to areal spe-

cialists. I would argue that a transition from capital punishment to revenge-based raiding (with social substitution) entailing a marked increase in the distribution and frequency of war should be reflected in the material conditions of existence and thus in the archaeological record. In other words, the significant question concerns the development of an intensity of warfare that alters social life, and this is readily answerable.

22. There are interesting questions of the similarities and differences between human and chimpanzee patterns of intercommunity violence. These would most usefully be taken up in a separate publication. However, several points may be noted here. An earlier comparative study, conducted by Manson and Wrangham (1991:369–90), examines forty-two foraging societies. However, four of the total of six unsegmented foraging societies that are included in their sample are not coded for the variables under consideration due to source problems or coder disagreement (and in all eleven of forty-two societies were uncoded) (Manson and Wrangham 1991:375). This means that the similarities and differences adduced are based almost entirely on segmental foraging societies. A comparison with unsegmented societies would lead to rather different conclusions (cf. Knauft 1991). For example, intergroup aggression among chimpanzees differs from that typically found in unsegmented societies in being deliberate (rather than spontaneous), productive of decisive outcomes of group annihilation (vs. stalemate), and characterized by high mortality rates (vs. low rates).

23. Unsegmented foraging societies in open environments manifest homicide rates on the order of about 40 per 100,000 per year (as exemplified by the !Kung, Mbuti, and Semang cases). Although this is comparatively high in cross-cultural terms, this rate would result in only 1 homicide every 100 years within a local group of 25 persons. Most social actors would thus experience homicide as an event that occurred once a generation among neighboring local groups.

Bibliography

Anzar, José Camón
1954   *Las Artes y Los Pueblos de la Espana Primitiva.* Madrid: Espasa-Calpe.
Asch, Michael I.
1981   Slavey. In *Handbook of North American Indians,* vol. 6, *Subarctic,* ed. June Helm, 338–49. Washington, DC: Smithsonian Institution.
Balikci, Asen
1970   *The Netsilik Eskimo.* Garden City, NY: Natural History Press.
Benedict, R.
1935   *Patterns of Culture.* London: Routledge and Kegan Paul.
Bodley, John H.
1985   *Anthropology and Contemporary Human Problems.* Palo Alto, CA: Mayfield Publishing Company.
Boehm, Christopher
1984   *Blood Revenge: The Enactment and Management of Conflict in Montenegro and Other Societies.* Philadelphia: University of Pennsylvania Press.
Bose, S.
1964   Economy of the Onge of Little Andaman. *Man in India* 44:289–310.
Bové, G.
1884   Fuegia and the Fuegians. *South American Missionary Magazine* 18:187–91.
Bridges, Thomas
1884   Moeurs et coutumes des Fuégiens. [Translated by Hyades from a MS. Prepared 1866.] In *Bull. Soc. d' Anthr. de Paris,* ser. 3, vol. 7, Paris.
1886   El confin sur de la República: La Tierra del Fuego y sus habitantes. In *Boletin del Instituto Geográfico Argentino,* tomo 7, cuaderno 9, Buenos Aires.
1893   La Tierra del Fuego y sus habitantes. In *Boletin del Instituto Geográfico Argentino,* tomo 14, cuadernos 5–8, Buenos Aires.
Briggs, Jean L.
1970   *Never in Anger: Portrait of an Eskimo Family.* Cambridge: Harvard University Press.
1978   The Origins of Nonviolence: Inuit Management of Aggression (Canadian Arctic). In *Learning Non-Aggression: The Experience of Non-Literate Societies,* ed. Ashley Montagu, 54–93. New York: Oxford University Press.
1982   Living Dangerously: The Contradictory Foundations of Value in Canadian Inuit Society. In *Politics and History in Band Societies,* ed.

Eleanor Leacock and Richard B. Lee, 103–31. Cambridge: Cambridge University Press.

Burbank, V. K.

1990 Sex, Gender and Difference: Dimensions of Aggression in an Australian Aboriginal Community. *Human Nature* 31:251–78.

1994 *Fighting Women: Anger and Aggression in Aboriginal Australia.* Berkeley: University of California Press.

Burch, Ernest S., Jr.

1984 Kotzebue Sound Eskimo. In *Handbook of North American Indians,* vol. 5, *Arctic,* ed. David Damas, 303–19. Washington, DC: Smithsonian Institution.

Cantrell, Eileen M.

n.d. Gebusi Gender Relations. Ph.D. dissertation draft, Department of Anthropology, University of Michigan.

Carneiro, Robert L.

1988 The Circumscription Theory: Challenge and Response. *American Behavioral Scientist* 31 (4): 497–511.

1994 War and Peace: Alternating Realities in Human History. In *Studying War: Anthropological Perspectives,* ed. S. P. Reyna and R. E. Downs, 3–27. Amsterdam: Gordon and Breach.

Census of India, (3)

1901 *The Andaman and Nicobar Islands.* Calcutta: Office of the Superintendent of Government Printing.

Chakraborty, Dilip Kumar

1990 *The Great Andamanese Struggling for Survival.* Calcutta: Seagull Books.

Childe, V. Gordon

1941 War in Prehistoric Societies. *Sociological Review* 32:127–38.

Cipriani, Lidio

1966 *The Andaman Islanders,* ed. and trans. D. Tylor Cox. New York: Praeger.

Collier, Jane Fishburne

1988 *Marriage and Inequality in Classless Societies.* Stanford: Stanford University Press.

Collier, Jane F., and Michelle Z. Rosaldo

1981 Politics and Gender in Simple Societies. In *Sexual Meanings: The Cultural Construction of Gender and Sexuality,* ed. Sherry B. Ortner and Harriet Whitehead, 275–329. New York: Cambridge University Press.

Cooper, Z.

1985 Archaeological Explorations in the Andaman Islands. *Bulletin of the Indo-Pacific Prehistory Association* 6:27–39.

1987 "A Report on Archeological Investigations in the Andaman Islands (1985–1986)," manuscript, submitted to the Homi Bhabba Fellowships Council, Bombay.

1988 Shell Artifacts from the Andaman Islands. *Australian Archaeology* 26:24–41.

1989   Analysis of the Nature of Contacts with the Andaman Islands during the Last Two Millennia. *South Asian Studies* 5:133–47.

1990a   Archaeological Evidence for Resource Exploitation in the Andaman Islands. *Man and Environment* 15 (1): 73–81.

1990b   The Problem of the Origins of the Andamanese. *Bulletin of the Deccan College Post-graduate and Research Institute* 49:99–104.

1990c   The End of 'Bibipoiye' (Dog Not) Days in the Andamans. In *Hunter-Gatherer Demography Past and Present,* ed. B. Meehan and N. White, 117–25. Sydney: Oceania Monographs 39.

1992   The Relevance of the Forager/Collector Model to Island Communities in the Bay of Bengal. *Man and Environment* 17 (2): 111–22.

1993a   The Origins of the Andaman Islanders: Local Myth and Archaeological Evidence. *Antiquity* 67:394–99.

1993b   Abandoned Onge Encampments and Their Relevance in Understanding the Archaeological Record in the Andaman Islands. In *Living Traditions: Studies in the Ethnoarchaeology of South Asia,* ed. B. Allchin, 235–63. New Delhi: Oxford and IBH Publishing Co.

n.d.   "Salient Features of Site Location in the Andaman Islands." Manuscript.

Damas, David
1984   Central Eskimo: Introduction. In *Handbook of North American Indians,* vol. 5, *Arctic,* ed. David Damas, 391–96. Washington, DC: Smithsonian Institution.

Davie, M. R.
1929   *The Evolution of War: A Study of Its Role in Early Societies.* Reprint, Port Washington, NY: Kennikat Press, 1968.

De Laguna, Frederica, and Catharine McClellan
1981   Ahtna. In *Handbook of North American Indians,* vol. 6, *Subarctic,* ed. June Helm, 641–63. Washington, DC: Smithsonian Institution.

Dentan, Robert K.
1968   *The Semai: A Nonviolent People of Malaya.* New York: Holt, Rinehart and Winston.

1978   Notes on Childhood in a Nonviolent Context: The Semai Case (Malaysia). In *Learning Non-Aggression: The Experience of Non-Literate Societies,* ed. Ashley Montagu, 94–143. New York: Oxford University Press.

1979   Fieldwork edition. *The Semai: A Nonviolent People of Malaya.* New York: Holt, Rinehart and Winston.

Dickson, D. Bruce
1990   *The Dawn of Belief.* Tucson: University of Arizona Press.

Dutta, P. C.
1978   *The Great Andamanese: Past and Present.* Calcutta: Anthropological Survey of India.

Elkin, A. P.
1938   *The Australian Aborigines.* Sydney: Angus and Robertson.

Ember, Carol R.
    1978   Myths about Hunter-Gatherers. *Ethnology* 17:439–48.
Ember, C., and M. Ember
    1992   Resource Unpredictability, Mistrust and War: A Cross-Cultural
           Study. *Journal of Conflict Resolution* 36:242–62.
Ericksen, Karen Paige, and Heather Horton
    1992   "Blood Feuds": Cross-Cultural Variations in Kin Group Vengeance.
           Behavior Science Research 26:57–86.
Erickson, P., and S. Beckerman
    1975   Population Determinants in the Andaman Islands. *Mankind* 10 (2):
           105–7.
Fabbro, David
    1978   Peaceful Societies: An Introduction. *Journal of Peace Research* 15 (1):
           67–83.
Ferguson, R. Brian
    1984   Introduction: Studying War. In *Warfare, Culture, and Environment,*
           ed. R. B. Ferguson, 1–79. New York: Academic Press.
    1992   A Savage Encounter: Western Contact and the Yanomami War Com-
           plex. In *War in the Tribal Zone: Expanding States and Indigenous War-
           fare,* ed. R. B. Ferguson and N. L. Whitehead, 199–227. Santa Fe:
           School of America Research Press.
    1997   Violence and War in Prehistory. In *Troubled Times: Violence and War
           in the Past,* ed. Debra Martin and David Frayer, 321–56. Amsterdam:
           Gordon and Breach.
Fortes, Meyer
    1969   *Kinship and the Social Order.* Chicago: Aldine.
Frayer, David W.
    1997   Ofnet: Evidence for a Mesolithic Massacre. In *Troubled Times: Vio-
           lence and Warfare in the Past,* ed. Debra Martin and David Frayer,
           181–216. Amsterdam: Gordon and Breach.
Fried, Morton H.
    1967   *The Evolution of Political Society.* New York: Random House.
Fromm, E.
    1973   *The Anatomy of Human Destructiveness.* New York: Holt, Rinehart
           and Winston.
Gabriel, Richard A.
    1990   The Archaeology of War. In *The Culture of War: Invention and Early
           Development,* 19–34. Westport, CT: Greenwood Press.
Gamble, Clive
    1982   Interaction and Alliance in Paleolithic Society. *Man* 17:92–107.
Giedion, S.
    1962   *The Eternal Present: The Beginnings of Art.* Bollingen Series
           XXXV.6.1. New York: Pantheon Books.
Gillespie, Beryl C.
    1981a Territorial Groups before 1821: Athapaskans of the Shield and

MacKenzie Delta. In *Handbook of North American Indians,* vol. 6, *Subarctic,* ed. June Helm, 161–68. Washington, DC: Smithsonian Institution.

1981b Mountain Indians. In *Handbook of North American Indians,* vol. 6, *Subarctic,* ed. June Helm, 326–37. Washington, DC: Smithsonian Institution.

Goodale, Jane

1986 *The Chimpanzees of Gombe: Patterns of Behavior.* Cambridge: Harvard University Press.

Gough, Kathleen

1976 The Origin of the Family. In *The Evolution of Human Adaptations,* ed. John Poggie, Gretel Pelto, and Pertti Pelto, 205–24. New York: Macmillan.

Greenberg, J.

1971 The Indo-Pacific Hypothesis. *Current Trends in Linguistics* 7 (1): 807–71.

Gusinde, M.

1931 Die Fuerland-Indianer, vol. 2, Die Yamama, Mödling (English translation of vol. 2, pp. 365–1185, 1278–1500 only, for the HRAF by Frieda Schutze).

Harrold, Francis B.

1980 A Comparative Analysis of Eurasian Paleolithic Burials. *World Archaeology* 12 (2): 195–211.

Hobbes, Thomas

1958 [1651] *Leviathan Parts I and II.* New York: Liberal Arts Press.

Holmberg, A. R.

1969 *Nomads of the Longbow: The Siriono of Eastern Bolivia.* Garden City, NY: Natural History Press.

Honigmann, John J.

1946 Ethnography and Acculturation of the Fort Nelson Slave. *Yale University Publications in Anthropology* 33. New Haven: Yale University Press.

Howell, N.

1979 *Demography of the Dobe Area !Kung.* New York: Academic Press.

Kang, Gay E.

1979 Exogamy and Peace Relations of Social Units: A Cross-Cultural Test. *Ethnology* 18:85–99.

Keeley, Lawrence H.

1996 *War Before Civilization.* New York: Oxford University Press.

Kelly, Raymond C.

1977 *Etoro Social Structure: A Study in Structural Contradiction.* Ann Arbor: University of Michigan Press.

1985 *The Nuer Conquest: The Structure and Development of an Expansionist System.* Ann Arbor: University of Michigan Press.

1993 *Constructing Inequality: The Fabrication of a Hierarchy of Virtue among the Etoro.* Ann Arbor: University of Michigan Press.

Kent, Susan
  1989   And Justice for All: The Development of Political Centralization among Newly Sedentary Foragers. *American Anthropologist* 91:703–12.
  1990   Kalahari Violence in Perspective. *American Anthropologist* 92:1015–17.
Knauft, Bruce M.
  1985   *Good Company and Violence: Sorcery and Social Action in a Lowland New Guinea Society.* Berkeley: University of California Press.
  1987   Reconsidering Violence in Simple Human Societies: Homicide among the Gebusi of New Guinea. *Current Anthropology* 28:457–500.
  1988   On Reconsidering Violence in Human Evolution. *Current Anthropology* 29:620–33.
  1989   Sociality versus Self-Interest in Human Evolution. *Behavioral and Brain Sciences* 12:712–13.
  1990   Violence among Newly Sedentary Foragers. *American Anthropologist* 92:1013–15.
  1991   Violence and Sociality in Human Evolution. *Current Anthropology* 32:391–428.
  1994   Culture and Cooperation in Human Evolution. In *The Anthropology of Peace and Nonviolence,* ed. Leslie Sponsel and Thomas Gregor, 37–68. Boulder, CO: Lynne Rienner.
Koch, Klaus-Friedrich
  1974   *War and Peace in Jalemo: The Management of Conflict in Highland New Guinea.* Cambridge: Harvard University Press.
Lal, Parmanand
  1976   *Andaman Islands: A Regional Geography.* Anthropological Survey of India, Memoir 25. Calcutta: Government of India Printers.
Lambert, Patricia
  1997   Patterns of Violence in Prehistoric Hunter-Gatherer Societies of Coastal Southern California. In *Troubled Times: Violence and Warfare in the Past,* ed. Debra Martin and David Frayer, 77–110. Amsterdam: Gordon and Breach.
Lapicque, L.
  1894   Photographies Relatives aux habitants des Iles Mergui (les Selon). Quelques Observations Anthropologiques et Ethnographiques sur cette Population. *Bulletins de la Société d'Anthropologie de Paris,* Feb. 15 and March 1, 1894, 219–31.
Lee, Richard B.
  1968   What Hunters Do for a Living, or, How to Make Out on Scarce Resources. In *Man the Hunter,* ed. R. B. Lee and I. DeVore, 30–43. Chicago: Aldine.
  1979   *The !Kung San: Men, Women and Work in a Foraging Society.* New York: Cambridge University Press.
Lee, Richard, and Irven DeVore, eds.
  1968   *Man the Hunter.* Chicago: Aldine.

Leroi-Gourhan, André
1968   *The Art of Prehistoric Man in Western Europe.* London: Thames and Hudson.

Lévi-Strauss, Claude
1971   The Family. In *Man, Culture and Society,* ed. Harry Shapiro, 333–57. Oxford: Oxford University Press.

Levinson, D.
1989   *Family Violence in Cross Cultural Perspective.* Newbury Park: Sage Publications.

Lothrop, Samuel K.
1928   *The Indians of Tierra Del Fuego.* Contributions from the Museum of the American Indian, Heye Foundation, vol. 10, New York.

Loudon, J. B.
1970   Teasing and Socialisation on Tristan da Cunha. In *Socialisation: The Approach from Anthropology,* ed. P. Mayer, 293–331. London: Tavistock.

Lowie, Robert H.
1924   *Primitive Religion.* New York: Boni and Liveright.

Malhotra, R.
1989   *The Indian Islanders.* New Delhi: Mittal Publications.

Malinowski, Bronislaw
1941   An Anthropological Analysis of War. *American Journal of Sociology* 46:521–50.

Man, E. H.
1885   *On the Aboriginal Inhabitants of the Andaman Islands.* London: Royal Anthropological Institute of Great Britain and Ireland (1932 reprint).

Manoharan, S.
1983   Subgrouping Andamanese Group of Languages. *International Journal of Dravidian Linguistics* 12 (1): 82–95.

Manson, Joseph, and Richard Wrangham
1991   Intergroup Aggression in Chimpanzees and Humans. *Current Anthropology* 32:369–90.

Marshall, L.
1965   The Kung Bushmen of the Kalahari Desert. In *Peoples of Africa,* ed. J. L. Gibbs, 241–78. New York: Holt, Rinehart and Winston.

Mason, J. Alden
1946   *Notes on the Indians of the Great Slave Lake Area.* Yale University Publications in Anthropology, no. 34. New Haven: Yale University Press.

Mead, M.
1961   *Cooperation and Conflict among Primitive Peoples.* Boston: Beacon Press.

Meggitt, Mervyn J.
1965   *The Lineage System of the Mae-Enga of New Guinea.* New York: Barnes and Noble.

1977   *Blood Is Their Argument: Warfare among the Mae Enga Tribesmen of the New Guinea Highlands.* Palo Alto, CA: Mayfield.

Murdock, George P.
    1949   *Social Structure.* New York: Free Press.
    1981   *Atlas of World Cultures.* Pittsburgh: University of Pittsburgh Press.
Murdock, George P., and D. R. White
    1969   Standard Cross-Cultural Sample. *Ethnology* 8:329–69.
Murdock, George P., and S. Wilson
    1972   Settlement Patterns and Community Organization: Cross-Cultural Codes. *Ethnology* 11:254–95.
Naroll, Raoul
    1966   Does Military Deterrence Deter? *Trans-Action* 3 (2): 14–20.
    n.d.   "Warfare, Peaceful Intercourse and Territorial Changes: A Cross-Cultural Survey." Manuscript.
Newcomb, W. W., Jr.
    1960   Toward an Understanding of War. In *Essays in the Science of Culture in Honor of Leslie A. White,* ed. Gertrude E. Dole and Robert L. Carneiro, 317–56. New York: Thomas Y. Crowell.
Ortner, Sherry B.
    1990   Gender Hegemonies. In *Discursive Strategies and the Economy of Prestige,* ed. Bruce Lincoln and Richard Leppert, 35–80. *Cultural Critique* 1989–90 (winter).
Osgood, Cornelius
    1958   *Ingalik Social Culture.* New Haven: Yale University Press.
Oswalt, Wendell
    1962   Historical Populations in Western Alaska and Migration Theory. *Anthropological Papers of the University of Alaska* 11 (1): 1–14.
Otterbein, Keith F.
    1968   Internal War: A Cross-Cultural Study. *American Anthropologist* 70:277–89.
    1970   *The Evolution of War: A Cross-Cultural Study.* New Haven: HRAF Press.
    1973   The Anthropology of War. In *Handbook of Social and Cultural Anthropology,* ed. John J. Honigmann, 923–58. Chicago: Rand McNally.
    1986   *The Ultimate Coercive Sanction.* New Haven: HRAF Press.
    1987   Comment on: Reconsidering Violence in Simple Human Societies, by B. Knauft. *Current Anthropology* 28:484–85.
    1991   Comment on: The Human Community as a Primate Society, by L. Rodseth et al. *Current Anthropology* 32 (3): 245–47.
    1993   *Feuding and Warfare: Selected Works of Keith Otterbein.* New York: Gordon and Breach.
    n.d.   "The Origins of War." Manuscript.
Otterbein, Keith, and Charlotte S. Otterbein
    1965   An Eye for an Eye, a Tooth for a Tooth: A Cross Cultural Study of Feuding. *American Anthropologist* 67:1470–82.
Pandit, T. N.
    1990   *The Sentinelese.* Calcutta: Seagull Books.

Pandya, Vishvajit

1993   *Above the Forest: A Study of Andamanese Ethnoanemology, Cosmology and the Power of Ritual.* Delhi: Oxford University Press.

Portman, M. V.

1899   *The History of our Relations with the Andamanese.* 2 vols. Calcutta: Government Printing Office.

Power, Margaret G.

1995   Gombe Revisited: Are Chimpanzees Violent and Hierarchical in the "Free" State? *General Anthropology: Bulletin of the Council for General Anthropology* 2 (1): 5–9.

Radcliffe-Brown, A. R.

1964   [1922] *The Andaman Islanders.* New York: Free Press of Glencoe.

1933   Primitive Law. In *Encyclopedia of the Social Sciences* 9:202–6. New York: Macmillan.

Rasmussen, K.

1931   *The Netsilik Eskimos.* Report of the Fifth Thule Expedition to Arctic North America, vol. 8. Copenhagen: Gyldendalske Boghandel, Nordisk Forlag.

1932   *Intellectual Culture of the Copper Eskimo.* Report of the Fifth Thule Expedition to Arctic North America, vol. 9. Copenhagen: Gyldendalske Boghandel, Nordisk Forlag.

Redmond, Elsa M.

1994   *Tribal and Chiefly Warfare in South America.* Memoirs of the Museum of Anthropology, University of Michigan, no. 28. Ann Arbor: University of Michigan Museum of Anthropology.

Rogers, Edward, and James G. E. Smith

1981   Environment and Culture in the Shield and Mackenzie Borderlands. In *Handbook of North American Indians,* vol, 6, *Subarctic,* ed. June Helm, 130–45. Washington, DC: Smithsonian Institution.

Roper, Marilyn Keyes

1969   A Survey of the Evidence for Intrahuman Killing in the Pleistocene. *Current Anthropology* 10 (4): 427–58.

1975   Evidence of Warfare in the Near East from 10,000–4,300 B.C. In *War: Its Causes and Correlates,* ed. Martin A. Nettleship et al., 299–343. The Hague: Mouton.

Ross, Marc Howard

1983   Political Decision Making and Conflict: Additional Cross-Cultural Codes and Scales. *Ethnology* 22:169–92.

Sandars, N. K.

1985   *Prehistoric Art in Europe,* 2d ed. Harmondsworth: Penguin.

Sarkar, Jayanta

1990   *The Jarawa.* Calcutta: Seagull Books.

Service, E. R.

1966   *The Hunters.* Englewood Cliffs, NJ: Prentice-Hall.

Singh, N. I.

1978   *The Andaman Story.* New Delhi: Vikas Publishing House Pvt. Ltd.

Sipes, R. G.
    1973   War, Sports and Aggression: An Empirical Test of Two Rival Theo-
           ries. *American Anthropologist* 75 (1): 64–82.
Snow, Jeanne H.
    1981   Ingalik. In *Handbook of North American Indians,* vol. 6, *Subarctic,* ed.
           June Helm, 602–17. Washington, DC: Smithsonian Institution.
Sorokin, P.
    1962   *Social and Cultural Dynamics.* 4 vols. New York: Bedminister Press.
Sponsel, Leslie E.
    1994   The Mutual Relevance of Anthropology and Peace Studies. In *The
           Anthropology of Peace and Nonviolence,* ed. Leslie Sponsel and
           Thomas Gregor, 1–36. Boulder, CO: Lynne Rienner.
Steenhoven, Geert Van Den
    1959   *Legal Concepts among the Netsilik Eskimos of Pelly Bay, N.W.T.*
           Ottawa: Northern Co-ordination and Research Centre, Department
           of Northern Affairs and National Resources, NCRC-59-3.
Steward, J. H.
    1968   Causal Factors and Processes in the Evolution of Pre-Farming Soci-
           eties. In *Man, the Hunter,* ed. R. B. Lee and I. DeVore, 321–34.
           Chicago: Aldine.
Steward, J. H., and Louis C. Faron
    1959   *Native Peoples of South America.* New York: McGraw-Hill.
Tacon, Paul S., and Christopher Chippendale
    1994   Australia's Ancient Warriors: Changing Depictions of Fighting in the
           Rock Art of Arnhem Land, N.T. *Cambridge Archaeological Journal*
           4:211–48.
Testart, Alain
    1982   The Significance of Food Storage among Hunter-Gatherers: Resi-
           dence Patterns, Population Densities, and Social Inequalities. *Current
           Anthropology* 23:523–37.
Thomas, Elizabeth Marshall
    1959   *The Harmless People.* New York: Knopf.
Turnbull, Colin M.
    1961   *The Forest People.* Garden City, NY: Natural History Press.
    1965   *Wayward Servants: The Two Worlds of the African Pygmies.* Garden
           City, NY: Natural History Press.
    1978   Death by Decree: An Anthropological Approach to Capital Punish-
           ment. *Natural History* 87 (5): 50–67.
Tylor, E. B.
    1889   On a Method of Investigating the Development of Institutions;
           Applied to Laws of Marriage and Descent. *Journal of the Anthropolog-
           ical Institute* 18:245–69.
Vencl, Sl.
    1984   War and Warfare in Archaeology. *Journal of Anthropological Archae-
           ology* 3:116–32.
Voltaire, François M.
    1959   The Huron, or Pupil of Nature. In *Voltaire,* ed. Edmund Fuller,
           173–234. New York: Dell.

Wendorf, F.
    1968   Site 117: A Nubian Final Paleolithic Graveyard near Jebel Sahaba, Sudan. In *Prehistory of Nubia,* vol. 2, ed. F. Wendorf, 954–95. Dallas: Southern Methodist University Press.

Wendorf, F., and R. Schild
    1986   The Wadi Kubbaniya Skeleton: A Late Paleolithic Burial from Southern Egypt. In *The Prehistory of Wadi Kubbaniya,* ed. Angela Close. Dallas: Southern Methodist University Press.

Whallon, R.
    1989   Elements of Cultural Change in the Later Paleolithic. In *The Human Revolution: Behavioral and Biological Perspectives on the Origins of Modern Humans,* vol. 1., ed. Paul Mellars and C. B. Stringer. Edinburgh: Edinburgh University Press.

Wiberg, Hakan
    1981   JPR 1964–1980—What Have We Learned about Peace? *Journal of Peace Research* 18 (2): 111–48.

Wiessner, Polly
    1982   Risk, Reciprocity, and Social Influences on !Kung San Economics. In *Politics and History in Band Societies,* ed. Eleanor Leacock and Richard B. Lee, 61–84. Cambridge: Cambridge University Press.

Wiessner, Polly, and Tumu Akii
    1998   *Historical Vines: Enga Networks of Exchange, Ritual and Warfare in Papau New Guinea.* Washington, DC: Smithsonian Institution Press.

Wolf, Eric R.
    1987   Cycles of Violence: The Anthropology of War and Peace. In *Waymarks,* ed. Kenneth Moore. Notre Dame: University of Notre Dame Press.

Woodburn, James C.
    1979   Minimal Politics: The Political Organization of the Hadza of North Tanzania. In *Politics in Leadership: A Comparative Perspective,* ed. William A. Shack and Percy S. Cohen, 244–66. Oxford: Clarendon Press.

    1980   Hunters and Gatherers Today and Reconstruction of the Past. In *Soviet and Western Anthropology,* ed. Ernest Gellner, 95–117. New York: Columbia University Press.

    1982   Egalitarian Societies. *Man* (n.s.) 17:431–51.

    1984   Stability and Flexibility in Hazda Residential Groupings. In *Man, the Hunter,* 2d ed., ed. Richard B. Lee and Irven DeVore, 103–10. New York: Aldine.

    1988   African Hunter-Gatherer Social Organization: Is It Best Understood as a Product of Encapsulation? In *Hunters and Gatherers,* vol. 1. *History, Evolution and Social Change,* ed. Tim Ingold, David Riches, and James Woodburn, 31–64. Oxford: Berg.

World Archaeology
    1986   Weaponry and Warfare. In *World Archaeology* 18 (2).

Wrangham, Richard, and Dale Peterson
    1996   *Demonic Males: Apes and the Origins of Human Violence.* New York: Houghton Mifflin.

Wright, Quincy
    1942   *A Study of War.* Chicago: University of Chicago Press.
Zide, Norman, and Vishvajit Pandya
    1989   A Bibliographical Introduction to Andamanese Linguistics. *Journal of the American Oriental Society* 109 (4): 639–51.

Index

Adoption, 118, 160, 171
Aggression. *See* Violence
Agriculture. *See* Economic organization, and war
Andaman Islanders, 53, 67, 73,
 129–30, 146, 172
 armed conflict among, 52, 63, 66, 78,
 87–92, 95–107, 136–38, 141–47,
 168
 Bea tribe, 82, 87–92, 95–101, 134,
 138–39, 142–46
 and depopulation, 88–90
 economy of, 92–97
 Jarawa tribe, 78, 87–92, 95–101, 134,
 138–39, 142–46
 and linguistic relationships, between
 tribes, 77–78, 80–81, 169–70
 peacemaking ceremony of, 85–86,
 97, 105–8, 112, 116–19, 124–25,
 160
 population density of, 71–73, 89, 92,
 105, 173
 tribal territories of, 77, 79, 87–90,
 95–96, 169
 vengeance patterns among, 55, 61,
 96, 101–7
Andaman Islands
 colonial history of, 81–91, 170–71
 geography of, 77
 location of, 78
 prehistory of, 80–81
Archaeological evidence. *See* Prehistory, warfare in
Armed conflict, 3, 135. *See also* Capital punishment; Feuds; Homicide;
 Raiding; Violence; War
 spontaneous shoot-on-sight attacks,
 91–92, 95–101, 103–5, 107,

136–44, 146–47, 149, 151–53, 156,
 158–60

Balikci, A., 29–30, 33–34, 42, 152,
 173
Bands, 14, 16, 92, 95–96, 104, 106, 132,
 163, 172
Bodley, J., 131–32
Boehm, C., 163–64
Brideservice, 48, 166
Bridewealth. *See* Marriage
 payments
Briggs, J., 30
Burch, E., 125
Burials, 148–52, 156–58

Cantrell, E., 28
Capital punishment, 5–10, 41–43,
 55–56, 58–60, 75, 101–5, 123,
 128, 130, 136–40, 143, 147,
 151–52, 156, 158–60, 163–64,
 174. *See also* Vengeance
Carneiro, R., 65, 136
Casualty rates, 100–101, 106, 134, 138,
 145, 148, 158–59
Chakraborty, D., 88–89
Child socialization, 14–22, 29
 and war, 37, 165
Circumscribed environments, 76, 81,
 91, 96, 105, 129, 136, 141, 143–47,
 151, 158–60
Compensation, 56, 160
Competition. *See* Resource competition
Conflict, 4, 102–5, 129, 136–37, 141,
 143, 160. *See also* Armed conflict;
 Conflict resolution; Violence,
 interpersonal

Conflict resolution, 9, 14–15, 38, 42,
    65, 77, 119, 138, 144, 160–61. *See
    also* Peacemaking practices
Cooper, Z., 80–81, 92–93
Cross-cultural samples, 49–51
Cross-cultural studies, 43, 50, 53–56,
    131–33, 163, 167–68

Defense, 68, 131–33
Dentan, R., 13, 20–22, 34, 38, 49,
    141
Dickson, D., 127–30, 132, 174
Dutta, P., 80, 93–94, 129, 170

Ecological zones, and armed conflict,
    92–101, 145–46, 150–51
Economic organization, and war, 1–3,
    14–16, 68–71, 92–97, 135
Egalitarian societies, 14, 20, 36, 103,
    126, 172
Ember, C., 2, 43, 54, 123, 163
Enga, 134
Environment. *See* Circumscribed envi-
    ronments; Ecological zones, and
    armed conflict; Resource competi-
    tion
Eriksen, K., 54–56, 59, 62, 167–68
Eskimo
    Central, 20–22, 29–30, 33–34, 38,
    41–42, 152
    Copper, 13, 15, 17–18, 20, 28, 31, 37,
    49, 51–52, 55, 61, 63, 66, 70, 72,
    76, 141, 165, 168, 171, 173
    Netsilik, 29–30, 32–35, 41, 42, 165,
    173
Ethnographic analogy, 127–33,
    150–51
Evolution of war, 1–3, 11, 19, 43,
    56–64, 73, 75, 118, 125, 129–61.
    See also War and society, coevo-
    lution of
Exchange, 45, 64, 95, 104, 108, 135,
    138, 160. *See also* Marriage, as
    exchange between groups
Exogamy. *See* Intermarriage

Fabbro, D., 11–19, 31, 37–39, 41–43,
    49–50, 64, 67, 164

Family, 34–35, 44–45, 126, 128, 136,
    140, 160
Famine, 68, 134, 157
Female infanticide, 33
Ferguson, R., 157–58, 173
Feuds, 5–7, 43, 56, 59–60, 62, 96, 104,
    106–7, 129, 130, 132, 151–52, 156,
    159, 163. *See also* Vengeance; War
Food storage, 20, 68–71, 73
Foraging societies, 50–51, 55–56, 62,
    64, 70, 72. *See also* Hunter-
    gatherers
Fraternal interest groups, 48–49,
    168
Frayer, D., 157–58

Gamble, C., 125
Gebusi, 7–10, 20–22, 28, 30–31, 37, 56,
    58, 164–65, 171, 174
Gideon, S., 153–54
Gillespie, B., 157, 173
Gough, K., 126

Harrold, F., 156
Hobbes, T., 121, 124, 160, 164
Homicide, 4–5, 18, 21, 25, 29, 32–34,
    37, 41–43, 56–60, 102–5, 136, 148,
    151–52, 156– 60, 163
    rates, 21–22, 28, 31, 37–39, 165, 168,
    173–75
Howell, N., 35
Human nature, 121
Hunter-gatherers, 14, 16, 20, 39, 50,
    56, 65, 67, 69
    armed conflict among, 125, 130,
    132–51
    basic model of, 127–30, 132
    frequency of war among, 1–3, 43–44,
    50–52, 63–64, 76
Hutterites, 13, 15–19, 49

Ingalik, 32, 52, 55, 61, 63, 66, 70, 72,
    76–77, 142–43, 169, 173
Intermarriage, 60, 62, 63, 73, 138, 160,
    168

Jebel Sahaba (Nubian site 117),
    148–51, 155–56, 159

Keeley, L., 71, 125, 134, 142, 156–58, 163, 173
Kinship, 38, 126, 128, 160
  terminologies, 47
  and vengeance obligations, 54–62
Knauft, B., 7–10, 19–22, 28, 31–33, 37, 41, 126, 160, 164–65, 171–74
!Kung, 13, 15, 17–18, 20–25, 28, 30–35, 38, 41–42, 49, 51–52, 55, 58, 61, 63, 66–67, 70, 72, 141, 159, 165, 167–69, 173

Lal, P., 77, 80, 89–90
Lambert, P., 152
Land resources. *See* Resource competition; Territory
Lee, R., 24–25, 28, 32, 35, 58–59, 166–67

Malhotra, R., 88
Manson, J., 35, 122, 175
Marriage, 28, 33–35, 47, 62, 102. *See also* Intermarriage; Marriage payments
  as exchange between groups, 48, 60, 62
Marriage payments, 48, 60–62. *See also* Brideservice
Mbuti, 13, 15, 17–18, 20–22, 26–35, 38, 41–42, 49, 51–52, 55, 61, 63, 66–67, 70, 72, 136–37, 141–42, 165, 169, 171
Military organization, 4, 12, 92, 106–7, 136, 155
Monoharan, S., 169
Mortality. *See* Casualty rates; Female infanticide; Homicide

Origin of war. *See* Evolution of war
Otterbein, K., 6, 10, 20, 123, 130–32, 152, 163, 168, 172

Paleolithic (2,900,000 to 10,000 B.P.). *See* Prehistory
Pandya, V., 80, 169–70
Peace, 2, 12, 16, 18, 108, 116, 118–19, 124, 135, 146, 160–61

Peaceful societies, 11–39, 41–43, 49, 51, 67, 102, 160, 165
Peacemaking practices, 85–86, 97, 105–8, 112, 116–19, 124, 135, 138, 144, 146, 160–61. *See also* Conflict resolution
Plunder, 131–32
Population decline, 89–90, 142–43, 170
Population density, 20, 89. *See also* Resource competition
  and war, 71–73, 92, 105, 127, 133, 136, 141–48, 158, 173
Population growth, and war, 134, 151
Prehistory
  social organization forms in, 125–28, 133–34
  warfare in, 1–3, 125, 130, 133–36, 146–61, 163, 174–75
Prestige, and participation in war, 4, 131–33

Raiding, 4, 60, 68–69, 71, 97, 99–100, 105–7, 136, 138, 143, 147–52, 156, 158
Recruitment of participants in warfare, 4–5, 106
Resource competition, 11, 91–105, 129, 131–50, 158–60
Revenge. *See* Vengeance
Roper, M., 1, 158
Ross, M., 50–51, 53–54, 56, 123–24, 169

Sarkar, J., 88, 91
Sedentarism, and war, 1–3, 11, 63, 65–71, 73
Segmental organization, 45, 50–51, 56, 62, 64, 67, 71, 73, 75, 105–6, 128, 134–35, 141, 143, 146–48, 152
Semai, 13, 15, 18, 21–22, 24, 30–34, 37–38, 41–42, 49, 165
Semang, 49, 51–52, 55, 61, 63, 66–67, 70, 72, 141–42, 169
Settlement pattern, 63, 65–71, 73, 76, 92, 166
Singh, N., 113, 170
Siriono, 13, 15, 18–19, 22–24, 28–36, 38, 41–42, 49, 164–65, 167

Slave, 52–53, 55, 61, 63, 66, 70–72,
    76–77, 141, 167–69, 171, 173
Social organization, 44–48. *See also*
    Family; Marriage; Unsegmented
    societies
    and war, 1–2, 12, 43–44, 49–51, 54,
    62, 64, 71, 73, 75, 130–32, 141–42,
    159
Social substitution, 5–7, 41, 43–44,
    46–49, 75, 105, 139–40, 143, 147,
    150, 164
Sponsel, L., 11

Tacon, P., 174
Territory. *See also* Resource competi-
    tion; Trespass
    conflict over, 27, 95–96, 100–105,
    137, 144, 169
Testart, A., 68–70
Trade. *See* Exchange
Trespass, 95–96, 100–105, 137–43,
    153–54, 158
Tristan de Cunha, 13, 15–19, 49

Unsegmented societies, 44–73, 81, 103,
    105, 125–30, 133–47, 158–61, 166,
    170, 172
Upper Paleolithic (35,000 to 10,000
    B.P.). *See* Prehistory

Vengeance, 5–6, 41–43, 73, 75, 96,
    101–7, 130–31, 139, 148–52, 155,
    160, 163, 166–67, 172, 174. *See
    also* Feuds
    variations in, 54–62
Violence, 12, 19, 36, 172, 175. *See also*
    Homicide
    interpersonal, 14–38, 42–43, 102–3
    as a unitary phenomenon, 37
    and war, 21

War. *See also* Armed conflict; Casualty
    rates; Defense; Ecological zones,
    and armed conflict; Economic
    organization, and war; Evolution
    of war; Feuds; Military organiza-

tion; Population growth, and war;
    Prehistory, warfare in; Raiding;
    Recruitment of participants in
    warfare; Sedentarism, and war;
    Social organization, and war; Vio-
    lence, and war; War and society,
    coevolution of; Weapons;
    Women, and war
    causes of, 21, 76–77, 96–97, 105,
    130–33, 159
    definition of, 3–10, 122–23, 140, 142,
    163–64
    frequency of, 2–3, 43–44, 50–52,
    62–65, 73, 76–77, 122–25, 130,
    133, 135–42, 148, 167–68,
    172–73
War and society. *See also* Social orga-
    nization, and war
    coevolution of, 7, 68–69, 71, 73, 121,
    131–45, 159–61, 174
Warless societies, 31–39, 41–43, 49–53,
    64, 66, 124–25, 131, 143, 148, 155.
    See also Peaceful societies
    distinctive features of, 75
Warrau, 52, 55, 61–62, 63, 66, 70, 72,
    148, 169–70
Weapons, 106, 109, 136, 148, 151–52,
    156
Wendorf, F., 1, 148–50, 174
Whallon, R., 125–26, 128, 133
Wiessner, P., 134
Women
    and conflict resolution, 9, 97, 105–8,
    112, 116–19
    and domestic violence, 22–24,
    26–28, 30–34, 36, 166, 171
    violence between, 17–19, 24, 27, 29,
    32–33, 35–38, 102–3, 165, 171
    and war, 100–101, 105–7, 148–50
Wrangham, R., 35, 172, 175

Yahgan, 32, 52, 55, 58, 61, 63, 66, 70,
    72, 136–37, 141–42, 147, 156, 158,
    160, 168–69, 174

Zide, N., 80, 169